ILLUSTRATED PLAYBILLS

Playbill for ARTISTS' AMATEUR PERFORMANCE, St James's Theatre (May 1850),
courtesy of the Bodleian Library, University of Oxford

ILLUSTRATED PLAYBILLS

by Derek Forbes

A study together with a reprint of
*A Descriptive Catalogue of Theatrical Wood
Engravings* (1865)

Motto for Illustrated Playbills
'Now to the Drama turn – Oh! motley sight!
What precious scenes the wondering eyes invite!'
Lord Byron, *English Bards and Scotch Reviewers*

The Society for Theatre Research
2002

First Published 2002
by the Society for Theatre Research
c/o The Theatre Museum, 1E Tavistock Street,
Covent Garden, London WC2E 7PA

ISBN 0 85430 072 4

General Editor of Publications: Richard Foulkes
Volume Editor: Catherine Haill

Designed & Pageset by: Blot Publishing
www.blot.co.uk

Printed by: E&E Plumridge Ltd
41 High Street, LINTON, Cambridgeshire, CB1 6HS

Contents

Illustrations

FRONTISPIECE. Playbill for ARTISTS' AMATEUR PERFORMANCE, St James's Theatre (May 1850), courtesy of the Bodleian Library, University of Oxford

IN TEXT, PART-PAGE OR FULL-PAGE

Introduction

Many thousands of playbills have come down to us. Of those that were printed during the first sixty years or so of the nineteenth century a few, a very few, were illustrated with one or more woodcuts relevant to the action of the piece being advertised. To be kind, most of these illustrations lack artistic distinction. To be blunt, some look pretty awful. Even so their rugged force demands reluctant respect. Certainly they serve the purpose of catching the eye, and there are, besides, occasional examples that possess decorative appeal. Too often dismissed as unimportant if sometimes amusing, for various reasons the illustrations on playbills repay careful consideration and deserve a degree of analysis. They can make a contribution to our understanding of the theatrical practice of the time.

This is a greatly expanded version of a paper on illustrated playbills tabled at the conference on "Picturing Performance: graphic representations of the nineteenth-century theatre" held at the University of Kent at Canterbury, 3-5 July 1997. It rounds off a personal evaluation of art-work on British playbills of the first half of the nineteenth century which has already resulted in two earlier papers. These are 'The Earliest Grossmiths and their Pictorial Playbills' in *Scenes from Provincial Stages*, ed. Richard Foulkes (STR, 1994), 65-87, and 'Colour and Decoration on Nineteenth-century Playbills', *Theatre Notebook* LI/1 (1997), 26-41.

The study accompanies and introduces a reprint in photocopied facsimile of the little-known but intriguing *Revised Descriptive Catalogue of Theatrical Wood Engravings* from the Whitechapel 'Steam Printing Works' of E.J. Bath, circa 1865. The owner of the original copy (possibly the unique copy) is a distinguished authority on the theatre of the nineteenth century. His unreserved generosity in allowing it to be reproduced and discussed here is most deeply appreciated.

The catalogue provided a register of hundreds of woodcuts presented for sale as illustrations on the bills of plays and pantomimes. Over 200 titles were identified by name and many further theme-based designs were available for more general suitability. Interesting in themselves, their descriptions could be of value in future work on the early Victorian popular stage.

An abstract of the 700 numbered catalogue-entries has been prepared on a database. Visit the website of the Society for Theatre

Research for details (http://www.str.org.uk). A printout of the database, sorted to give an alphabetical index of Bath's entries by play or theme, forms the final part of this publication.

Acknowledgements

More than I can say is owed to David Mayer. Amongst other kindnesses he was so good as to cast his eyes over my initial paper in advance of its presentation at Canterbury and make helpful suggestions. I am grateful to Louis James for encouragement both at that time and subsequently, and to Jack Reading for help with contacts. I am beholden to further fellow-members of the Society for Theatre Research, in particular Graeme Cruickshank, Frances Dann, David Gowan, Howard Loxton, Susan Solomon and George Speaight, for sharing their knowledge and in some cases for generously allowing me information about material in their own possession and the reproduction of it here. As always, my wife Adrienne has been a constant support, and helped to compile the abstract of catalogue-entries.

I am indebted to a number of other individuals and the staff of institutions in which, over the years, I have conducted investigations leading to this study. People who have gone to particular trouble on my behalf include Rosemary Bennett, formerly of Hertford Museum; Chris Blanchett of Littlehampton, an independent scholar and tile historian; Mrs Diana Clunes; Susan Crabtree of the Templeman Library, University of Kent at Canterbury; Sarah Cuthill, formerly of the University of Bristol Theatre Collection; Claire Hudson of the Theatre Museum; Ann Kent of the Tyne and Wear Archives Service; John Lambert, Hertfordshire county conservator; Richard Russell, a director of Messrs Stephen Austin and Sons Ltd and a typographical specialist; Michael Twyman of the University of Reading; and David Withey of the Finsbury Reference Library, London Borough of Islington. I have also been helped by members of staff of Aberdeen University Library, the British Library and British Museum, the Guildhall Library (City of London), Hertfordshire County Library (especially the Central Resources Unit and Hertford branch library), the John Johnson Collection of the Bodleian Library, the National Picture Library (Victoria and Albert Museum), the Shropshire Records and Research Unit, and archivists or local studies librarians of the City of Westminster and the

London Boroughs of Lambeth and Southwark. The staff of the Hertford branches of Messrs Prontaprint and CallPrint have taken care over some delicate reproduction needs. Further help with particular cruces is acknowledged in the notes. To all, my sincere appreciation.

I am most obliged to my knowledgeable, meticulous and generously cooperative editor, Catherine Haill of the Theatre Museum, and similarly obliged to the STR's general editor of publications, Richard Foulkes, whose supportive wisdom never fails. Leonie Blows of Blot Publishing deserves equal gratitude for her exercise of page-setting and designing skills.

I wish also to offer thanks to the printing firm with which I have dealt over many years both on behalf of the Society for Theatre Research and independently, namely Messrs E. and E. Plumridge of Linton. I have found Tim and Oliver Plumridge and their staff to be unfailingly obliging and to give good guidance where it is needed. It is a pleasure to add to my acknowledgements a personal tribute to the printer's helpfulness and attention.

No apology is made for the variable quality of the reproductions, which is not the fault of the owners of the original items nor that of the book's producers. Perfection of examples has not been sought. The variability is an apt reflection of the standards of the printed engravings on bills up to two centuries old – some being faint, some clear, and others muzzy or sullied. A few of the illustrations are my own or in the public domain. Most, credited to their source, come from institutional or private collections; I am grateful for the courtesy of permission to reproduce them.

Derek Forbes
Hertford 2002

Illustrated Playbills

PART ONE

1. Definitions and Early Examples

The pictorial representation of characters, action and setting on illustrated playbills provides one of the sources for visual images of the drama in the first half of the nineteenth century. In considering these, together with some sideways glances at comparable sources when relevant, this essay will also include discussion of the little-known *Revised Descriptive Catalogue of Theatrical Wood Engravings* published about 1865 by the London printer E.J. Bath. Like other categories of theatrical iconography, illustrations on playbills may be far removed from what was actually presented on stage, but can equally well provide interesting material for speculation, amusement and sometimes enlightenment.[1]

'Playbills'? Yes, to employ the term conventionally stretched to include showbills of any size from handbills upwards for advertising theatrical and kindred entertainments, even for circuses and equestrian shows– until the 1860s or so, when 'posters' (outside) and 'programmes' (inside) started to take over the playbill's dual function. 'Illustrated'? That is, an advertising bill for a theatrical or similar entertainment which includes a picture featuring the act or acts being publicised. Emblems such as badges, heraldic arms and other small images as part of headings or titles are not to the point here and have already been considered in a previous paper.[2]

The illustrations on playbills are usually woodcuts (that is, normally on box-wood or pear-wood end-grain, using a broad graving tool) or wood engravings (that is, normally on side-grain using a finer graving tool), rather than engravings on metal. Even after Bewick introduced the alternative technique of 'white-line' engraving at the end of the eighteenth century, it takes an expert eye to discern the difference between woodcuts and wood engravings, especially in reproduction. The terms 'cut' and 'engraving' were in any case used loosely. So, in this study, the terms 'woodcut', and 'cut' (short for woodcut), and 'engraving' (for wood-engraving), and 'block' (for the process) are used interchangeably for prints from matrices engraved on wood, to adopt the relaxed practice of Bath's trade catalogue discussed below. In practice, Bath's offerings seem likely to be restricted to 'woodcuts' rather than to include 'wood engravings'. So far as can be ascertained, Cruikshank's work, where cited for comparison in due course, is the sole example of engraving on steel, and the illustration of Master Betty's characters the sole copperplate.

The examples discussed focus on the theatre of the British Isles. A comparison with European, American or colonial practice could be fruitful and illuminating but would need a width of attention beyond the present scope. The period under discussion is the first sixty years or so of the nineteenth century. Soon after the mid-century playbills gave way to colourful wall-posters, and placard composition became subject to new techniques.

There are certain ambiguous woodcuts from the eighteenth century to deal with first. The animal-trainer Laurent Spinacuta or Spinacuti presented an act featuring his monkey Turco, 'Le Chevalier des Singes', at Sadler's Wells Theatre under the management of Rosoman in the period 1766-68, according to accounts by Dennis Arundell and in *A Biographical Dictionary of Actors, etc., 1660-1800*. There is an undated engraving illustrating the monkey's feats (see illustration). Several prints of it exist in landscape format (that is, sideways on the sheet), both in playbill size and in a smaller handbill size. The most obvious explanation is that the design was supplied by Spinacuta for the decorative print market, though it is possible that the prints were reproduced from a published source for the same purpose. Nonetheless to an admittedly non-specialist eye they give the appearance of having a use as fly-sheets as well or rather than as wall-prints. The design consists of four rows of eighteen small woodcuts of the monkey in action and one bigger central cut of the trainer holding it on high. The wording at the top is crucial: 'The Curious and Uncommon Performances of A MONKEY as they will be introduc'd every evening at Sadler's Wells by Signor Spinacuta'.[3]

The exact nature of these prints remains unclear. What might seem to be a side-issue must be briefly noticed. Prints of this multi-boxed type exist for further eighteenth-century entertainments. It seems possible that they had some association with the fashion for decorative tiles, either as tile designs to start with or taken over for tile design following publication as prints. The matter is deferred to the appendix where the genre is discussed in more detail and further examples are identified, such as that for 'The Famous Polander' of 1788.

3

Regardless of a possible association with decorative tiles, the existence of at least four examples of the Spinacuta engraving is evidence that copies were run off, even if, as can be shown to be the case with the print of 'The Famous Polander', the design had its origin as a plate in a journal. The wording that heads the Spinacuta pictures refers to '...Performances of A MONKEY as they will be introduc'd every evening...'. Aside from any other function, these prints may, then, have operated as advertising bills. Should this be the case, Spinacuta's prints, and conceivably those of other eighteenth-century entertainers noticed in the appendix, would give us uncommonly early examples of theatrical advertisement in the form of pictorial fliers.

The style represented by the Spinacuta design is not based on the normal playbill practice of the day in which the bill consisted of written description and doubled as both poster and programme. Spinacuta's substance is devoted to pictures, with a minimum of text. In this it is unlike the illustrated playbills in what became the standard style of the nineteenth century. When managers started to commission the printing of a woodcut on their bills, the fashion developed for it to be fitted in amongst the written text, usually centrally, to catch the eye and inform the illiterate but with most of the space still occupied by wording. The very few nineteenth-century exceptions that we will come across in which a 'normal' playbill is almost entirely pictorial, and almost certainly meant largely for wall-posting, date from the 1830s onwards. These can be regarded as pointing the way to the specialist advertising poster, predominantly graphic or in large type, that at first only supplemented the outdoor function of playbills but then steadily replaced it thirty years later.

Circuses give us our earliest unambiguous examples of illustrated bills. An advertisement for Pidcock's Travelling Menagerie, c.1795, is held by the Theatre Museum and reproduced in *Images of Show Business*. The bill's mid-text cuts of an elephant, a zebra and a lion by the inimitable Thomas Bewick make it delightful to the eye but hardly typical of what followed. A.H. Saxon reproduces a bill of 30 May 1799 for the benefit of Peter Ducrow at the Olympic Circus, Shaw's Brow, Liverpool. This contains two simple cuts of balancing acts side by side at the very top, followed by performance details in normal playbill style. The placing of cuts at the head of the sheet above all text gives a top-heavy effect. Although some managers, or printers, continued using similar positioning for illustrations at times, a more satisfactory placement was

For the BENEFIT
OF THE
HULL
General Infirmary.

At the New Circus, in the Market-Place,

On THURSDAY Evening next, 16th June, 1803.

A GREAT VARIETY OF

New ENTERTAINMENTS.
HORSEMANSHIP.
By a CAPITAL TROOP of PERFORMERS.

Mr. FROST,
Will go through a Number of surprising Feats, and throw a Somerset from the Horse in Full Speed.

Mr. JONES.
Will perform several wonderful Feats on a single Horse, in particular he picks up FOUR HAND-KERCHIEFS from the Ground without dismounting, with the Horse in perfect Cadence.

STILL VAULTING with Surprising LEAPS.
Master CIMEX's Horseman's Agility,
With the much admired STIRRUP TRICKS.
THE ASTONISHING
POLANDER's PERFORMANCES,
WITH
The GEOMETRICAL LADDER,
Grand Trampoline Tricks,
𝔊round and 𝔏ofty 𝔗umbling.

2. Playbill for horsemanship act, Frost and Smith's Circus, Hull (1803),
courtesy of George Speaight

achieved by setting a woodcut in the midst of text. This became the standard style. It can be seen in an advertisement from the George Speaight collection that shows a flag-waving performer standing one-footed on horseback (see illustration). It is one of several bills for Frost and Smith's 'New Circus' at Hull in May and June 1803. The text also reveals that 'the astonishing Polander' was still active, despite his last sighting in the *Biographical Dictionary* being given as 1795. Further illustrations on bills in this six-week series include a rope dancer and the rousing vision, as described by George Speaight in a personal communication, of 'a man standing on his head on an exploding firework'.[4]

So far as is known, these examples from *c*.1795, 1799 and 1803 are the earliest functioning showbills with illustrations, though previous examples may await discovery or disclosure. It then took nearly twenty years for such illustrated bills to become less rare and even then they remained uncommon.

Uncommon, yes, but to what degree is hard to estimate. Anyone who has leafed through gatherings of playbills knows not only the rarity of those with illustrations but also their varied infrequency. With student assistance, twenty-odd years ago the writer compiled a census of the summer-season Sadler's Wells bills at Finsbury Library for 1800-1837. This identified 200 bills between 1800-1820 of which none were noted as illustrated, and 225 between 1821 and 1837 of which two were illustrated. At the other extreme Astley's Amphitheatre, pictorially the most prolific house of all, put out an average of one illustrated bill in every five or six after 1825. To leave out Astley's as a special case and, for what it is worth, to make a subjective generalisation: the field as a whole might be assessed at about one bill in a thousand illustrated before 1820, hardly more than ten (and probably less) in a thousand 1820-30, and twenty or more in a thousand in 1830-50 with a further increase in the 1850s and 1860s. These figures might well be an over-estimate.

With its centralised picture the bill for Hull of 1803 sets the standard style for lay-out. In addition it foreshadows the subject for the majority of illustrated playbills that have survived from the years that ensued, by virtue of featuring an animal. The woodcuts of this majority of extant bills display feats of horsemanship and related acrobatics, while yet more extend the circus image to other animals whether in the amphitheatre or the playhouse. It seems as if managers considered images of the creature world more important than any other type of pictorial device on their bills. As well as the more superficial appeal of the exotic it may be that a nostalgic, even an atavistic, instinct was at work here, perhaps as a subconscious counter to the loss of involvement with the 'natural' creation that accompanied the onset of industry, urbanisation and steam power at this time.

The next decade throws up bills picturing a monkey in a play of 1815 and a lion-act in 1816, recurred to below; 'Toby, the Sapient Pig' in the Royal Promenade Rooms in 1817; and acrobats on horseback again as seen on Aberdeen bills for 'Ord's Horsemanship' in 1817 and the 'Olympic Circus' in 1818. The 'Fashionable Amusements' of Cooke and Bridges (touring from Astley's) picture their equestrian and other delights in Bridgnorth's Royal Hotel Yard on six illustrated bills between 30 October 1819 and 1 May 1820. These comprise a trick horse with its forelegs up a ladder; male and female performers upright on horseback with the Union flag being waved; nine acrobats in a tier mounted on three horses; the head and shoulders of Hay, the clown; an acrobat of 'Herculean Power' supporting a frame on which are ten further acrobats in two tiers; and five 'Tyrolean Peasants' dancing on stilts. Despite the fact that three out of the six in this catena sport human images alone, it is generally found that acrobats by themselves, unaccompanied by horses, appear less often in such illustrations.[5]

The examples given in this paper mostly come as a result of leafing through a limited number of playbill collections and are by no means comprehensive. Knowledgeable readers will have their own perception of illustrated bills and know of others beside those mentioned here. A brief breakdown of the field into subject-types, with examples, may be helpful and will have consequence when we come to survey the significance of the catalogue of the theatrical printer E.J. Bath.

2. Animal subjects

Horses

As can already be inferred, equestrianism led the way. Astley's Amphitheatre has provided the greatest number of illustrated hippodrama bills for any one venue. The earliest seem to be for a horse-racing drama, *The High Mettled Racer,* for which eleven illustrated bills are extant between March and June 1823, each normally with two or three small cuts. The Theatre Museum's magnificent redaction of Astley's bills on forty-eight microfiches has an average of thirty bills on each. In merely nos. 2-15 of these fiches, covering 1826-38, there are over eighty illustrated bills, giving an average of six per fiche. Many of these bills show a development into more than one image, either connected to make a complex whole or in separated blocks on the sheet. In the case of the long-popular *Mazeppa* the engraving gets refined over the years: this is discussed in more detail later. A selection of Astley's illustrated bills for other spectacles shows 'Paul Pry' on horseback with six action frames (12 June 1826) and another of 'Paul Pry caught in a shower of rain' on horseback with an umbrella (May 1828); a line of ten cavalrymen in *The Invasion of Russia* (August 1828); in 1830 two horses jumping a hurdle with 'Mr Ducrow as The Sportsman' upright with one foot on each; six cuts between them on two bills for *St George and the Dragon* (May 1833); and on 11 August 1834 one cut, printed high on the bill, of knights on horseback for *The Tournament of London* with a second cut lower down of Dick Turpin on Black Bess leaping the tollgate in *Turpin's Wonderful Ride.* 'Puss in Boots' on horseback is pictured three weeks later. There are five illustrated bills with epic (and hippic) views of *The Siege of Jerusalem* and *The Battle of Waterloo* between June and October 1835. A total of no less than eleven complex engravings on bills during the 1837-38 season, an outstanding year for Astley's advertising, may be exemplified by the entirely blue-printed bill for *Epsom Races* in which the centre of the sheet is devoted to an oval cut of Ducrow's 'Infant Jockeys and Fiery Coursers'.

Astley's occasionally gave precedence on its bills to the human element though never without accompanying beasts. There are sundry individual frames of mounted performers on bills that advertise benefits. Amongst these Andrew Ducrow features large, for example on a bill for the Benefit Performance of William West in 1831 which carries a framed engraving of 'Mr Ducrow as the Centaur combating the Lion'.

An exceptional Astley's playbill for *The Wars of Wellington* (n.d., 1838) has a central engraving of the general inscribed 'The Hero of Our Times', surrounded by action pictures in red and green with the bare minimum of text. Attractively designed, this is one of the rare bills given over almost entirely to illustration.[6]

A strip across the width of the bill normally occupies only a quarter or less of the available height of the sheet, as in the panoramic engraving for Astley's 'May Day Revels' which was the first-act prelude to *The Fire of London* (1836). The scene centres on a maypole to show the populace at play, but inevitably draws on the stables to illustrate pig-sticking and jousting games in the background as can be seen.

3. 'May-day Revels' from a playbill for Astley's Amphitheatre (1836), courtesy of Minet Library, London Borough of Lambeth

Other venues during the 1820s-30s have similar equestrian activity pictured on the bills, whether a Ducrow spectacular on tour or companies like Cooke's visiting the provinces with acrobats on horseback. A series of bills for Cooke's Circus at Dundee in February-March 1835 shows various balancing acts. One features a cut of Gulliver and Lilliputians but even this also pictures a rider balancing on one foot. Horse-racing is pictured on one of the very rare illustrated bills for Sadler's Wells (September 1826), while Vauxhall Gardens has a cut to advertise a race between three Roman chariots, each with two horses in hand (July 1839).

Cornered or framing illustrations can be found from 1825, if not before. A good example is the alluring playbill put out in black and red by the Theatre Royal, Drury Lane, for Ducrow in 'The Grand Equestrian and Romantic Drama of *St George and the Dragon*' on Boxing Day 1833, with cuts in each corner concentrating on the dragon and knights on horseback. The engravings ignore the fact that the programme also included 'Mr Stanfield's Splendid Diorama exhibiting The Great Cataracts of the Nile'.

Theatre Royal, Drury Lane.

☞ The Unprecedented Success

Which has attended the
Production
OF
The Grand Equestrian
and Romantic Drama of

St. George and the Dragon

IN WHICH TAKES PLACE

A Grand Old English Cavalcade,

INTRODUCING

Authorities of Coventry,	Morris Dancers,
Knights with their Pages,	Heads of the different Trades,
Squires and their Ladies,	Minstrels and Bards,
Men-at-Arms,	Gentry, Peasants, Mob, &c. &c.

An Egyptian Marriage DIVERTISEMENT!

Mr. STANFIELD's

SPLENDID DIORAMA!

EXHIBITING

The Great Cataracts of the Nile.

Dragon's Haunt by Moonlight.

Mr. DUCROW's

Extraordinary Combat.

THROUGH THE

Excavated Temples of Ghirsheh. Caverns of Abou Samboul. Ascent of a Pyramid.

Triumphal Entry into the City of Memphis

CONSISTING OF

King Ptolemy in his Chariot,	Prince of Morocco in his Car,
St. Denis, of France, with Deer,	St. David, of Wales, with Trophies,
St. Antony, of Italy, with Trophies,	St. Patrick, of Ireland, with Giant's Head.
St. James, of Spain, with Wild Boar,	St. Andrew, of Scotland, with Swans,

THE PRINCESS SABRA UNDER A GORGEOUS CANOPY!

Zebra with Gold Dust,	Soldiers with Banners,
Dancing Girls,	Knights carrying Trophies,
Slaves bearing Presents,	Members of the Royal Band,
Knights on Horseback,	Ladies on Horseback.

St. GEORGE mounted on his Charger Bayard, with the Conquered
Dragon lying at his Feet.

And owing to the
**Nightly
Overflows,**
immediately after the
opening of the Doors, it

Will be Performed every Evening !!!

W. Wright, Printer, Theatre Royal, Drury Lane.

4. Playbill for *St George and the Dragon*, Drury Lane (1833),
courtesy of the Trustees of the National Picture Library, Victoria and Albert Museum

10

Earlier in the year the fourteen-year-old Princess Victoria had been so taken with *St George and the Dragon* when she saw it at Astley's that she recorded impressions of it in her sketch-book. A later image of St George spearing the dragon (Cooke's Circus, 1840) is included under 'Conclusions and Questions' below. Another play to cast a horse in disguise as a dragon was *The Dragon of Rhodes* of which there is an illustrated bill for 'The Royal Equestrian Circus' at Aberdeen in 1835.[7]

Dogs

The next most popular animal act for illustration is dog-drama.

Dogs had long trodden the boards, though the earliest ones like Launce's 'Crab' in *The Two Gentlemen of Verona* were not called upon to do much acting. An illustrious early example can be named. Garrick's mastiff Dragon, normally his Hampton house-dog, was once haled to, and hailed on, the Drury Lane stage. The eighteenth century saw the appearance of trained animals. Christopher Smart's 'Mrs Midnight' entertainments at the Haymarket included 'Mrs Midnight's Animal Comedians', which were dogs and monkeys 'brought from Italy by Sig. Ballard'. They performed on and off from 11 December 1752 until 10 March 1753. The act in which the dogs attacked 'battlements' defended by monkeys, all in uniform, was the subject of an amusing drawing of which the central section is shown herewith. Later, Scaglioni's fourteen-strong pack of canine bravos, under their famed pack-leader 'Moustache', performed in

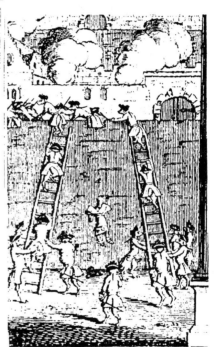

5. 'Mrs Midnight's Animal Comedians' from a print (c. 1752-3), courtesy of Mrs Diana Clunes and Messrs Cassell.

The Deserter at Sadler's Wells in 1784. (Those interested in a general survey of stage-animals can find a useful summary in Bamber Gascoigne's *World Theatre*). In the Theatre Museum there is a flier in a style comparable to that of Spinacuta's 'Chevalier des Singes' which displays Moustache and his thespian kennel-mates. Even if the main purpose of the 'Mrs Midnight' and Scaglioni prints was for wall-decoration, we cannot rule out their indirect advertising influence during the period of performance.[8]

Frederick Reynolds set the trend for nineteenth-century dog heroes with his play *The Caravan; or, the Driver and his Dog* involving a watery rescue at Drury Lane in 1803, when The Dog Carlo played the diving divo. Charles Dibdin the Younger's first dog-drama using the tank that he installed within the stage at Sadler's Wells was actually *The Ocean Fiend* of 1807. A later one of 1816 was his most successful, *Philip and his Dog; or, Where's the Child?* Pictures from other sources for this legendary aqua-drama represent the range of graphics that illustrated bills were beginning to join. One is a 'Twopence Coloured' sheet published in October 1816 by Whittle and Laurie with eight scenes in which Philip's excellent and eponymous 'Bruin' features large. This sheet was taken over for the Juvenile Drama by Jameson. Bruin was such a favourite that Luke Clint's painting of the animal was honoured by the Royal Academy and hung in 1817 (no. 341). It was also engraved.

Another image was on a music cover which has a large engraving showing the noble beast about to rescue Little Adelaide from drowning (see illustration). This is comparable to woodcuts that were beginning to appear on playbills but much better engraved and printed.[9]

6. 'Bruin' saves Little Adelaide from drowning, from a music cover for *Philip and his Dog* at Sadler's Wells (1817), courtesy of Finsbury Library, London Borough of Islington

A representative early playbill picturing a dog shows the animal attacking a victim's assailant on a bill for *The Rival Indians; or, the Sailor Boy and his Dog* at Bath in May 1824, and for the same piece at Warwick in September 1826, now crediting 'Mr Wood and his Wonderful Dog Bruin'. The Noble and Sagacious Bruin inspires a dog-image on a number of bills, whether carrying a lantern, rescuing a prisoner, acting in a lion-skin, or, of course, leaping for the throat of aggressors – 'taking the seize'. This manœuvre is figured here from that prolific source of nineteenth-century theatrical illustration, the juvenile drama.[10]

7. Skelt's toy-theatre image of Bruin taking the seize

The early dog-illustrating bills concentrate upon 'Bruin'. Perhaps we see here the promotional hand of W.F. Wood, the dog's master. Bruin (or a successor of the same name) is still in evidence in the 1830s. He stars in *The Foulah Slave* at Warwick in October 1833, when the cut on the playbill is of an attacking lion. There are appropriate woodcuts on the bills for a rapidly-changing series of roles for Bruin at Waterford in March and April 1835, when he is pictured in *The Grateful Lion* (Lion: Bruin), *The Knights of the Cross* and *The Exile of Erin* as well as in that most enduring of all canine dramas *The Dog of Montargis; or, the Forest of Bondy,* a play we come back to in the case-studies below.

At first the Leading Dog star in nineteenth-century canine drama was Bruin, though he sometimes acted with Hector as Supporting Dog, for example in *The Cherokee Chief; or, the Dogs of the Wreck* at Sadler's Wells in May 1834 for which the bill shows a picture of snake, sailor, and palm tree as well as dog. Then in due course Hector rose to the lead. The names of Bruin and Hector were marketable. In 1844 an illustrated bill for Wellington advertises 'Mr H. Smith and his Celebrated Dogs' naming this pair again, or rather, perhaps, their replacements or imposters. The *nom-de-chien* of Hector in the cast list survived into the 1870s.

There is less evidence for illustration on playbills when other dog-stars of the 1820s-40s are named in the cast, such as Captain, Carlo, Lion, Napoleon, Neptune, Tyger and Wolf (eponymous appellations, perhaps, and used even when, as sometimes happened, the dog was suspected of being a bitch). The bill for *Cato; or, the Planter and his Dog, and the Slave's Revenge* at Bury St Edmunds in November 1841 has a full-width cut of a floored planter, a knife-wielding slave standing over him and a large dog attacking the slave, but does not name the dog-star.

Nor, perhaps more understandably, does it seem that the enchanting and versatile actress Eliza Vincent (once 'The Little Pickle', now graduated to being billed as 'the Acknowledged Heroine of Domestic Drama') allowed a likeness to appear on the bills for her performance in the name part of Moncrieff's *Caesar, the Watch Dog of the Castle; or, the Sword of Whitefriars,* which her manager and lover Osbaldiston persuaded her to play 'in a revealing dogskin' at the Royal Victoria Theatre in 1844. Perhaps Eliza took on this uncomfortable role to continue assuaging the feelings of the Old Vic audience, which had booed her, favourite though she was, when her liaison with the already married Osbaldistone became known.

Commenting on *Caesar, the Watch Dog* in *The 'Revels' History of Drama,* Robertson Davies confirms 'the strong chthonic element in the play— what Englishman can doubt the moral grandeur of a dog?' Thus, if sardonically, he sums up much of the appeal of the iconography of canines as well as their performances. In the 1850s-60s, the Bower Saloon made a feature of canine cuts on its bills for dog-drama. The images of dog on playbills were idealised— not portraits of the actual animals, though the usual reproduction of a Labrador-like creature seems to have stemmed from Mr Wood's first Bruin. A poster-sized playbill of 1853 (double crown, 20 x 30in., 50 x 75 cm) for *The French Spy; or, the Arab and his Dog* represents the apogee of such portrayal (see illustration). In its profusion of small cuts the bill echoes the style of publicity for human juveniles dealt with below.[11]

The occasional mutations when horses acted dragons and bulls, or dogs acted lions and wolves, should not obscure the enormous popularity of horses and dogs in their own personae, both in performance on stage and in the generalised pictures on the bills. This reflects a historical feature of human culture that is still with us, though in different forms. Beneath Robertson Davies's mockery lies some truth. To the human mind, horses and dogs plumb a well of association that goes beyond

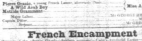

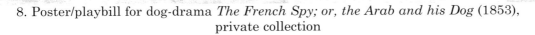

8. Poster/playbill for dog-drama *The French Spy; or, the Arab and his Dog* (1853), private collection

familiarity or sentiment, and far beyond their aptitude for being trained. There are deep motives to account for their supremacy in animal-based show business.

Large and small cats

Other animals appearing on the nineteenth-century stage which were pictured in the bills include an early lion in 1816 for Polito's Travelling Menagerie. Such menagerie-shows were put in the shade in the late 1830s by Isaac van Amburgh's large cats, comprising lions, tigers, leopards and a cheetah together with Supporting Lamb. At least two different cuts of the act were pictured on the playbills, of which this figure is representative.

9. 'Van Amburgh's large cats' on an Astley's playbill (1839), courtesy of Minet Library, London Borough of Lambeth

Van Amburgh's was another entertainment much admired by young Queen Victoria (or perhaps rather its trainer's muscles and mastery). She had come to the throne in 1837 at the age of eighteen. In 1839, as George Rowell has told us, she attended Van Amburgh's show seven times. The discipline and control that Van Amburgh exercised also had its fascination for the Duke of Wellington, accustomed though he was to dominating a different article. Another to whom the act appealed was Landseer, who painted it.[12]

The clown Richard Usher (and his daughter 'Miss Usher', one of a large brood) used domestic felines on stage in their 'Celebrated Stud of Real Cats', which Usher also harnessed to a little chariot and paraded in the streets for advance publicity. A splendid bill for Usher's Benefit Performance at the Bristol Theatre Royal on Friday 14 September 1827 is unusual for a touring company of its time, indeed any company, in having two distinct illustrations. The upper one shows Usher's carriage drawn by his four 'Thorough-bred Mousers' Tibby, Tabby, Toddle and Tot, while the other just below mid-sheet is a round 'moon' enclosing figures for his 'Clown in the Moon' act. As the bill included *Harlequin Dog Star* and an unnamed Man-Monkey, almost certainly Garcia, together with Dicky Usher's Canary Concert (an 'admired imitation of the Feathered Creation'), Bristolians had their fill of the bestiary that night– though these are only part of the generous evening's programme.

Interestingly Usher's bill for 14 September 1827 exists in two versions. The one reproduced contains extra side-lined text to advertise Usher's Benefit, while the other version lacks the side-lining and was presumably intended mainly for distribution to the audience. Further lavish publicity was provided by a new bill being put out for the following night, Saturday 15 September, rather than the two nights (or more) being advertised on one bill. The cat-carriage woodcut is repeated on the second bill. Usher's bill for 14 September is given in full here as an example of a high standard, applied as comparatively early in the half-century as 1827, to show the care that could be taken over text as well as illustration. It becomes apparent that some managers, perhaps only a few but certainly some, were picture-minded, and moreover went to unusual trouble and expense to see that their playbills were designed and printed attractively.

Irresistibly at this point we divert for a moment. It is to be assumed that Usher's cats behaved better than the hard-done-by animals on the occasion described by 'Old Wild' nearly thirty years later, when for his Benefit Performance the clown (Boardman) offered to 'be drawn across the stage by fifty-four cats in a blaze of fire'. Fifty of the team 'were not forthcoming', but four cats were cast from many aspirants brought to the stage-door. Once on stage, says Sam Wild, terrified by their harnesses and the fireworks the demented creatures engaged in 'an unaffected struggle for liberty' until the closure of the curtain enabled 'a timely rescue of the revolters'. Poor beasts. This scene was not captured for the playbills. Nor, so far as known, was another renowned animal act first exhibited by Usher (see his account on the playbill) and subsequently copied by Nelson, when to publicise a benefit the clown sailed along a stretch of river in a washing-tub drawn by geese. This sight was said to have rendered even the Thames watermen speechless, which took some doing.[13]

Laurent, another clown, also used a live cat on stage. For the most part, however, domestic felines represented on stage were cats in pantomimes such as *Puss in Boots* (illustrated on the bill already

10. Playbill for Usher's cats and clown act, Theatre Royal, Bristol (1827), upper section

CATS,

FOUR-IN-HAND SEVERAL TIMES ROUND THE STAGE.

The Evening's Amusements will commence with a Comic Extravaganza, as performed in London for upwards of 50 nights, called the Clown in the Moon.

IN THE COURSE OF WHICH

Harlequin Dog Star!

Will take off his head and carry it under his arm.

Mr. USHER will exhibit his astonishing deception of Swallowing his own Head.

Takes several Leaps apparently through the Ceiling, and in one instant return through the Earth—magnify himself to the size of the late O'Brien eight feet high—with various other surprising Feats, which must be seen to be credited.

After which the admired Play of

She Stoops to Conquer,
Or the Mistakes of a Night,

Tony Lumpkin, Mr. WOULDS,
Young Marlow, Mr. BEVERLY.—Mr. Hardcastle, Mr. SMOLLET.
Hastings, Mr. FORDE.—Sir Charles Marlow, Mr. HAMERTON.
Diggory, Mr. KING.—Landlord, Mr. FISHWICK.—Jack Slang, Mr. WITHERS.
Tim Twist, Mr. ENNIS.— Robert, Mr. DALVILLE.
Miss Neville, Miss PITT.—Mrs. Hardcastle, Miss BANNISTER.
Pimple, Mrs. CORNWALL.—And Miss Hardcastle, Miss MORDAUNT.

TO WHICH WILL BE ADED THE FARCE OF THE

WEATHERCOCK,

Tristam Fickle, Mr. WOULDS.
Briefwit, Mr. SMOLLET.—Old Fickle, Mr. KING.—Sneer, Mr. ENNIS.
Gardiner, Mr. GLOVER.—Barber, Mr. FISHWICK.—Servant, Mr. WITHERS.
Ready, Mrs. CORNWALL.—Variella, Miss PITT.

To finish with a Grand

MASQUERADE.

Among other characters of first rate celebrity, that surprising

MAN MONKEY,

who gained such universal admiration in London, will exhibit his astonishing GYMNASTIC FEATS.

Mr. HOWELL,

Of the Theatre Royal, Drury Lane, will personate the character of a BRITISH SAILOR, and with Miss Lancaster introduce a Jig and Irish Minuet. A comic Dance, in character, by Mr. Fishwick. And Mr. Usher will introduce his

Lancashire Hornpipe, in real Brewers' Clogs.

He will also give his admired Imitation of the FEATHERED CREATION, which was performed by him at the splendid Masquerade, Vauxhall Gardens London, and conclude with his grand

CANARY CONCERT.

The whole to conclude with a grand Antipodean Feat, surrounded by a brilliant display, representing a Palm Tree in

FIRE WORKS.

Doors open at 6, and Commence at 7 o'Clock.

Boxes, 4s. Pit, 2s. 6d. Gallery, 1s. 6d. Tickets to be had at the Theatre, where Places for the Boxes may be taken from 11 till 3.

11. Same bill, lower section. Courtesy of Trustees of the British Library

mentioned for Astley's in 1834, for example). Then as now pantomime cats were played by actors or juveniles in skins. Unlike today, though, their frequency in the nineteenth century was dwarfed by the popularity of the simian creation, both on stage and in images on the bills.

Monkeys and others

The surge, or resurge, of ape-plays and man-monkey acts during the first half of the nineteenth century can be accounted for by anthropomorphism as well as entertainment value, long before Wallace's and Darwin's bombshell papers delivered to the Royal Linnaean Society and the publication of *The Origin of Species* in 1859. Many playbills can be found from all over the country advertising one or other of the

12. Man-monkey as Jocko the Brazilian Ape in a bill for Usher's troupe at Hertford (1826), courtesy of Hertford Museum

dozen or more skin actors from Mazurier onwards. Quite a number are illustrated, as for 'Master Kellar' in *Pérouse* as early as 1815 and 'Signor Garcia' (an acrobat in Richard Usher's troupe) named for *Jocko, the Brazilian Ape* in 1828 on one of Usher's bills. The player of Jocko is not named on another of Usher's bills from which the figure here is taken, but is almost certainly Garcia. The feline head, it is to be hoped, is an aberrant mask or engraver's incompetence rather than a likeness.

Acted by first one and then a second player, 'Mons. Gouffé, the English Mazurier' *(sic)* was the most renowned of the troupe of man-monkeys. This character inspired an ape-picturing bill for the Sans Souci in June 1825, others at Belfast in 1828, Canterbury in 1831 and so on. Again, the figures of the ape blocked on the bills are stereotypes – and pretty hideous to our eye, at that – though the feats displayed may genuinely reflect stage-action.[14]

Further assorted beasts pictured on the bills include reptiles and an elephant. Concerning *Tippoo Sahib,* an enormously popular enactment at Sadler's Wells in 1791-92 of the Seringapatam campaign, one would like to know how the manager (Wroughton) staged that part of the spectacle in which the bills repeatedly described how 'a detachment of Sepoys... particularly signalized themselves by the Capture of an ELEPHANT'. There is no reference to the elephant being real. The first performing elephant on the English stage appears to have been 'Chuny' from Cross's Menagerie at London's Exeter Street Exchange with a début at Covent Garden on Boxing Night 1811 in *Harlequin and Padmanaba*. The Drury Lane machinist, Johnson, went to a performance. When he saw the animal on stage he is said to have exclaimed, 'I should be very sorry if I could not make a better elephant than that.' No bills picturing Chuny have emerged, but cuts of a performing elephant adorn Astley's bills in 1831 and 1838-39. A snake we have already noticed, shown on the bill for *Cato; or, the Planter and his Dog* at Bury. The bill for a freak show at Aberdeen in 1833 ('Beautiful Spotted Indian', 'The Hottentot Venus' etc.) has a cut of characters together with a boa constrictor and a crocodile.[15]

These last examples pose a question. Perhaps the reptiles were merely in the picture for exotic colour, but it is possible that they were part of the show, real or fudged or skin-acted. As we find throughout our investigation, such illustrations on playbills can be entertaining and may be revealing but should not necessarily be taken at face value. We need to exercise the same caution as in considering the famous stage-direction in *The Winter's Tale*, 'Exit, pursued by a bear.'

13. The clown Paulo as the Giant Killer on a playbill for the Theatre Royal, Hull (1851), private collection

3. Human Subjects

Coming to a consideration of playbills with illustrations of wholly human characters and action, wholly human situations and enterprise, we are forced to recognise that they are scarce in contrast to those that feature or include animals.

Individuals

Sam Wild, the Yorkshire actor-manager who recorded the cat-contretemps just mentioned, was one of quite a few performers whose portraits, in or out of character, were illustrated on playbills. Jo Harrop reproduces a Halifax bill of 1837 showing him as Mat Meriton in *Every Inch a Sailor*. Wild provides evidence, should we need it, that players could keep their own blocks by them for their bills. 'I lent him my block' he says about Templeton in 1857, another fit-up manager and one 'in a state of great need', so that it could enhance his playbill by being printed 'at the foot of the synopsis of scenery and incidents of the first piece'. Wild's image as Mat Meriton epitomises the cuts of further Jack Tar actors such as T.P. Cooke, or the likes of Ducrow on horseback. Attention has already been drawn to two such character-studies above, namely the clown Hay on a Bridgnorth bill for 'Hay's Night' in 1819 and Ducrow as the Centaur in 1831. Two others which have been featured in an earlier paper are worth bringing forward again: namely Hallam's tinted portrait occupying the entire top half of a bill for his benefit on 15 April 1822 at Ashbourne, not a crude woodcut but clearly something special and capable of being detached and independently mounted; and the formally dressed master of ceremonies of Vauxhall Gardens, Mr Simpson, who was pictured large on a bill for his benefit in July 1834 in an image which, when much reduced in size, was then used in place of a heraldic emblem at the top of subsequent bills. Performing as the Giant Killer, the clown Paulo is figured here from a bill of 1851 for the Theatre Royal, Hull.

Further individuals include Grimaldi as a Chinese on a Sadler's Wells print for *Whang Fong,* c. 1812; Crisp as Paul Pry on a bill for Bridgnorth on 24 March 1827; a silhouette on a bill for 'Mr Seville's Likenesses', c. 1825, boasting a 'scissor-cut' of the fiddler Blind Willie, no doubt Scott's Wandering Willie from *Redgauntlet;* and a portrait of Ira Aldridge at the top of a Dundee playbill of 1848 with additional smaller cuts of action, reproduced and referred to in more detail later.

Another useful visual signal could be given by a Harlequin figure, who appears on some pantomime bills such as one for Exmouth in 1850 in which he displays a scroll of announcements. As Dennis Arundell tells us, Almar's publicity for *The Skeleton Hand; or, the Vampire* of 1834 pictured 'a devilish female pouncing on a man'. The image was graced with a caption which could not fail to impress:

Ha! she comes – oh! she seizes me – oh, God! – Lorks, she clutches my throat. Crikey – oh! she chokes me! ah! ah! oh! – I die – ie – ie – ie! oh – ie – oh – ie – oh! oh! oh! COME EARLY.[16]

As with types such as Harlequin and Almar's vampire, portraits of individual stars on playbills usually characterise them in attitude and costume. A spirited example is displayed on an Adelphi Theatre bill of 1838 for 'The Metempsychosian Performer Signor Hervio Nano, as the Gnome Fly', with images of him as Gnome, Baboon, and Fly (see illustration).

Nano's images are in pictorial roundels engraved in black on white, but the eyefulness of the whole is dilated by the orange-hued background (dark in the plate) and by the bill being double size, 14 by 21 inches (36 by 54 cm). It is a costly and colourful attention-grabber to which most unusually the engraver, Dorrington, proud of his work, has inscribed his name. 'Signor Hervio Nano' was actually Leach, a dwarf. 'As the ape,' accoladed a contemporary reviewer, ' he exceeds even Gouffé and Mazurier'.

Another citrous portrait was produced on a poster for the Surrey Theatre's *Orange Girl,* a play by Leslie and Rose about which *The Times* reported on 27 October 1864:

For some days past the walls of our streets have been decorated with a remarkable wood engraving representing a young lady's head placed in the centre of a large yellow disc. This... symbolizes the production at the Surrey Theatre of a new drama entitled *The Orange Girl.*

Colour was much cheaper to reproduce on this flier than for Nano at the Adelphi, because the Surrey's printer could take advantage of aniline dyes which had been introduced to this country in 1856. At some time in the early 1860s the Surrey began to sell programmes. An example for *The Orange Girl,* complete with advertisements for 'Teeth

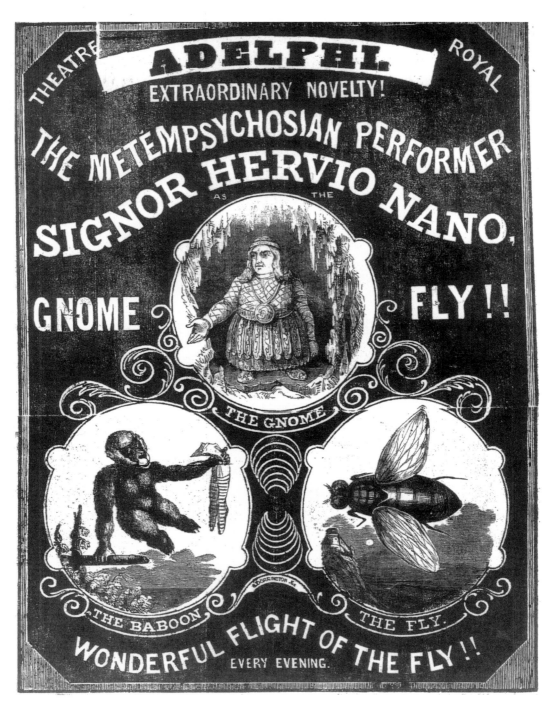

14. 'Signor Hervio Nano' as the Gnome Fly on an Adelphi Theatre playbill (1838),
courtesy of City of Westminster Archives Centre

without springs' and Sarsaparilla, etc., is one of the earliest extant.
The Surrey's wall-advertisement noticed by *The Times,* then, was a
'poster', with a separately printed 'programme' being sold to patrons at
the door. The playbill's duality was on the way out at this trend-setting
'minor' theatre.[17]

Exhibitions

A subordinate class of the human enterprise group can be noticed before we proceed to bills showing more spectacular dramatic action.

The presenter of a scientific or technical exhibition mounted as a stage show could generate publicity very much in the theatrical style, as in the deliberately dramatic example herewith of a spectral illusion featured on the bill as one of the excitements to be demonstrated in 1827 by 'The Original and Much Improved Ergascopia'.

15. Spectral illusion from a bill for the magic show *Ergascopia* (1827), private collection

At least one showman-magician, J.H. Anderson, advertised his exhibition with successive illustrations on his bills, as Catherine Haill tells us: 'Known as "The Wizard of the North", Anderson's brilliance as a performer was matched by his flair for publicity. Each magical feat is described in antiquated or pseudo-scientific language that conjures up a sense of mystery, and the illustrations on the bills were changed regularly to publicize his many tricks.'

Other showmen, or salesmen, included illustrations on their bills by which they exploited the enticement of their properties. For example a bill for a lecture by 'Mr Franklin' concerning his 'Grand Transparent Orrery' at Bridgnorth in 1831 contains two detailed cuts of spectacular instruments in addition to much descriptive text. An elegant illustration for this genre can be seen here on a bill advertising T.B. Dancer's exposition of glass working in miniature, c. 1830.

The picture occupies one-fifth of the sheet, with text above and below to describe Dancer's demonstration and the many glass objects available for sale or capable of being blown to order.

CURIOSITY HIGHLY GRATIFIED
FOR A SHORT TIME ONLY.

T. B. Dancer,
ARTIST IN GLASS,
(FROM LONDON,)

HAVING had the honour of receiving distinguished Approbation in the principal towns in Norfolk, Suffolk, and Essex, respectfully announces to the Ladies and Gentlemen of HERTFORD and its Vicinity, that he intends making a short stay in this place, to exhibit his most curious, pleasing, and interesting process of

GLASS WORKING,
IN MINIATURE,
Far surpassing any thing of the kind ever yet done by any other Artist.

Glass Spinning, Blowing, Variegating, Twisting, & Linking,
Is now exhibiting in a great variety of articles,
IN A COMMODIOUS ROOM AT

Mr. Austin's, Printer, Fore Street, Hertford:
Where Ladies and Gentlemen may be admitted at ONE SHILLING each, between the Hours of 11 and 4 in the Afternoon, and from 6 to 9 in the Evening ;
For which every Person may receive an Article to the amount of Admission.

Mr. Dancer makes various kinds of Devices, in all colours of Glass, before the Company, for Sale ; and forms Birds and Quadrupeds while the Glass is in a fluid state, without the use of any kind of Instrument whatever. Also makes Necklaces, Feathers, Bandeaus, Baskets of Flowers, ornamental Pens and Points for manifold Writing, Anchors, Crosses, Rings, Cupids, Figures, &c. Blows and forms Imitations of Decanters, Wine Glasses, Tobacco Pipes and Stoppers neatly ornamented, Segar Tubes, Smelling Bottles, Microscopes, Pulse Glasses, and Glasses to imitate the Circulation of the Blood, from Apparatus of his own construction. Mr. D. is enabled to spin out of One Pound of Common Window Glass, 4,000,000 and 30,000 Yards, at

Two Thousand Yards in One Minute,
which, from long experience and intense application, he has brought to the highest degree of perfection, and has had the honour of performing before the first Nobility in the kingdom, and has received universal approbation for his skill in this Art. Mr. Dancer challenges any contemporary Artist to equal the Variety of his Workmanship ; and if ever the like was performed in this Place, by any other person, he will forfeit

FIVE HUNDRED GUINEAS.

Austin, Printer, Hertford.

16. 'Glass-working by T.B. Dancer' on an exhibition bill (c. 1830), courtesy of Hertford Museum

At the other end of the scale, immense panorama exhibitions were popular in the early nineteenth century and their advertisements commonly carried an illustration, either on small scale in the text or as an adjunct. Sometimes the complete panoramic design was included on the bill, relegating the publicity to a footnote. Notable examples of this style are for *The Battle of Trafalgar* and *The Battle of Waterloo* at Barker's

17. Circular panorama on a flier for *The Battle of Trafalgar*, Leicester Square Panorama (early 19th century), courtesy of Hertford Museum

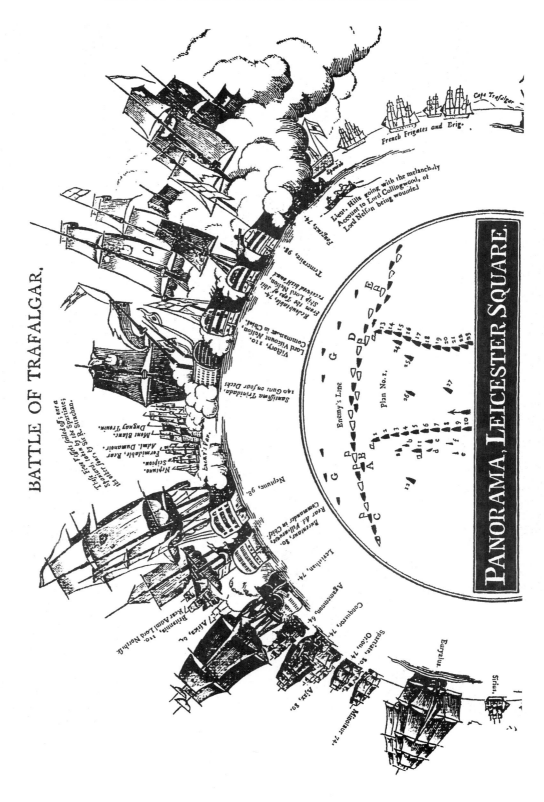

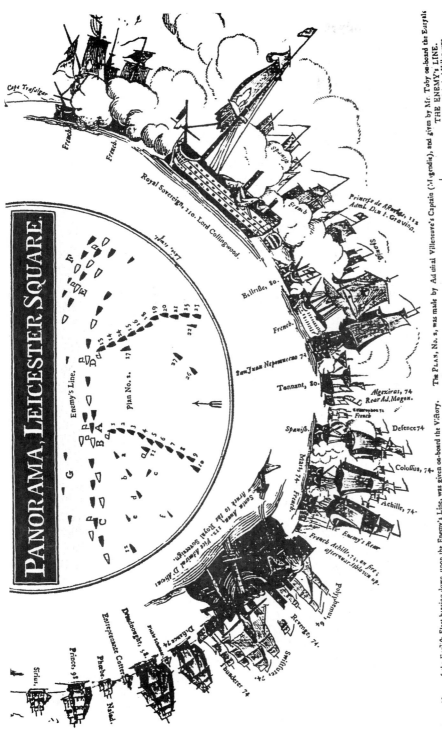

PANORAMA, LEICESTER SQUARE.

THE ENEMY'S LINE.

A Bucentaur, 10 guns, Admiral Villeneuve.
B Santissima Trinidada, 140 guns, Rear-Admiral Cis...
C Formidable, 80 guns, Rear-Admiral Dumanoir.
D Santa Anna, 112 guns, Vice-Admiral D'Alive.
E Principe de Asturias, 112 guns, Vice-Admiral Gravina.
F Squadron of Observation.
G Frigates and Brigs.

The PLAN, No. 2, was made by Admiral Villeneuve's Captain (Magendie), and given by Mr. Toby on-board the Euryalis.

The PLAN, No. 1, of the English Fleet bearing down upon the Enemy's Line, was given on-board the Victory.

REFERENCE TO THE ENGLISH LINE OF BATTLE.

1. Victory, 110 guns, the Right Hon. Lord Viscount Nelson, K.B. Vice-Admiral of the White; Captain J. M. Hardy,
2. Temeraire, 98 guns, Captain E. Harvey.
3. Neptune, 98 guns, Captain J. F. Freemantle.
4. Leviathan, 74 guns, Captain J. Pellew.
5. Conqueror, 74 guns, Captain Sir E. Berry, Bart.
6. Agamemnon, 64 guns, Lieutenant J. Pelfold.
7. Ajax, 80 guns, Lieutenant J. Pilfold.
8. Orion, 74 guns, Captain E. Codrington.
9. Minotaur, 74 guns, Captain C. J. M. Mansfield.
10. Spartiate, 80 guns, Captain Sir F. Laforey, Bart.
11. Britannia, 110 guns, Rear-Admiral Earl Northesk; Captain E. Bullet.
12. Africa, 64 guns, Captain H. Digby.
13. Royal Sovereign, 110 guns, Vice-Admiral Lord Collingwood; Captain E. Rotherham.
14. Belleisle, 80 guns, Captain Hargood.
15. Tonnant, 80 guns, Captain C. Tyler.
16. Bellerophon, 74 guns, Captain J. Cooke.
17. C I flut, 74 guns, Captain J. N. Morris.
18. Achille, 74 guns, Captain Richard King.
19. Polyphemus, 64 guns, Captain Robert Redmill.
20. Revenge, 74 guns, Captain Robert Moorfom.
21. Swiftsure, 74 guns, Captain W. E. Rutherford.
22. Thunderer, 74 guns, Lieutenant J. Stockham.
23. Defiance, 74 guns, Captain P. C. Durham.
24. Mars, 74 guns, Captain G. Duff.
25. Defence, 74 guns, Captain G. Hope.
26. Dreadnought, 98 guns, Captain — Conn.
27. Prince, 98 guns, Captain Richard Grindall.

Frigates.
a Euryalus
b Sirius
c Phoebe
d Naiad
e Pickle Schooner.
f Entreprenante Cutter.

HENRY ASTON BARKER, as Proprietor of the PANORAMA, LEICESTER-SQUARE, takes the liberty of informing the Public, that the various VIEWS, and other Subjects which have been exhibited in it, were taken by him, and painted under his sole Management, during the Life of his Father. He therefore hopes, that the Panorama has for so many Years been honoured, give Satisfaction, by strict and faithful Representation, will entitle him to a Continuance of that Patronage with which the Panorama has for so many Years been honoured.——N. B. A Person always attends to explain the Painting.

Open from Ten till Dusk—Admittance to each Painting, One Shilling.

J. Adlard, Printer, Duke-street, Smithfield.

Leicester Square Panorama. The former has two plans of the sea fight in progress as well as the main 360-degree view of ships in the line of battle (see illustration). As a chart of the engagement in its own right, one can imagine the bill being prized and pored over. Perhaps today's reader may find that it still exerts its fascination even in scaled-down reproduction.[18]

Profuse illustration (juvenile troupes) and bills in series

We have noted already from a number of examples that when illustrated playbills have only one woodcut, whatever the subject, the block usually dominates the sheet from a fairly central position. As also observed, a lesser number have two cuts; fewer still have three or four, usually at the side or in the corners. A modification to this style occurs where some bills contain many cuts, usually very small and concentrating on the star rather than on wider action. Perhaps because juveniles performed acts of the 'Mr Mathews at Home' type which involved jumping in and out of a series of roles, or at least stereotypes, their managers delighted in the sort of advertising in which the text of the bills was accompanied by multiple tiny illustrations. This practice was also adopted, as we have seen, on the dog-drama bill of 1853 for *The French Spy*.

18. 'Master Betty and his Characters' from a contemporary print (c. 1804-5)

By Permission of the Right Worshipful the Mayor and Magistrates.
And patronised, when at Windsor, by her Royal Highness the PRINCESS AUGUSTA.

THEATRE, SHREWSBURY.
FOR TWO EVENINGS ONLY,
On WEDNESDAY, the 10th, and FRIDAY the 12th of August 1825.

Mr. GROSSMITH, Sen. takes this opportunity of laying before the Public the following encomium passed on his Son, kindly pointed out to him by a Clergyman of Dudley; the numerous and repeated Paragraphs which have appeared in all the London and Provincial Papers cannot have escaped the eye of any one; but the work quoted below may probably escape the perusal of many.

Extract from the New Monthly Magazine, No. 45, July 1, 1825, (Page 299.)

" Master Burke betokens a dramatic instinct, which can scarcely be mistaken; but we saw in the country, the other day, a CHILD SEVEN YEARS OLD, " named GROSSMITH, who displayed even a *deeper vein of natural humour*; actually revelling in the jests he uttered and acted : singing droll songs with the " truth of a Musician, and the vivacity of a Comedian; and speaking passages of Tragedy with an earnestness and grace, as though the *dagger* & the *bowl* had " been his playthings, & Poetry his proper language."

Characters in the Introduction which Master Grossmith imitates.

Characters in Pecks of Troubles, which Master Grossmith personates.

1   2   3   4   5   6   7

THE CELEBRATED
INFANT ROSCIUS,
MASTER GROSSMITH,
From Reading, Berks,
ONLY SEVEN YEARS AND A QUARTER OLD,
Intends giving TWO EVENINGS AMUSEMENTS, when he feels confident he will meet with that support he has never failed to experience, in all the Cities and Towns he has visited.

The Infant Roscius will commence his Performance with his
ADVENTURES in the READING COACH
When he will imitate the following Characters, namely,
A Frenchman—a Fat Lady—an Affected Lady—a Tipsy Politician—a Stage Manager— two Candidates for the Stage—and his own Success.

Master Grossmith will then go through the humorous and laughable Comedy of
Pecks of Troubles:
OR, THE
DISTRESS OF A FRENCH BARBER.

(1) Miss Deborah Grundy, (an old Maid in love) .... Master GROSSMITH!
(2) Spindleshanks, (a dandy fortune hunter) .... Master GROSSMITH!!
(3) Monsieur Frizeur, in a Peck of Troubles about cutting old Grundy's face, (with a Song)............ Master GROSSMITH!!!
(4) Old Grundy, in search of the Frenchman to give him a Receipt in full for his Carelessness .... Master GROSSMITH!!!!
(5) Betty the Housemaid, in love with Corporal Rattle, with a Song, "Yes, aye for a Soldier's wife I'll go." Master GROSSMITH!!!!!
(6) Corporal Rattle, as hot as gunpowder, in love with Betty....................... Master GROSSMITH!!!!!.
(7) Timothy Clodhopper, a Servant of all work to old Grundy, bewailing his unfortunate love for Betty, who has run off with Corporal Rattle, with the laughable Song of "The Washing Tub," (which finishes the Peice.) .... Master GROSSMITH!!!!!!

ROLLA.   RICHARD III.

After which, " BETSY BAKER," with other Comic songs.

Part II. Will consist of Scenes from the MERCHANT OF VENICE, DOUGLAS, PIZARRO, MACBETH, RICHARD III. ROLLA, and HAMLET. The INFANT ROSCIUS will on the first night go through the Tent Scene of Richard III. The Scenes will be changed each night, and he will conclude his Performance with a Piece (composed in two Parts expressly for him) on

The Musical Glasses.
The whole of the Scenery, Wardrobe, and Preparations, which are very extensive, with the Grand Diorama, 560 feet in length, will pass through the Precenium during the intervals of Master G.'s Performance, consisting of views in Italy, &c.

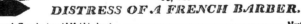

BOXES, 3s.—PIT, 2s.—GALLERY, 1s.

Doors to be opened at half past seven, and the Performance to commence at eight o'clock.—Children under twelve, and Schools, half-price to Boxes and Pit only.—Tickets and Places for the Boxes to be had of Miss Carkswell, Nardol Head.— Tickets may also be had of Master G. from ten to one o'clock on the Days of Performance.

Watton, Printer, Shrewsbury.

19. Various cuts of Master W.R. Grossmith on a bill for Shrewsbury (1825), courtesy of Shropshire Records & Research Unit and the Trustees of the late A.C. Eyton

The trend may have been encouraged by the engraving of 'Master Betty and his Characters' which was produced for the print-sellers when that young phenomenon took the stage by storm in 1804 (see illustration). No less than three subsequent Infant Roscius (or Roscia) troupes can be identified– perhaps there are more– whose publicity embodied a prolific use of illustrative miniatures.

The series of playbills for the touring act of the Grossmith juveniles is the most ambitious of the three. Over the life of the troupe between 1825 and about 1840, in which father William Grossmith presented first one son and then brought in a second, no fewer than eight different designs for their playbills were produced, each displaying anything up to twenty-four small pictorial cameos, or up to three small strips of character effigies with further side pictures. Additionally, most of the eight basic designs had sub-variations. The whole string has been discussed and six of their bills reproduced in an earlier study, the earliest shown there being of 1826. An earlier bill for 10-12 August 1825 containing twenty small images of the 'Infant Roscius, Master Grossmith' has come to light and joins the gallery here to show its pattern. 'Very primitive' (though quaint) the cuts may be, as the boy's descendant George Grossmith observed, but their profusion is remarkable for its day. The pictorial designs developed a decided sense of form and improved in sophistication during the troupe's fifteen-year active life.[19]

The promoter of 'Miss M.H. Carr, the Celebrated Infant Roscia' imitated the design of the playbills established for the Grossmith juveniles. Three bills for her act at Bridgnorth between 29 November and 8 December 1828 each show a similar prolific combination of strips and side-panels. The design re-emerges with images of Adelaide Biddles as the 'Infant Taglioni' at the Bower Saloon in 1846. These show her in twenty-two small cuts at the sides and foot of the bill. There are comparable illustrations for her return act in 1852.[20]

When they played in the same town for a number of days, playbills in series were the norm for the touring juvenile act whether that of the Grossmiths or Miss Carr. The manager slightly varied the number and placing of pictures on his bills for the different perform-ances, as he varied the repertory, though the 'house style' of his playbills stayed recognisably the same.

Beside juveniles, there were adult touring companies that put a sequence of different woodcuts on their playbills for a run of perform-ances in the same locality. When we see such a sequence it is presented in larger woodcuts, one (or rarely two) to a bill rather than in the scattered multiple small images of the juveniles. Examples already mentioned in the text are the six bills for Hull in 1803 of which an example is given earlier, the six 'Fashionable Amusements' of Cooke and Bridges at Bridgnorth between 30 October 1819 and 1 May 1820, and the four representations of the Dog Bruin on the bills for Waterford in March and April 1835; there are more examples in the notes. This was clearly the practice of some permanent theatres with a policy of muscular spectacle like Astley's.

The proprietors of such shows were not only in a position to be open-handed when it came to publicity but were more picture-orientated than their fellows, and, who knows, perhaps more successful.

A profusion of small-scale pictures on illustrated playbills seems to be generally restricted to entertainments featuring those small-scale beings, children or dogs. The picture size enlarges as we move from juveniles to multi-illustrated or large-scale vistaed playbills featuring the human activities of adult performers. A transitional bill has already been mentioned and is now reproduced, that of Ira Aldridge for the Dundee Theatre Royal on 2 June 1848. The upper part of the bill contains a large full-width portrait of 'The Celebrated African Roscius' in triptych-style, while there

20. Various cuts of Ira Aldridge on a bill for Dundee (1848), courtesy of Trustees of the British Library

33

are five smaller cuts in mid-page of action in *The Sicilian Mariner* and *The Virginian Mummy* and three at the foot for *Robinson Crusoe*. A similar pictorial abundance appears on his following bills for 10 and for 12 June.

Large-scale illustration (adult players)

It can be observed that benefits, festivals and other special events sometimes inspired extensive illustration. Jerrold's *Rent Day* and Coleman's *Poor Gentleman* were presented in aid of the Artists' General Benevolent Institution at the St James's Theatre in May 1850. The ARTISTS' AMATEUR PERFORMANCE of these pieces would have had to reach a high standard to match the outstanding quality of illustrations, decoration and typography on their playbill. Though admittedly *sui generis,* it is reproduced as evidence of the peak that could be reached in playbill design of the mid-nineteenth century (see frontispiece). In passing, we note that the performers included such famous names as George Cruikshank, who was approaching the end of his career, and John Tenniel at the beginning of his. The manner in which the cast lists are printed breaks away from the traditional playbill pattern and prefigures the style soon to become standard in the theatre industry's separate 'programmes', though it is not the first to do this; the Theatre Museum has an equally sumptuous cast-listing bill with text in a similar layout which was produced by Charles Kean for the Royal Command Performance at Windsor in 1849.

Apart from such creative and atypical examples, the craze for ballooning in the 1830s spawned several airship illustrations. The 'First Aerial Ship' *The Eagle* appeared on various bills in June 1835, for viewing at the European Aeronautical Society's premises and elsewhere. In 1845 Cremorne Gardens advertised its night-time venture with a picture of a balloon ascent, as can be seen in the reproduction here.

Large pictures of ballooning were aired by the Royal Vauxhall Gardens on a series of bills from 1831 onwards and include cuts of ascents and a two-balloon race. They culminated in an opulent view of the Gardens' own 'Royal Vauxhall Nassau Balloon' in June 1837 ('Seats in the car for ten persons – Gentlemen, 20 gns; Ladies, 10 gns'). The shows at the Vauxhall Gardens come second only to Astley's for the amplitude of their pictorial advertising. The bill for 'Fancy Fair' in 1832 shows us a wide Abbey scene, while not to be outdone in the field of multiple illustrations Vauxhall Gardens devotes an entire half of the large bill for its family fête in July 1831 to a dozen cuts of the rotunda, fireworks, and posturing cherubs.[21]

IT WILL BE MOONLIGHT!

CREMORNE GARDENS

KING's ROAD, CHELSEA.

NIGHT ASCENT

GREEN'S

MONDAY NEXT, AUGUST 18th, 1845,

MR. GREEN, the intrepid Æronaut,

Will make his SECOND ASCENT from these Gardens,
At **TEN O'CLOCK AT NIGHT,** in his

BALLOON!

With the CAR MAGNIFICENTLY ILLUMINATED!

The Amusements of the Evening will be of varied and interesting character, including the surprising ASCENT and DESCENT of

Master LIONEL HERBERT,

Amid Showers of LIQUID FIRE, to and from the Topmost Bough of one of the loftiest Trees surrounding the Illuminated Lawn.

A CONCERT, BALLET and BALL,

Under the Direction of **Mr T. MATTHEWS**, the celebrated Clown of T.R.D.L.

On SUNDAY, the Car which Mr. GREEN made his bed-room and sitting-room for the night, in the turnip-field in Kent, will be placed in the grounds for the view and inspection of the scientific and curious. The following Extract referring to this interesting descent is taken from the 'GLOBE' of August 9th, 1845 :—

" It was Mr. Green's object to alight where he was likely to cause the least possible injury to the produce. He made a few attempts to descend, and at the same time displayed some Bengal lights, but which drew no one to his assistance, when, about 20 minutes past 11, he made choice of a large turnip-field three miles on the other side of Farningham, Kent, the property of Mr Russell, of Horton Kirby, on which he fixed his grappling iron, after having been in the air about 40 minutes. Having got out of the car, and discovering that there was no one nigh, Mr. Green immediately took measures to relieve the balloon of its gas, the first time he had been compelled to do so unassisted. After he had effected that, he made himself a TEMPORARY RESIDENCE FOR THE NIGHT IN HIS CAR. From five to six o'clock in the morning he was employed in walking about, looking for assistance, when he came to the farm-house of Mr. Russell, who, upon being informed by his servant of the visit paid to him, got up immediately and went to the spot where the balloon had alighted. Mr Green arrived at Cremorne Gardens yesterday afternoon about three o'clock, where the greatest anxiety was manifested on account of his long absence."

On SUNDAY no charge for admission is made, but every visitor is expected to take Refreshment to the amount of Sixpence.

Admission on MONDAY, to the Fete! Fun! Balloon Inflation! Ascent! Fireworks! &c. only ONE SHILLING!

The Original Iron Steam Boats from London Bridge and all parts of town, will land passengers right into the Gardens, fare 4d. Omnibusses from every part of London, Islington, Bethnal Green, Mile-end-road, &c fare 6d, Omnibusses in attendance to convey passengers to town to the last hour.

The Fire-works accompanying Mr GREEN in his Ascent by Mr SOUTHBY.

S. G. FAIRBROTHER, Printer, 31, Bow Street, Covent Garden.

21. 'Night Ascent' pictured on a ballooning handbill for Cremorne Gardens (1845),
courtesy of Susan Solomon

FORGET IT NOT.
FRIDAY, June 22nd, 1832,
EDWIN'S
BENEFIT,
Who will for that Evening only appear as
Clown.

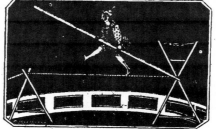

For the first time this season

Edwin's BUFFO GROTESQUE,
AND
COMIC TREMBLING FIT.
Allowed to be one of the most Laughable Scenes ever beheld.

Mr. Edwin will also perform the whole of his Aerial Flights, in particular he will turn a most surprising Somerset through

6 BALLOONS
Over, a number of the Beautiful Coloured Horses.

And lastly a Flying Ascent through a

VOLCANO of FIRE.
FIRST APPEARANCE IN SHREWSBURY OF
Miss EDWIN, 3 Years Old ! !
IN THE CHARACTER OF THE
EMPEROR NAPOLEON,
Mounted on his splendid War Charger.

As this is only intended as an announcement of the above Evening, a full Programme with particulars of Performances will be given in the Bills for Friday.

Cooke's Royal Equestrian Circus, Bridde Street, June 20th, 1832.

FRANCE, PRINTER, MARDOL, SHREWSBURY.

22. Advance pictorial flier for Edwin's clown act, Shrewsbury (1832), courtesy of Shropshire Records and Research Unit and the Trustees of the late A.C. Eyton

The engravings appeal not only to the illiterate but of course to the public at large. The managers' intention is to whet the appetite by showing various intriguing or sensational aspects of the production being advertised. Further bills of this extensively illustrated sort are sometimes seen for particular plays. *The Guerillas,* for example, was publicised on a double-size bill with a full-width spread of large cuts of action scenes which comprise Storming of St Sebastian, Rescue of Julietta, Battlefield by Moonlight and three others.[22]

In the unusual situation where most of the space is taken up with pictures and the text is minimal, as for Astley's *Wars of Wellington* mentioned earlier and the reproduced flier for Signor Hervio Nano at the Adelphi, the bill may have a special function. It may be a poster in advance of the regular playbill– an early foretaste to excite. Revealingly, the pictorially replete example for Edwin's benefit at Shrewsbury on Friday 22 June 1832 informs the viewer that 'As this is only intended as an announcement of the above Evening, a full Programme with particulars of Performances will be given in the Bills for Friday'. Here is the significant and declared début of a graphic poster for advance publicity, as opposed to the normal advertising playbill containing 'particulars of performances'. This example occurred thirty years before the divergence between poster and programme became at all common.[23]

An effort of a similar kind from Sadler's Wells overreaches all the pictorial bills so far mentioned. The eleven cuts on this multi-illustrated flier have been listed as follows:

1st, exterior of the 'Crown and Crozier' public house; Harry Halyard standing over Black Brandon, whom he has felled to the earth, Sam Snatcher standing by him with his hat over his eyes; Watchful Waxend upon a table with a pipe and pot in his hand, Old Sam Sculler and waterman looking on. 2nd, exterior of Dame Halyard's cottage; two of the press-gang pressing Harry Halyard in the king's name; Mary Maybud clinging round his neck, his mother standing by his side. 3rd, quarterdeck of the 'Polyphemus'; Captain Oakheart reprimanding Harry Halyard; officers on each side. 4th, between decks of a slaver; Watchful Waxend firing a pistol out of a cask at Black Brandon, who is in the act of stabbing Harry Halyard in the back with a dagger. 5th, exterior of a fort; general fight between sailors and pirates;

a sailor, with sword in hand, waving the standard on top of the fort. 6th, a mail-coach drawn by four horses, crowded with sailors; one on the top with a purse in his hand, dancing; another with the union jack. 7th, exterior of Mary's cottage, with distant view; Harry Halyard in conversation with Mary; she having read an account of his supposed death, has married his friend Joe Tiller, the knowledge of which she endeavours to keep from him. 8th, a room; Joe Tiller lying dead in the centre; Harry Halyard and Mary kneeling hand-in-hand; watermen and villagers looking on. 9th, full length figure of a sailor, with sword in hand. 10th, full length figure of a waterman. [11th,] Full length figure of a sailor, with a purse in his hand.

This is a description of engravings for Haines's *My Poll and My Partner Joe* (1835) on a showbill which is probably the most comprehensively illustrated of any during the first half of the nineteenth century, as can be judged from the copy herewith.

The bill has been reproduced before.[24] However the provenance of the engravings for it has not been known and can now be divulged. They stem from 'No. 407 – Eleven Engravings for the drama of *My Poll and My Partner Joe*. Forming a crown sheet, to work in two colours, 15in. by 20in.' This is as given in E.J. Bath's *Revised Descriptive Catalogue of Theatrical Wood Engravings,* the detailed entry of which for this play has just been quoted.

23. Flier for *My Poll and my Partner Joe*, Sadlers's Wells Theatre (c. 1840), courtesy of the Trustees of the National Picture Library, Victoria and Albert Museum

39

4. Introducing Bath's Catalogue

About 1865 the Steam Printing Works of E.J. Bath, 'Theatrical Printer' of 26 High Street, Whitechapel and formerly of 43 Leman Street, Whitechapel, London E., published *A Revised Descriptive Catalogue of Theatrical Wood Engravings.* A rare if not unique copy of this catalogue recently came into the hands of one of the few people guaranteed to recognise its value. A leading authority in the field of nineteenth-century theatre, the owner has extended generous good-will in allowing it to be discussed here and reproduced from photocopy.[25] While the catalogue is not itself pictorial, it contains descriptions of over one thousand engravings made available for illustrating posters and playbills. There are about 700 effective numbered entries. The majority deal with a single engraving. A sizable minority of entries, however, describe multiple engravings. Some of these comprise a few only. Others, like no. 407 just quoted for *My Poll and My Partner Joe,* list as one numbered entry up to a dozen separate woodcuts or even more. Many single entries are collages of more than one scene, exemplified by no. 401 for *Mary Clifford* headed 'One engraving embracing three incidents'.

Trade practice

E.J. Bath heads his catalogue by drawing attention to the 'Present Reduced Price List, which... will be found so unprecedentedly low as to defy competition', and goes on:

> E.J.B., in addition to his already large connexion, anticipates an increase in Business in consequence of the Extraordinary Low Prices at which he offers to take every description of printing, and having immense facilities and requisite materials for this class of work above any other House in England, feels assured that his intention of small profits and quick returns will compensate him for the GREAT REDUCTION he has made in the Prices, and place him beyond doubt now the Cheapest Theatrical Printer in London.

The preliminaries give details of marketing practice and prices. Two pages give a schedule of prices.[26] Tickets could be printed for 1s. 2d per 100 white or 1s. 3d coloured. 'Announce bills' in four sizes range from three shillings per 100 on 4to. double-crown slips, 10in. by 15in., to 4s. on double-demy slips, 11in. by 36in. 'Full bills' in two sizes are 4s per 100 on double foolscap, 17in. by 27in., and 5s on double crown, 20 in. by 30in.

Small 'posters' are in two sizes, 7s per 100 on double crown and 8s 6d on double demy, 22in. by 36in., while large posters scale up to '4-sheet', 60in. by 40in. The bills and posters are offered on white and coloured paper for the same price and a price-reduction is given for larger numbers ordered, up to 1,000. Printing in coloured inks costs more, requiring 'a small advance' on the price given for black ink. We can sympathise with the request that 'the copy be plainly written, and as perfect as possible'.

The large engravings are charged separately, in price-brackets per 25, or 50, or 100 copies, ranging from 4s. per 25 for a 1-sheet engraving of 20in. by 30in. to £1-12s per 100 for a 4-sheet engraving of 40in. by 60in. These big pictures occupy Bath's entries nos. 1-370 and are meant for wall-posters. Playbill evidence shows that some of them inspired uncatalogued copies on a smaller scale. Nearly half of Bath's entries, nos. 371-720, come after the heading 'List of small engravings' and can be inserted on bills commissioned from the press 'without extra charge'. Small as some of these are, 3in. by 3in. or so, others are sized for crown or double foolscap. We can take it that these are the woodcuts for playbills (Bath's 'announce bills' and 'full bills') rather than for the huge wall-sheets. Some are duplicates in reduced size of the engravings offered for posters.

It will be noted that this catalogue, being 'revised', is at least a second edition. It appears to retain the same numerical basis and most of the engravings of the previous issue(s), but some old ones are cancelled and it may be assumed that some new entries are added. Predominantly, the plays are popular pieces for the lower end of the market, from roughly the late 1820s onwards. The year *ad quem* is 1865, which was the date written by hand on a sticker on the original thick-paper cover of the catalogue though there is no printed date of publication. This is supported by internal evidence, where Prince Albert (d. 1861) is 'the late' but Lord Palmerston (d. 1865) is not.

The printer preceded the price-lists with an address to managers, professionals and benefit-takers, telling them:

> ...The Wood Engravings will be found adapted (or nearly so) for
> every Play, Pantomime, or Burlesque, on record; this alone will be
> a great saving to Actors and others, who wish to illustrate their
> bills,... thereby saving them the expense and delay of ordering
> wood-cuts expressly. Woodcuts of future pieces engraved to order....

Bath's knowledge of what was 'on record' does not extend to many classic plays. Shakespeare appears in emblematic or burlesque form more often than in his true colours, Sheridan only in *Pizarro*. Certainly as far as melodrama and harlequinades are concerned the range is wide. There are woodcuts for many stage-adaptations based on novels from Scott and Dickens downwards, and on many plays from the French. The dramatic repertory for which Bath offered illustrations was popular rather than polished, and by criteria of 1865 was well-tried rather than up to the minute.

The Engravings

We can now come to details of the engravings, described on 107 close-printed pages of which the last page in the copy-document is a torn fragment only. Essentially they are intended for theatrical use, though some, such as engravings of the royal family, were clearly intended for sale as cheap prints to decorate the home. Of the 720 entries catalogued numerically, 312 are for about 210 plays and pantomimes mentioned by title ('about 210' titles because inconclusive nomenclature sometimes prevents an exact count). Dozens more are for named acts such as those of Bedouin Arabs or Van Amburgh or are identifiable from the naming of a character such as Jem Crow or Mrs Caudle. Twenty-seven entries are not described but marked 'destroyed'. Some entries are late additions to the numbering system, being inserted with 'half' added as a fraction, for example '355½' following the existing 355. The remaining entries, close on 400 of them, are associated with no particular play, act or pantomime but introduce the details with a phrase such as 'Represents the interior of a Cottage', or 'Three Engravings: Nautical', or 'Sylvan retreat of the Fairy Queen'.

Database

An abstract of the catalogue has been entered into a database. Using this, a printout has been prepared that is appended to Part Two. The 700-plus entries have been summarised and sorted alphabetically according to the play-title where known. Entries where the title is not given then follow, sorted in alphabetic order of theme or genre derived from the written description of the engraving(s). For this the following designations are introduced: acrobatics; adaptation; American (+ /slavery); animal act; Arctic; ballooning; biblical; burlesque &c.; circus; crime (+ /historical; /Scottish; /Turkish); dance; dog-drama; domestic (+ /crime); emblematic (+ /Shakespearean; /African &c.); equestrian; foreign (+ /French; /oriental &c.); gold rush; gypsy; historical (+ /domestic; /religious &c.); London;

magical; maritime; masquerade; military (+ /Turkish &c.); migration; minstrels; mythological; pantomime (+ /circus); portrait; Punch; religious; riverine; rustic; Scottish; snowbound; sporting; supernatural; temperance. These are very rough-and-ready designations somewhat imperfectly accomplished, with much overlapping between, for example, 'crime' and 'historical', and with its own ambiguities in variants such as 'Scottish' and 'Crime/Scottish'. Such an abstract would be of limited value without the catalogue itself, but it has the purpose of witnessing to Bath's wide range of topics and can alert researchers quickly to references to a particular play or genre.

The Society for Theatre Research has made the database available free of charge on its website (http://www.str.org.uk). There are no restrictions on non-commercial use, though acknowledgement to Bath's Catalogue, this book and the Society for Theatre Research will be expected in any publication making use of the material for academic purposes. For commercial use in any medium application must be made in advance to the General Editor of Publications, the Society for Theatre Research.[27]

Readers who explore Bath's entries for their own purposes may well wish to amend and extend the present abstract. Anyone using this material in a database program can of course sort the fields *ad lib,* and evoke information from keywords according to interest. Others who may not be able to download the database for any reason, but wish to augment or modify the abstract by hand, should feel free to make a personal-use photocopy of it and work on that if they wish not to mark the book copy.

The list of summarised descriptions on the database is necessarily brief in the extreme. For example, Bath's entry no. 436 appears in the catalogue as follows:

> One engraving for the drama of *The Wreck of the Royal George,* 7x5in. The open sea; the Royal George sunk, all but the rigging and sails, to which seven seamen and an officer are clinging, some waving their hats for signals of distress; a boat with a female and two men inside, saving some of the crew from a watery grave; also a boat the other side, with two men in it, one throwing out a rope.

Much as this vivid picture deserves to be treated with respect, the one-line compression of the database reduces it to '436 / Wreck of the Royal George / maritime / Royal George all but sunk'. It is open to those who download or rework the database to fill out the descriptive field for themselves.

5. Case studies of selected plays and their illustrations

Some of the playbill illustrations already mentioned have an origin in Bath's catalogue. As well as that for *My Poll and My Partner Joe,* others are for Van Amburgh's act with his large cats (Bath's entries no. 282 and no. 496, one cut equating with the illustration reproduced), and for *The Guerillas* (Bath's entries no. 42, no. 376 and no. 377). Some plays and their illustrations relating to the catalogue invite more extensive treatment.

Mazeppa

The couplet given as a motto at the beginning of this book was written with unwitting prescience some years before a version of *Mazeppa; or, the Wild Horse of Tartary* was adapted from Byron's poem by Henry Milner and first performed at the Coburg Theatre in 1823, followed by the lastingly-popular revised version for Astley's Amphitheatre in April 1831.

Over the next thirty-odd years at least three motley sights illustrating the identical precious scene from the piece were put out on the bills. They show an uncomfortably supine Mazeppa tied to the back of his homesick charger during its unstoppable Wild Career over the steppes from Poland to its Tartar birthplace, this being young Mazeppa's punishment for making up to his master's wife (so Byron; his master's daughter, Milner). Reproductions of the series here show that the earliest picture has the crudest finish. First put out by Astley's in May 1831, it went on being used for years by various theatres; it is illustrated here from an almost precise copy on a later provincial playbill. It did not satisfy the Royal Amphitheatre's management for long. Ducrow and West replaced it with the second picture of 1833 onwards (shown from an Astley's bill of 1836), which is a more refined version of the first basic image to display the vulture circling more viciously and with an addition of rocks to the middle ground on the right.

Later still the playbill picture of this scene was again replaced. It is shown here from an Astley's bill, undated but about 1864-65. Its new setting includes the shrubs, rocks and water in the foreground and forest in the background as before, together with accompanying wolves; but the lightning and vulture are missing, the Wild Horse looks even wilder going in the opposite direction from the earlier bills and appears to be entering the water rather than leaving it, while Mazeppa, unexpectedly androgynous, is without his breeches and has every right to look concerned about the security of his G-string. Naked, certainly, Mazeppa was supposed to be. That state was described by Byron in a neat oxymoron ('Thus bound in nature's nakedness') and bluntly ('tout nu') in the poem's inspiration, a brief passage from Voltaire. The playbills, and no doubt the productions, of the 1830s-50s at least allowed Mazeppa a pair of drawers. No such prudishness swayed the American dancer-actress Adah Isaacs Menken, for it was she who starred in Astley's 1864 revival and whose superb physique the playbill-artist discreetly suggested. She played the episode of the ride with 'magnificent audacity' (reverent phrase) in what spectators descried as a 'state of virtual nudity'. Of course she wore fleshings, but soft theatrical gaslight allowed much play to the imagination.

The headlong course of the animal was mocked in a short *Punch* review of two *Mazeppas* in 1851, simultaneously presented at Astley's Amphitheatre on the south bank and at the Marylebone Theatre in Church Street, Paddington. The writer pretended not to understand how it was that, on the same night,

> the wild horse of the desert has been urging on his wild career through the Steppes of Tartary near the steps of Westminster Bridge, as well as some other Steppes that have been lately got up, for the purpose, at Paddington.... Such... [is] theatrical life.... We can imagine, however, some little difficulty among the unaccustomed horses, for *Mazeppa*, entrusted to the hands or legs of a new stud, will entail the necessity for a new study. We can, nevertheless, imagine the groom, with a few yards of pack-thread, enticing the unaccustomed animal into a 'wild career', and the stage carpenter behind the brute with a couple of property wolves in profile....

We can view that satiric fancy, with the addition of a bird of prey worked from the flies. It was enshrined in late 1851 by John Tenniel in one of the earliest cartoons that he drew for *Punch* at the outset of his fifty years as a contributor.[28]

The second Astley's *Mazeppa* playbill of 1836 is an obvious refinement of the first of 1831. Its third of 1864, though a new picture, shares a correspondence with the others. Significant entries for this scene are listed by E.J. Bath.

The catalogue has three entries for *Mazeppa*. Nos. 209 and 231 are poster-scenes of the bound victim on horseback. No. 209 is simply described as '"Mazeppa" bound to the Wild Horse', to which no. 231 adds 'figures restraining the horse, rocky mountains in distance'. Entry no. 462

24. (above) 'The Wild Career' established: the earliest illustration for *Mazeppa*, first introduced on playbills for Astley's Amphitheatre in May 1831 and shown here in a close copy on a later provincial playbill, private collection. 25. (below) 'The Wild Career' refined: from a bill for *Mazeppa*, Astley's (1836), courtesy of Minet Library, London Borough of Islington

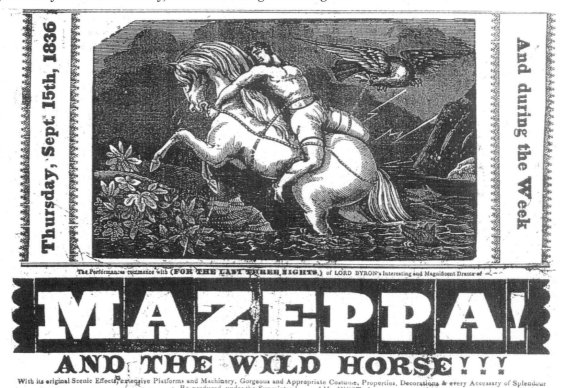

26. (above) 'The Wild Career' surpassed: Adah Isaacs Menken on a playbill for *Mazeppa* at Astley's (c. 1864), courtesy of Templeman Library, University of Kent at Canterbury

27. (below) 'The Wild Career' revealed: backstage at *Mazeppa* in a cartoon by Tenniel from *Punch* (1851)

describes three smaller woodcuts of which the second and third scenes relate to the Astley's playbills of 1831 and 1836. In full, the entry reads:

No. 462 – Three engravings for the drama of *Mazeppa*. **1st,** 6in. by 4½in., A forest with large trunk of a tree lying across.... **2nd,** 6½in. by 4in., A forest; horse partly in a pool of water, madly plunging onwards, bearing on his back a man bound with cords; two wolves following him; an eagle hovering above him; lightning. **3rd,** 2in. by 1½in., Ditto.

The catalogue entry for '2nd' refers to 'forest' but no rocks. It therefore seems to relate to the playbill illustration's earliest edition of 1831. Modifications such as were made to the *Mazeppa* illustration are not listed in the catalogue, unless they silently replaced the earlier woodcuts. This leaves wide open the questions both of revision and also of authorisation (or more likely lack of it) once Bath's original had been supplied.

Sadler's Wells was another theatre that went to town with *Mazeppa*. A fragile example of its bill of 1843 has kindly been made available for reproduction here. Mention is made of the scenic master Fenton's panorama in front of which the Wild Career will take place (with

28. End of 'The Wild Career': from a *Mazeppa* playbill for Sadler's Wells (1843), private collection

48

the horse presumably on scruto fitted over or inset into the lid of the Sadler's Wells tank), and we observe a new engraving for the Career's climax when 'The Exhausted and Worn-out Steed... sinks Beneath his Fatigue'. By the look of it, Mazeppa in his bonds will be lucky to get free without his leg being crushed by the collapse of the Worn-out Steed.

Despite *Mazeppa's* reality in performance being inevitably different from the stirring pictures on the bills, audiences found the piece profoundly satisfying, both here and across the Atlantic where, again, illustrations for *Mazeppa* seem to have been in demand. An engraving for the popular Wild Career scene is given in the specimen-book of theatrical cuts distributed by the Ledger Job Printing Office, Philadelphia, c. 1875. The posture of the horse and body on the American *Mazeppa* poster is very close to the Templeman Library's example of c.1864-5, and the direction and foreground also have affinities with the Astley's bills. In this case the similarities may be a coincidence. On inspection, most of the American posters for the plays pirated from Britain seem to be original compositions. Nonetheless it is evident that British models were used occasionally, for example an imitation of the picture on a bill for Andrew Halliday's *Notre Dame; or the Gipsy Girl of Paris* (1871) – and indeed models, it may be, in earlier cases from Bath's press.[29]

The Dog of Montargis

Bath's catalogue entry no. 76 reads as follows:

No. 76 – 4-sheet, 60in. by 40 in. On the right is a dog with a lantern in its mouth, on the left, Dame Gertrude is looking amazed. Engraved for the *Dog of Montargis*.

This woodcut appears on a number of bills for the play at various theatres, though much reduced in size from its '4-sheet' original. Illustrated here from a Hartlepool bill of *c.* 1840, it provides another case of use being made by managers of an illustration that seems to issue from the Bath catalogue.

The play's full title is *The Dog of Montargis; or, the Forest of Bondy*. It was alternatively known as *The Forest of Bondy; or, the Dog of Montargis* – an example of a piece of which the title and sub-title were thought to be equally appealing at the time and used in either order with little apparent discrimination.

William Barrymore rendered Pixérécourt's *Le Chien de Montargis* (1814) into English soon after it was first given at Paris. Translation into German followed. Goethe had been appointed to the directorship of the Weimar Court Theatre in 1791 with a mission of dramatic reform. He withdrew in 1814– 'The stage is for people, not dogs!'– when provoked by an intrigue against him in which the Hund von Montargis was a poodle appearing in a comic version of the play. Subsequently Goethe blew the gaff on the way that stage-dogs were trained to take the seize: by seeking a lump of sausage-meat hidden under the flesh-coloured collar or neck-scarf of the one to be pounced upon.

The robust appetite of the British public kept *The Dog of Montargis* in the repertory until at least 1880, when the piece was given in the last week of the Royal Victoria's life as a theatre before Emma Cons got the place going again as a music-hall. It has yet to be established how soon after 1814 the play's *soi-disant* 'Dragon', Dog of Montargis, was pictured on the playbills for the piece.

The reproduction of Dragon bounding to the rescue with lantern in jaws is taken from a printer's copy for Hartlepool. This copy includes cast-amendments for a subsequent production but with Dragon continuing to be played by 'the Wonderful Dog Hector'. This is the best known though not the only image printed on playbills for this play. As with *Mazeppa,* later productions were thought to need a new picture. In keeping with the showman's desire for continual novelty even the sub-title of the play received a going-over. A black-printed poster on bright yellow paper for a production in 1874 at the Coxhoe Theatre near Newcastle-on-Tyne tells us that the play is now called *The Dog of*

29. 'Dragon to the Rescue': from a playbill for *The Dog of Montargis,*
Hartlepool (c. 1840)

Montargis; or, the Murder in the Wood though it still stars the ageless 'Wonderful Performing Dog Hector' as Dragon. The picture on the Coxhoe poster shows a dramatic climax at pistol-point in which Dragon is taking the seize. The new picture loses the background of the earlier one but has the clarity that better reproductive techniques were bringing to this form of popular art.[30]

ON MONDAY EVENING, NOV. 30th, 1874,
Will be enacted

The DOG of MONTARGES
OR, THE MURDER IN THE WOOD,

30. 'Dragon taking the Seize': from a poster for *The Dog of Montargis*, Coxhoe (1874), courtesy of Tyne and Wear Archives Service

Dick Turpin

The celebrated Turpin was never far from the public consciousness. Astley's presented *Richard Turpin the Highwayman* in 1819. The story took off again with Harrison Ainsworth's gothic pastiche *Rookwood* (1834) which included the novelist's invention of the highwayman's ride to York to establish an alibi– or, rather, the

51

31. 'Leaping the Tollgate': from a playbill for *Dick Turpin* (c. 1835-40), courtesy of Templeman Library, University of Kent at Canterbury

novelist's working of an old myth into Turpin's scenario. Dramatisation followed fast, notably at Astley's again, where *Dick Turpin's Ride to York* opened in August 1834. This was another Milner piece, for which, as has already been mentioned earlier under 'Horses' at Astley's, there was a playbill with an engraving of Turpin and Black Bess leaping the tollgate at Hornsey. Later Powell, Ducrow's successor, played it on tour. The *Dick Turpin* spectacular, or G.D. Pitt's stage version of Ainsworth as *Rookwood,* stayed popular in the suburban and provincial playhouses for at least the next two decades.

The first illustration for *Dick Turpin* here closely equates with Bath's description of a woodcut for it. It is reproduced from a playbill *circa* the late 1830s for an unnamed theatre. Entry no. 463 in the *Catalogue* itemises 'Eight Engravings for the drama of *Dick Turpin'* of which the first is described thus:

> 1st, 8-in. by 6-in., Exterior of the toll-house; Dick Turpin mounted on his mare, Black Bess, who is leaping the gate; toll-keeper looking at him in an attitude of astonishment; two officers pursuing him in the distance.

The second version here of this playbill illustration, from around the 1840s, is owed to Robert Wood, *The Victorian Provincial Printer and the Stage,* from the same press as the Hartlepool bill for *The Dog of*

32. 'Leaping the Tollgate' rehashed: from a playbill for *Dick Turpin*, Hartlepool (c. 1840)

Montargis above. The *Turpin* pictures are almost identical, but Wood's loses the 'two officers pursuing him in the distance' and is slightly cruder in finish. It seems to be a copy redrawn from the Bath original, though unlike the first and second *Mazeppa* playbills the second *Turpin* picture is less refined than the first. Its existence implies that not only theatre managers and artistes but also printers elsewhere– in this case Hartlepool– were purchasing, or pinching, Bath's engravings.

Ainsworth's *Rookwood* went quickly into a number of editions, with illustrations by Sir John Gilbert and others. One of these editions was issued in 1836, 'a beautiful volume with designs by George Cruikshank' as Laman Blanchard tells us in his memoir of Ainsworth. One of Cruikshank's steel engravings for *Rookwood*, 'The Hornsey Gate', is comparable to but not identical with the playbill's woodcut. Some of the remaining woodcuts of Bath's entry no. 463 follow Cruikshank's choice of scenes to illustrate, for example Black Bess at speed and the death of Black Bess in the forest, but without playbill examples no further connection can be hazarded.[31]

The Cruikshank element can however be pursued more closely in other stage-adaptations. Many of Cruikshank's series of etchings were highly dramatic, whether intended as conversation pieces or book illustrations. They influenced scene designers as well as theatrical printers.

Oliver Twist and Jack Sheppard

Dramatisations that drew on Cruikshank's work for illustration of one sort and another included versions of Dickens's *Oliver Twist* and another Ainsworth romance, *Jack Sheppard*. E.J. Bath was not far behind.

Bath's *Catalogue* has four entries for *Oliver Twist*. Two are essentially emblematic, being simple portrait figures of 'a boy with stick and bundle on his shoulder' (no. 295) and Bill Sikes with 'his celebrated bull-dog' (no. 323). However, readers possessing an edition of *Oliver Twist* that contains Cruikshank's engravings might like to compare three of them with Bath's playbill offerings. It is conceivable that the artist for Bath's entry no. 324, at Jacob's Well, took an interest in Cruikshank's book-picture entitled 'The Last Chance' but thought it was not good enough and vigorously proceeded to outdo it. Cruikshank contented himself with showing Sikes noosing a chimney stack on the rooftop and his dog perching unhappily on the ridge; Bath's description offers 'the Thames by moonlight', officers of justice gaining the roof and Sikes being haunted and then shot by Oliver. The dog is understandably omitted, but the greater detail of the Bath illustration would have had more pulling power on the playbills.

A closer parallel occurs in Bath's fourth entry for this play, no. 409. This is a demy-sheet of ten engravings, to be worked 'in two colours'. The descriptions of five of these bear resemblance to Cruikshank's originals, two of them closely. One of the two is of 'Oliver on the doorstep of Mrs Maylie's house, the door open, servants looking at him amazed'. The other is of the meeting under the bridge, captioned by Cruikshank merely as 'The Meeting'. Bath's cataloguer described the press's woodcut for this scene as 'Southwark side of London Bridge; steps leading down to the river; Nancy disclosing her secrets of Fagin to Rose Maylie and Mr Brownlow; Noah Claypole listening', terms which would do equally well to summarise the Cruikshank engraving.

The copying of Cruikshank's book-illustrations for the design of playbills was fully evident following the publication of Harrison Ainsworth's *Jack Sheppard* in 1839. Furthermore, the scenery in at least three of the stage versions that were rushed out owed much to Cruikshank. His influence is also seen in the frontispieces to the printed play-texts. The writer's separate study of '*Jack Sheppard* Plays and the Influence of Cruikshank' discusses the matter, and includes the reproduction of an exceptional playbill (currently on display in the Theatre Museum) for *Jack Sheppard* at the Adelphi Theatre which contains no fewer than twelve cuts of the action, closely modelled on Cruikshank's plates for Ainsworth's novel.[32]

E.J. Bath offered numerous examples of *Jack Sheppard* motifs, some clearly based on the great engraver's book illustrations. Typical of Bath's reflection of Cruikshank is a woodcut of the carpenter's workshop in which Jack Sheppard is carving his name on a beam. Cruikshank's original is a most harmonious realisation of Ainsworth's elaborate description and was apparently copied in detail by Bath, as follows:

No. 421. One engraving for the drama of *Jack Sheppard,* 4-in. by 6-in. Interior of Wood's workshop; a bench in the centre, with planes, a glue-pot, an oil-stone, &c., upon it: Jack standing upon a three-legged stool to reach the beam, upon which he is carving his name; Owen Wood behind a plank watching him; some saws, squares, compasses, &c., hanging against the wall, also various placards stuck about.

33. Cruikshank's engraving of 'The Name on the Beam' for Ainsworth's *Jack Sheppard*

Bath's entries for *Jack Sheppard* provide the most for any one piece. In this the *Catalogue* aligns with the excessive number of different dramatisations of the book– a dozen or more– that came out in the autumn of 1839. The large engravings for posters are no. 219 (the Tyburn hanging) and then nos. 318-322. A note added to no. 219 states 'Various other Engravings connected with this Drama may also be had', which may indicate that the extra cuts were catalogued subsequently to take advantage of the frenzied popularity of the play. Entry nos. 420-424 are of a size for playbills. Some identical pictures are offered in both large and small scales, for example no. 321 and no. 420(4). The famous name-carving scene first appears in 322(1) and then in 420(1) and 422 as well as 421 quoted above. Altogether ten scenes are included in nos. 420-424, all available 'without extra charge' on playbills printed by the firm. Bath cannot be accused of stinting his customers, though we do see that the blocking in of a woodcut might save some type-setting work.

The Bottle and The Drunkard's Children

We can notice two of Cruikshank's independent publications that inspired dramatisation and entries in Bath's catalogue. The *Bottle* series of etchings had a somewhat tortuous origin in four engravings that Cruikshank first produced for *The Blessings of Temperance*, a poem by John O'Neill. When Cruikshank took the pledge he re-worked and expanded this moral exercise. T.P. Taylor's abstinence play, *The Bottle* (1847), took its theme and its scenes from the eight Cruikshank *Bottle* engravings. Bath offers merely two poster-sized cuts for this play, nos. 38 and 183. The resemblance of the descriptions of these to the cartoonist's work is uncertain.

Cruikshank followed up with another eight-strong series in 1848 called *The Drunkard's Children,* immediately dramatised by Reynoldson for the Surrey Theatre. For this Bath offered two composite entries which do appear to offer homage to Cruikshank, no. 190 (six scenes of children's rise and fall) and no. 393 (eight scenes of principal incidents). Allardyce Nicoll says that Cruikshank directed the Surrey's production of *The Drunkard's Children.* It is a fair guess that even if he did not actually 'direct' it himself he was involved in the design and staging preparations, as he had been for the Surrey's *Jack Sheppard.* The illustrations for *The Drunkard's Children* described in Bath's catalogue, especially the long entry for the 'tableaus' in no. 393 *(q.v.),* may thus be taken as not only a reflection of the original Cruikshank engravings but a possible reflection of the actual staging at the Surrey Theatre.[33]

Scenic descriptions, and Don Caesar de Bazan

Some interest, then, stems from those entries of Bath's catalogue, such as those for adaptations from Cruikshank, which provide us with scenic descriptions. It seems immaterial whether the original performances were set against a panorama as with *Mazeppa,* or built pieces with a backing (drop or shutters) as with *My Poll and My Partner Joe,* or a combination of all as for *Dick Turpin.* Where woodcuts on particular bills can be assigned to Bath's engravings as with these three plays and others, they can be compared with the catalogue description. A high degree of correlation transpires, even (within the limitations of verbal description) exactitude. Should one take the bold but perhaps not entirely unjustified step of conjecturing that, even if conventionalised or exaggerated, the engravings may reflect or inspire the disposition of scenery, set-dressing and action of the play in production (which is, after all, the message they purported to convey to potential customers): then the catalogue's written descriptions of engravings can complement information from any other sources of illustration, and for pieces which are not known pictorially from other sources the catalogue may give useful pointers to what they looked like on stage.

A straightforward example of this appears in the catalogue for *Don Caesar de Bazan*. Bath's entry no. 192 ('Three-sheet, 60in. by 30in.') offers the following engraving to attract the customer's eye to publicity for the piece:

> Magnificent hall with lofty pillars, in the distance the city and lake by moonlight, groups of ladies and cavaliers ascending marble steps, in the centre of the hall a couch. R.H., table with splendid vases and flowers, chamberlain with wand, announcing a visitor. L.H., a table with writing implements upon it, Don Caesar starting up in chair with a paper in his hand. Duenna and lady looking on with astonishment, on either side of the figure of Don Caesar seated. Engraved for *Don Caesar de Bazan*.

The original French play was by Dumanois and Dennery, loosely based on Hugo's *Ruy Blas* to exploit the characters of Don César and Maritana. Rendered into half-a-dozen English versions between 1844 and 1865, the two leading adaptations were by Gilbert à Beckett and Mark Lemon for the Princess's Theatre, and by Boucicault and Webster for the Adelphi. Lesser figures worked the piece up for the Olympic, the Grecian, Marylebone and Sadler's Wells, among them Thomas Archer, Charles Webb, and Irving's friend and mentor Tom Mead. A metamorphosis by Fitzball produced the libretto for Wallace's opera *Maritana*. Should such a varied concatenation invite critical interest, the Bath description could be relevant.

Jonathan Bradford

Woodcuts may appear on some playbills that differ in substance from Bath's *Catalogue* even if it offers an apparently similar scene. Presumably these either emanate from a source other than Bath's Steam Printing Works or show a divergence from Bath's woodcut not included in the catalogue, like the *Mazeppa* variants noticed above. The renowned multiple setting for *Jonathan Bradford* as illustrated on Scottish playbills shows the 'Front section of the George Inn divided into four apartments'. In the top left a man (Caleb) is asleep on a chair beside a bed with a figure (Macraisy) outside the window. In the top right, another man (Hayes) is being attacked by an assailant (Macraisy). The ground-floor exterior of the George Inn appears below this first storey with sets of windows left and right

34. The 'four-in-one' scene from *Jonathan Bradford*, Edinburgh (1833), courtesy of the editors of Theatre Notebook

through which figures within can be discerned (see illustration).

A similar cut appears on a bill for Dundee in April 1834 with the following informative addition:

> The whole of the above scene is entirely new, and has been constructed from drawings made for the occasion by Mr Donaldson; the ingenious contrivance by which the action of the Drama is carried on in four different apartments, all under the view of the spectators at the same moment, has been honoured with the warmest approbation of the London audience, and a facsimile is now respectfully submitted to the notice of the public of Dundee.[34]

Fitzball's stage directions for the setting of act II, scene v in the printed script of *Jonathan Bradford* make the intention clear:

> Exterior of the Inn, divided into Four Apartments. (No. 1) [i.e. left upper]. A Two Bedded Room, with window opening to a tiled roof. One bed or sofa (practicable) the other just on; a chair, L; table near bed, with a written newspaper on it. (No. 2) [i.e. right upper]. A One Bedded Room, with a window opening to the same tiled roof; table R, and chair. (No. 3) [i.e. left lower]. Little Back Parlour; table and two chairs in centre seen through the window. (No. 4) [i.e. right lower]. The bar seen through window – punch bowl – glass of brandy and water, &c., on bar; in centre of all a door, and sign of the 'George Inn'.

Clearly echoing the first two and last of Fitzball's 'apartments', Bath's entry no. 221 (single sheet, 30in. by 20in.) offers:

> View of the 'George Inn', shewing, L.H., a sleeping apartment, Mr Hayes asleep in chair, Dan Macraisy entering window. R.H., apartment, bed, table, and chair, Mr Hayes dead on the floor. Beneath, bar of the innkeeper Jonathan Bradford. Bradford on his knees, Ann Bradford clasping her hands with grief, man shewing bloody knife, soldiers with muskets. R. and L., sign up, 'the George Inn'. Engraved for *Jonathan Bradford*.

The playbill for the Surrey Theatre's original production of *Jonathan Bradford* (12 June 1833) describes this scene, without woodcut, as:

Another View of the Inn, showing also the Inner Apartment:
In this peculiar scene, an effort will be made so to harmonize Four Actions, as to produce
ONE STRIKING EFFECT!
The Murder of Mr Hayes: – Arrival of the Soldiery: –Apprehension of Bradford.

We can correct the catalogue's lapses in the 'L.H.' description whereby Caleb is called 'Mr Hayes' and Macraisy is assumed to be entering rather than departing through the window– and note from these lapses that the description therefore appears not to have derived from the written text of the play. Otherwise Bath's engraving seems more graphic than the one on the Scottish playbills and is closer to the Surrey's written description of the four-in-one setting, while at the same time showing sequential episodes from the play's action.

This leads us to another caveat. Where stage directions in the playscript can be referred to, they may differ from the descriptions contained in catalogue entries for engravings. The last-discussed example has demonstrated that artist's licence might compress the actions on stage by showing, as though they are simultaneous, bits of business that take place separately.

Multiple Settings

The multiple setting of 1833 for *Jonathan Bradford* is the best known example of compartmental staging. It is rare but not unique. Fitzball came up with another one six months later, *Walter Brand; or, the Duel in the Mist,* as George Speaight has informed us. Some kind of multiple setting seems to be projected for *The Gamblers* (Surrey Theatre, 1823, attributed to Milner). It is definitely called for in Greenwood's *Jack Sheppard* for Sadler's Wells in 1839 in which the main escape scene effectively presents action in five contiguous Newgate locations.

E.J. Bath produces another instance of this intriguing genre, not previously noticed:

No. 254, Two-sheet, 40in. by 30in. Section of a house open to the audience. Upper chamber, L.H., man kneeling to a clergyman. Upper chamber, R.H., female lying on bed; rooms beneath filled with company. Engraved for *The Adventures of a Gentleman.*

This play by Mark Lemon (Olympic Theatre, October 1842) appears not to have been printed but can be found in the Lord Chamberlain's Plays. [35]

A further example may be provided by entry no. 37 for an unnamed play, to which we return in the last section below.

The Courier of Lyons

Action-illustrations like those just referred to are likely to use the multiple settings to display sequential episodes as though they

THE COURIER OF LYONS.

A DRAMA, IN THREE ACTS.

BY B. WEBSTER.

First Performed at the Adelphi Theatre, March 10th, 1851.

Dramatis Personæ.

[See p. 8.

Jerome Lesurques	(The innkeeper of Luisant)		Mr. O. Smith.
Joseph Lesurques	(His Son)		} Mr. Leigh Murray.
Dubosc	(The Assassin)		}
Didier	(Betrothed to Julie Lesurques)		Mr. G. Lee.
Joliquet	(Waiter at the Inn of Lieursaine)		Mr. J. Rogers.
Lambert	{ Friends of Lesurques and Brother }		Mr. O J. Smith.
Guerneau	{ Collegians of Courriol }		Mr. Hastins.
Daubenton	(A Magistrate)		Mr. Parselle.
Choppard	(A Horsedealer, alias The Irresistible)		Mr. P. Bedford.
Courriol	(A Fashionable)		Mr. C. Selby.

1,035. Dicks' Standard Plays.

35. Attack at the inn: frontispiece to The Courier of Lyons,
Dicks' Standard Plays no. 1035

are simultaneous. A less complex example than that of *Jonathan Bradford* would be of an illustration showing two sequential episodes within a single frame. A paradigm can be found in Webster's *Courier of Lyons* of 1851 (forerunner of Reade's *Lyons Mail* of 1877). The scene-setting for act I, scene ii of this play as given in Dicks' plays no. 1,035 is as follows:

Fore-part of an inn. Table near the door. The highroad at back. House bell. Chamber at the back with bottles, glasses; another door leading from it, three steps leading down to the cellar in sight of the audience. It is getting dark....

61

During the course of the scene the script enjoins that 'the mail[coach] is seen in the extreme distance coming'; presumably the author intended a panorama effect on the 'highroad at back'. The audience is to imagine it approaching when the noise of whips, wheels, horn etc. is heard increasingly loudly. The coach does not arrive on stage though, merely its postilion and the courier. Then the play's action develops, in sequence, as follows: first one, and then the other, of these two characters from the mail-coach are shot by the assassin Dubosc; his accomplices drag on a chest from off-stage after being understood to have robbed the coach; the proceeds get shared out; Jerome Lesurques makes an alarmed appearance and is shot 'through the shoulder' by Dubosc.

For this play Bath's catalogue shows 'no. 55. – Two sheet, 30in. by 40in.' of which the two engravings 'can be used singly if required':

> The top sheet represents the exterior of the Inn, at Lieursant, with cellar beneath; woody country with winding mail road; Dubosc in the act of shooting Jerome Lesurges [sic], the innkeeper, while his companions are robbing the Mail. The second sheet represents the Place de Grove (etc.).... Engraved for the *Courier of Lyons*. Room for name of Theatre and date.

No table, no rear chamber on the first sheet here, but a picture with the simultaneous view of two sequential events from the play, the shooting and the robbery, of which one is seen on stage and one is only described.

Identical compression to that shown in the description of Bath's woodcut can be seen on Dicks's title-page for this play. The background of this cut displays the coach being robbed (which is not seen on stage) while Dubosc, pistol in hand, stands over a fallen figure in the foreground (which is seen on stage). The correlation here between Bath's description and Dicks's realisation makes one wonder if there was some arrangement between the two printing houses.

More practically, we need to recognise a difference between illustrations of scenery and those showing stage action. The former may *(may)* be adequate pointers to the settings produced by the designers and scene-painters. However, while illustrative wood-cuts of action and business, and their written descriptions, also may *(may)* sometimes be adequate pointers to the action on stage, as seems to be likely for *Jack Sheppard,* an even more rigorous judgment must be exercised on images that juxtapose disparate events and represent an idealised over-view. These call for the most cautious dissection and evaluation.

The Battle of Waterloo

One more such idealisation from the catalogue is a case in point. In the text of Amherst's *Battle of Waterloo* (1824) a detailed scenario for the final 'Grand Battle' occupies the whole of 'scene last'. After much action this ends:

> ...The Cuirassiers approach [the Guards], are defeated, Bonaparte flies, and the Prussians arriving, the Victory is decided in favour of the English and Allied Troops.
> GRAND MILITARY TABLEAU.

Bath's catalogue offers this engraving as entry no. 355½ (that is, 355a after previous no. 355):

> Three sheet, 60in. by 30in. The field of Waterloo. English and French soldiers engaged in battle; on the left hand the Duke of Wellington and staff on horseback; in the centre, men and horses lying dead and wounded; on the right hand Napoleon and staff retreating, the whole forming a grand picture of *The Battle of Waterloo*.

While it is tempting to speculate that this may represent how Davis and Ducrow actually ended the 'Grand Battle' in performance at Astley's, it is safer to assume that Bath's massive engraving would have offered a view that is more of an imaginary construct than even nominal stage-picture. Hence the category 'emblematic' in the genres listed in the summary, to identify the woodcuts where this quality seems unarguable as well as the woodcuts whose purpose is clearly totemic, such as Bath's no. 300, simply entered in both catalogue and database as 'A flag'.

The Idiot of the Mountain

For our last case let us find a more positive correlation between stage and woodcut. We can be amused by the branch-hanging and perilously eavesdropping heroine on a Surrey Theatre handbill for W.E. Suter's *Idiot of the Mountain,* adapted from the French of Grangé and Thibout (see illustration).

The production itself showed 'one of those curious scenes in which the art of the painter becomes all-important in carrying out the intention of the author,' said *The Times* in its review following the play's opening on 7 September 1861. The review goes on to describe how the conversation of the two rival plotters, Caussade and the smuggler Ravel, is overheard by the heroine, Jeanne, who to get information

36. Flier for *The Idiot of the Mountain*, Surrey Theatre (1861), courtesy of Southwark Local Studies Library

helpful to her father 'is suspended from the branches of a tree which grows on the opposite side of the chasm, and almost reaches the rude dwelling'. Lightning strikes her branch, she 'falls into the abyss', clambers up hurt on the cottage side and falls into Ravel's hated hands. She is rescued by Claude, the idiot, after he 'ascends the crags to save her'. The reviewer sums up:

It should be remarked that the interior of the cottage and the exterior landscape are both shown at once, and that a complicated action is carried on with immense skill and with excellent effect.

64

The woodcut may overstate the scene as it appeared on stage, but thanks to *The Times* there is no reason to doubt that it recreates the essence of the actual setting and action.

Bath's entry no. 454 is offered 'for the drama of *The Idiot of the Cliff*'. The description runs 'Cottage in flames;... man supporting a female who has fainted; villagers,... a man falling headlong from the ruins; also a man in Scotch dress, who is seized at the back of a neck by a dog, whilst he is holding on by a rafter'. Suter's play has no such scene, nor does a second version brought out the following year for the City of London Theatre by Nelson Lee Jr. Unless Bath's piece is an otherwise unknown adaptation set in Scotland it shares no identity with *The Idiot of the Mountain*. Indeed it is short of identity altogether, as *The Idiot of the Cliff* does not figure in the Lord Chamberlain's Plays nor in the standard play lists. This case points the moral against jumping to conclusions brought about by a similarity of title, despite the fact that in other cases such confused titles for the same play do exist.[36]

New for Old

About 1875, a mere ten years or so after the date of Bath's *Catalogue,* the Ledger Job Office of Philadelphia offered show-printing specimens for a repertory that left Bath a long way behind– Savoy operas, *East Lynne* and *Lady Audley's Secret,* plays by Boucicault and Tom Robertson, *The Ticket of Leave Man, Frou-Frou, The Woman in White, Under the Gaslight* and, as we have seen, *Notre Dame.* Here is the new drama soon after the start of the second half-century. E.J. Bath's repertory represents the drama that it displaced.

The dual-purpose playbill continued for some years to come, especially in the regions. Even playbills luxuriously printed on silk but laid out in the traditional way made their appearance in the latter nineteenth century if not before. They were rarely illustrated, but personal information from Catherine Haill, the Theatre Museum's poster specialist, refers to 'an instance of a print showing two horses sitting at a table and eating, which we have in hand-coloured print form, being used as an illustration on a silk playbill....'[37] However, as garish wall-posters came into their own, managers moved towards the separately printed programme for informing their audiences about the details of performance– and for gaining extra income from the inclusion of advertisements.

If Bath's *Catalogue* of 1865 may be thought of as a swan-song to mark the onset of the playbill's terminal throes, let the genre have its due for being an unconscionable time a-dying. We can pay tribute to it for continuing to include occasional pictures as evocative as that on a bill for Astley's *Siege of Troy* (1883), which contains a central feature running the full length of the bill (with text columnised on either side) to show an overwhelming Trojan Horse and a human figure, no more than fetlock-high, standing beside it.[38]

6. Conclusions and Questions

Concerning Illustrated Playbills

During our period the more august managements seem to have put out few illustrated playbills. The suspicion arises that such naive and popular art might have been considered undignified by the theatres royal and by culturally ambitious impresarios like Samuel Phelps and Charles Kean. In the playbills of such managements the typography was normally more restrained anyway (even if the text was more extensive) than in the variety of fonts used by the printers for the more rumbustious theatres. We can see from the Drury Lane example for *St George and the Dragon* that they could illustrate with the best of them when minded, but in general they may have tried to appeal to patrons who were not so smitten by unsophisticated art-work as those of the suburban and provincial houses. The type of play may have affected the issue. The classics might well be thought never to need picturing. While Shakespeare and Sheridan played shoulder-to-shoulder at the theatres royal with *Bluebeard, Lodoiska* and *The Cataract of the Ganges* in the first quarter-century, this was the thinnest time for illustrated playbills. As illustration expanded a little in the next three decades, it may not have spread to the stateliest theatres because they began to adopt a somewhat weightier repertory. They also advertised daily in *The Times* and periodically in other newspapers (which the lesser managements by no means always did), so they did not need to make so much of a splash with their playbills.

Given a few exceptions, we cannot now regard most of the illustrations on playbills of the first half of the nineteenth century as having much beauty or style, and might on the contrary find many gauche or ridiculous or both. Artistic merit, if it existed, was not the main purpose. What impact did playbill illustrations have, then, on the people of the day to whom they were addressed? There can be no doubt about their eye-catching quality and some degree of attractiveness even if occasioned merely by variety and rarity. Their aim was at once to arrest attention to the advertisement as a whole, and to provoke further interest with an image, usually extravagant, that reflected the piece to be performed. In the first half of the nineteenth century such publicity probably had an even stronger effect on that majority of the country's population who found reading difficult or could not read at all.

We must also remember a factor that is not easily recognisable in our own day, so massively image-swamped as it is. In the period dealt with there were very few pictures about. Those that could be obtained or caught sight of were greatly valued. That is one reason why the independent panorama/diorama exhibitions were so successful early in the nineteenth century. For people who could afford to buy them, books and journals had some illustrations– the substantial sales of Bentley's monthly *Miscellany* in the 1830s were partly owed to the engravings of Cruikshank and his fellows– and from the 1840s *The Illustrated London News* and *Punch* and then others made increasing use of drawings and pictures. Producing and selling prints were major occupations, but like the products of drawing-boards and easels they were not for the poor except in very small quantities or long past first-hand. The existence of the broad-limned 'Penny plain, twopence coloured' and juvenile theatre sketches shows just how pictorially needy the poorer classes were, with an appetite that led to noses being pressed to the print-sellers' windows when a new series or spectacular single engraving came out.

Battered by the visual as we now are, we should bear in mind that until about a hundred and fifty years ago, when photography and other new reprographic methods started to bring a steady development, pictorial representations of any sort were scarce and when seen were subjects of pleasure and remark; even so, one dares to suggest, were the crude woodcuts on playbills for a large percentage of the population. Furthermore it was to feast the eyes that our forbears went to the theatre, and not merely the less affluent of them. (We still do, whether we realise it or not. We might ask each other, for example, 'Did you see Peter Brook's *Dream?'* By no deviation from normality, surely, would we talk about having managed to 'hear' *The Blue Room* rather than see it– despite being in the 'audience'. We are 'spectators'.) Personable players acting or dancing their hearts out, exciting and intriguing action, exotic spectacle, splendour of sets and costumes, clever transformations, painted cloths, brilliance of colour and light were no less and perhaps more important for many people when going to the play in the nineteenth century than other qualities like words, music, moral or intellectual interest, companionship and warmth. For the gallery if not the pit, illustrations on playbills might have acted like a magnet in providing a draw to the drama's deeply-sensed visual appeal.

It remains true that the majority of managers abstained from illustration, whatever the size or scope of their business. Playbills were expected to carry a lot of information. A packed evening's menu of pieces needed much text to do it justice. Because of this one can envisage managers not having it in mind to illustrate their playbills other than in exceptional circumstances. Another pressure must have been the need for economy. Bath's free engravings aside, artistes or printers who commissioned their own blocks saw the cost passed on to their playbills. What we cannot know now, and perhaps what no one could have worked out then, is the relationship between the added cost of printing playbills with an illustration, and the extra takings that might have been brought in by providing it. The market-research determinant must have been as variable as it was nebulous, though Bath based his operation on the persuasion that illustrations were worth having.

We may be making too much of the matter in implying a widespread degree of deliberate policy. The convention, by and large, was that playbills were not illustrated. Putting out an occasional illustrated playbill might simply have been thought a good thing to do, if it could be contrived without too much trouble, expense or sacrifice of text. For most managers there may have been no more to it than that.

Where a policy to illustrate playbills did exist, we can identify two factors at work. The first is that certain plays seemed to demand being pictured if possible. The obvious example is *Jonathan Bradford,* closely followed by the plays and acts that featured animals, whether it was the play that dominated the decision to illustrate as in *The Dog of Montargis* and the Dick Turpin plays, or the act, like that of Van Amburgh or the man-monkeys. Some of the clowns, skin-actors and animal-masters with performing beasts favoured having a woodcut on their bills. One such was Usher, who like the Grossmiths and others would have toured with his own blocks for each local printer to incorporate. The second factor is that of house-style. The two great homes of mass spectacle, Astley's Amphitheatre and Vauxhall Gardens, had a lavish policy regarding woodcuts on their bills compared to other London houses, though the Adelphi Theatre and the Bower Saloon came near to catching them up as the Victorian age advanced. Touring circuses were often keen to put pictures on their fliers, and still are. Far distant from the powerful treasuries of Astley's and Vauxhall Gardens, there were touring managers who had faith in the drawing-power of pictures and as we have seen have left us a few illustrated bills, even a few series of illustrated bills on which they rang the changes. Playbill enthusiasts can be glad of their enterprise and applaud it and hope it was rewarded.

Concerning Bath's Catalogue.

The catalogue gives us only an indirect insight to illustrations on playbills and posters because it describes its list without pictures. Nonetheless its birth of a thousand cuts possesses value in regard to the theatrical life of its period, essentially that of the second quarter of the nineteenth century with a few years either side. We register the abundance of the pictorial opportunities that the list offered to theatre managers and benefit-takers. We can identify Bath's descriptions with some of the illustrated playbills that have survived, and look for more. With great care, useful surmises concerning stage-realisation can be extrapolated from certain significant descriptions. Material on particular plays or genres may be found that could be helpful to researchers. Interesting comparisons can be drawn between the descriptions in the catalogue and the images to be observed from other sources such as the juvenile drama and the illustrations printed with play-texts. The plays and genres and episodes selected for illustration by Bath offer a new opportunity for evaluation of the popular repertory.

In a wider view, as the market at which the printer seems to be aiming is that of the suburban and country theatres patronised by audiences out for thrills and fun, the socio-cultural norms or expectations implied in the catalogue are capable of analysis and being related to other studies of early Victorian life and manners.

Taking it for what it is as a trade document, and intriguing though it is in many ways, it has to be conceded that E.J. Bath's catalogue is not free from shortcomings. In addition to being alert to mistakes of detail such as Hayes for the sleeping Caleb in *Jonathan Bradford,* the reader has to engage in occasional guesswork and redress. Sub-titles may or may not be given. Similar-seeming titles might be given for different plays, as we have seen for *The Idiot of the Mountain / Idiot of the Cliff.* Different titles might be given for what appears to be the same play: Bath's entry no. 456 is given as for *Cato; or, the Dogs of the Plantation* while the playbill described above under 'Dogs' (featuring a woodcut provided by or modelled on the Bath example) gives the play as *Cato; or, the Planter and his Dog, and the Slave's Revenge.* To be fair to Bath such rearrangements of play-titles were not uncommon and were usually caused by the meddling or carelessness of managers– who may well have been working from an unofficial script.

70

Erudition– or a craving to delve– well beyond that possessed for this purpose by the present writer is required to ascertain whether, for example, *The Murder at the Old Cross Roads* (Bath's entry no. 39) and *The Cross Roads* (no. 380) are the same; or *The Deserter and his Dog* (entry no. 234) the same as *The Deserter* (nos. 388 and 599), and whether the latter is Charles Dibdin the Elder's play of 1773 still thought worth a place in the catalogue in 1865 or possibly a newer adaptation of Sedaine's original *Déserteur* or something else altogether. Entry no. 258, 'Engraved for *Norval'* and containing a figure of Young Norval, is presumably a mistaken titling of *Douglas;* but is entry no. 429, 'One engraving for the play of *Rolla'*, describing 'Rolla with sword in hand, holding a child over his shoulder', a reference to *Pizarro* or to the recension of 1810 of which *Rolla* is actually the title? In this case the variance is admittedly without much import save as a confirmation of the famous pose's universality.

There are perplexities of these and similar kinds throughout the catalogue. Few authors' names are given and no dates for first performance or first printing. And what about omission of plays? If *Obi; or, Three-fingered Jack* (1800) is included as entry no. 547, why not *The Miller and his Men* (1813), popular for sixty years and more? The contemporary *Maria Marten,* even the old *Mayor of Garrat* were hardy perennials of some country companies, but Bath offers nothing for them by title. Were proven stagers like these left off because they offered little stirring action to portray in an illustration? Surely not in the case of the Exploding Mill or the Red Barn, and one would have thought the hen-pecked 'mayor' Jerry Sneak worth a cartoon. While the barnstormers had little money to spare for illustrations, sometimes not even for the printing of their bills (hand-written bills are known), these plays and other favourites that the catalogue surprisingly seems to ignore were also performed by the better-established circuit companies, who took their playbills seriously and were demonstrably in the market for Bath's engravings. However, Bath has more woodcut entries for action in unnamed plays than for named ones, which might account, for example, for the cataloguer not wishing to identify various nautical scenes with a particular play when they could equally apply to several.

What an editing opportunity Bath offers to an interested post-graduate or other researcher! Short of such a make-over, to the *aficionado* the manual offers amusement and a challenge. Any reader familiar with the early Victorian repertory can have fun in trying to identify some of the scenes featured in those 400 of the 700 entries that are not named for a particular play. For example, what about this:

No. 37. – Four sheet, 60in. by 40in. Five inches' room all round for line in type. On the right-hand side a farmhouse and orchard with water-butt, at the side a broom and pail. A ladder against the window, with full-sized figure of a man with his foot on the bottom rail, escaping with bag of money in his hand. On the left is two compartments – the top a sleeping-room, with bed, and a man lying in front, having been stabbed, with upright figure of the murderer bewildered against the doorway. The bottom part of the kitchen, with dresser; cloth laid for supper; female sitting at the table, an old man on the right standing in horror at the other female on the left shewing one of the plates on the table stained with blood.

Is this a compression for the poster of scenes shown separately on the stage, or do we have here another two-level multiple setting? And do the present writer's if not the reader's antennae (as well as sensitivities) start twitching because it strikes an irretrievably faint chord of identity? Or is that merely the result of a dim and unassignable 'Memory of *Susan Hopley,* Party treated most improply' and her shuddering ilk?– though in Susan's case it was not so much that she was boltered with blood as with a skeleton in the cupboard.

These are all minor riddles compared to two great mysteries.

The first can be introduced by referring to the last sheet of the summary printout. Here are the numbered catalogue entries that mention animals, provisional because there may be a few omissions. Twenty-one or more contain dogs, forty-three or more contain horses (including straightforward equestrian acts). Forty-seven entries record twenty-four further creatures from bear to wolf. Some of these categories overlap on the same bill, so that the actual number of entries containing mention of animals is not much over 100. About 600 of the 700 numbered and valid entries are therefore of human action or emblems with no animal content.

That proportion is directly opposite to experience of extant illustrated playbills. As intimated at the beginning of this discussion, for the most part the illustrated bills that representative trawls have fished up are for animal acts of one sort and another, whether in

The curtain will rise at 7-30 to Shakspere's Sublime Tragedy, entitled

HAMLET
PRINCE OF DENMARK.

37. Cut for *Hamlet* on a playbill for Snape's Royal Britannia Theatre, Cradley Heath (after 1851), private collection

circuses, travelling equestrian shows, spectacles of Astley's type, or dog drama and ape plays and the like in the standard playhouses.

The class of illustrated bills of which we would wish to have the most, namely graphic representations of interesting action and staging such as we can see in the cuts for *My Poll and My Partner Joe, Jonathan Bradford,* and *The Idiot of the Mountain* seem to be restricted to a few handfuls. Three more examples which must be mentioned are bills showing a cod duel in which one duellist is seated and the other upside-down for *The Poet's Last Shilling* (Warwick, 1825); the boy cowering against a wall for Ducrow's *Idiot Boy of Heilbergh* (1841); and the illustration here of the ghost scene from *Hamlet.*

The *Hamlet* cut is from a playbill, not dated but after 1851, for Snape's Royal Britannia Theatre at Cradley Heath. All told this is a handsome and generously printed bill. It shows that a playhouse in the developing outskirts of a provincial conurbation (Birmingham) could be up there with the best in the land. The cut for *Hamlet* is neatly executed. While being a classic pose for the encounter (one thinks of Benjamin Wilson's famous painting of Garrick), it may have some reference to the stage picture– though only, one suspects, if the actors

38. Splendour of engraving on a bill for *St George and the Dragon*, Cooke's Circus, Hull (1840), private collection

modelled their stance on that shown in the engraving. It contains a hint of being an original or pirated wall-picture with what seems to be part of a print-seller's stamp– 'McCALL PRINT'– in the bottom right-hand corner. In this it bears comparison with the romanticised picture of *St George and the Dragon* on a playbill for Cooke's Circus in 1840, also illustrated here and ascribed to 'TINKLER, HULL'– and further notable for the splendour of its seemingly white-line engraving (the polarity is not reversed).

Other than supposing that an engraving commissioned for the playbill was subsequently made available for sale, might we see here a practice whereby an enterprising manager seeking a playbill illustration in a hurry might turn to his local printshop for an existing block? Uncertainty about print-trade practice justifies no more than the merest speculation about this.

There is no uncertainty about the next illustration, which is of the delightful 'Old Wooden House of London Wall' for Almar's *Earl of Poverty* at the Surrey in 1838. It stems from the trade list central to this study, the *Revised Descriptive Catalogue of Theatrical Wood Engravings* of E.J. Bath's Whitechapel Steam Printing Works. The bill

74

states 'This Scene is from an Authority'. The cut on it is as described in Bath's entry no. 397 for this play, 'Two antique houses closed; old street in London; an old man leaning on a stick with a bag at his back'. It is exact even to the catalogued dimensions, which are '2-in by 2½ in'. These can be checked in the illustration against Bodley's rule.[39]

Whether or not from Bath's press, assuredly there are further illustrated playbills to be noticed of the type displaying human action and interesting settings. Nonetheless the dearth of bills with this sort of uberty for research is striking, the more so because the 'human' group may be considered to provide the great majority of scenes depicted in the thousand-plus woodcuts offered overall by E.J. Bath.

So here is the second great mystery. Where are Bath's (and others') illustrated bills?

Royal Surrey Theatre.

Under the Exclusive Management of Mr. DAVIDGE.

THE EARL OF POVERTY!

☞ The production of this Drama has fully realized the expectations of the Management; it being nightly received in the most enthusiastic manner by crowded and brilliant Audiences. The originality of its construction—beauty of Scenery—and correctness of the Costume, form together a *coup d'œuil* seldom met with in the Minor Drama.

FIRST NIGHT OF A NEW DRAMA.
First Appearance of Mr. WEEKES at this Theatre.

MONDAY, February 12th, 1838, & During the Week.

Will be presented a Local Drama of peculiar interest, exemplifying the customs & manners of the times, with New Music, Scenery, Dresses, &c., entitled The

EARL OF POVERTY!

OR, THE
Old Wooden House of London Wall.

Sathanas. Now then, thy lesson to continue,
Tyro.—I am ready, Master.

Sathanas. — Sins are like debts, always greater than we take them to be.

From an Ancient Mystery called " The Reasoning Devil."
Printed by Wynkin de Worde.

Tyro.—Is Poverty a Crime ?

Sathanas.—Poverty is akin to Sloth; and Sloth is the rust of Industry: therefore in most countries, Poverty is a crime; but most so in England.

Tyro.—Then will I make money my God.

Sathanas.—And if thou dost, it will plague thee like the Devil.

Sir Crispe Dunstan.........(of the Worshipful Guild of Fishmongers, and Lord Mayor   Mr. DILLON
        Magnus Mountfichet.........(a Mercer, keeping a House of Wares in the Minories).........Mr. DALE,
Hammond Mountfichet.........(Cousin to Magnus, and Partner in his Estates).........Mr. ELVIN,
        Master Lawrence Osgood.........(of Easte Cheape, a City Gallant).........Mr. DIXON,
Laud Glendillan, {A necessitous Juvenile, known under the soubriquet of the Earl of Poverty, a Scottish Gentleman of Noble Descent, but whose Family Estates have been sequestrated, living in a hovel, near Bishopsgate, at the base of London Wall, and exercising the humble avocation of a Scribe or Public Writer.} Mr. E. F. SAVILLE,

39. 'The Old Wooden House of London Wall', no. 397 from Bath's catalogue, on a playbill for *The Earl of Poverty* at the Surrey Theatre (1838), courtesy of the Bodleian Library, University of Oxford

True, it is hardly surprising that copies of the large-scale engravings offered in the catalogue's first section have not survived, because the wall-posters for which they were intended could have had but the briefest of lives before being pasted over. These huge sheets have never been convenient for collection or storing. That said, unexpected finds can turn up. The Dacorum Museum of Hemel Hempstead in Hertfordshire has a fascinating group of late nineteenth-century circus and theatre posters which were

40. Treasure trove and nightmare: a solidified block of ninety posters before separation and conservation, courtesy of John Lambert, Hertfordshire County Conservator

found abandoned in a stuck-together slab, sullied and apparently intractable (see illustration). The ninety items have been skilfully separated and preserved by John Lambert, the county conservator.[40]

The second part of Bath's catalogue offered 350 entries for illustrations on smaller fliers whose preservation is a different matter. Although they are ephemeral, playbills have always been collected. While Gordon Martin's study *The Playbill: the development of its typographic style* has limitations, this view is worth quoting:

> Far more playbills exist than do examples of other kinds of ephemeral or miscellaneous printing.... Playbills were kept by theatre devotees, the actor himself or his admirers, as well as by ladies who saved them as souvenirs of the occasion. Every theatre kept them as a matter of record, customarily binding them in books which were marked with the year....[41]

This is over-written but the basic premise remains true. Whether well or badly printed, and with or without illustrations, millions of playbills were produced and huge tranches have endured. There are few, though, with illustrations of any kind compared to the thousands without, and even fewer of human action pictured in scenes from straight drama.

76

Did E.J. Bath in reality not print many bills and posters for the profession, and could this have caused a minimal response to his offer of small illustrations 'without extra charge'? Was it in despair for sales that he advertised his new price list as 'unprecedently low'? We have seen that quite a few of his woodcuts did appear on playbills; and there will be more illustrated bills out there somewhere which can be identified with entries in the catalogue: but the evidence of extant examples that clearly derive from Bath is small compared to the hundreds of descriptions in his list. Did the firm prepare woodcuts on spec that were never or seldom utilised? Possibly. Did they advertise engravings that would be cut only on receipt of an order, leaving many uncut as hopeful ghosts in the catalogue? This seems unlikely, though one cannot discount the accumulation of drawn designs that might be catalogued in the hope of orders before actually being engraved. The changing style in the metropolitan repertory soon after mid-century might have caused some decline but had little immediate effect on the less ambitious market at which Bath aims. The wider use of engraving on metal, of photography, of colour after the arrival of aniline dyes, of the revival of lithography with grained paper could all have made a difference to a printer offering wood-engravings: but even if in such respects the Steam Printing Works did not move with the times in 1865, it had surely been busy in its heyday when at least one earlier edition of its now-revised list can be assumed to have been distributed.

If sales of woodcuts from their previous marketing had not thriven it seems unlikely that the firm would have published the 'Revised Descriptive Catalogue' at all, and certainly not in the business-like and quite respectable format in which we have it. Very much a working document, it gives every impression of successful promotion in the second quarter-century during the previous edition(s), before if not after the technical improvements around mid-century. So should we assume that there was an active take-up of illustrations for playbills for which the evidence is now inadequate?

Perhaps the inadequacy is the writer's, because this investigation has only scratched the surface and there are many collections unexplored. Will there be readers to point gently in the direction of significantly illustrated playbills without number? Let us hope so. If not, at least we have Bath's catalogue to show us what we have missed.

Appendix

Eighteenth-century theatrical prints and decorative tiles

To follow up the multi-boxed engraving of Spinacuta and his 'Chevalier des Singes' at Sadler's Wells (*c.* 1766-68), it is pertinent that further entertainments in the later eighteenth century were pictured in a similar form. Prints of at least one of these have been used as a model for decorative tiles.

The basic design was used to picture a balancing act at Sadler's Wells about 1785. There are two versions. In one case the little pictures are ranged in four rows down and in the other case five; both have six pictures across. One version is headed 'Representations of the Several Surprizing Performances of the Famous Polander as they are Performed every evening at Sadlers Wells'. This is the one that shows 24 feats. It is reproduced in *A Biographical Dictionary of Actors, etc.* from a British Museum copy said to be hand-dated as from the *Morning Herald* of 2 August 1785. A print of this is currently on display in the Theatre Museum. The 'Famous Polander' (who flourished on the British stage about 1780-1805) is designated 'The Famous Ballance Master' on the further version showing 30 of his 'Surprizing Performances' but without the publicity details of the other.

Both of these prints of the Famous Polander's balancing act are reproduced in a recent article on pictorial tiles by Jan Pluis in the journal of the Dutch National Tile Museum, Otterlo, where it is shown that they have been utilised as designs for decorative tiles as recently as 1880-1910.[42]

Performing artists were featured on tiles in the eighteenth century. For instance, Moody as Simon in *Harlequin's Invasion* and Mrs Ward as Rodogune are depicted in character on tiles now in the Thomas Grey Collection of the Manchester City Art Gallery. They were painted in the late 1770s or so by the firm of Sadler and Green; information from the tile authority Chris Blanchett indicates that Messrs Sadler and Green normally commissioned the engravings for their tiles. Of the various eighteenth-century actresses named Mrs Ward, this one was Sarah Hoare, Mrs Thomas Achurch Ward, *fl.* 1776-1812, who made her mark as Rodogune in Rowe's *Ethelinda; or, The Royal Convert* and was a favourite of Manchester audiences. The Rodogune tile is an exact copy of the frontispiece to the text of the play in Bell's British Theatre, vol. 7 (1776), a process of transference noted by George Speaight. The representations on tile of single examples of Moody and Mrs Ward suggest that they were part of a tile collection of different players, one per tile, rather than a series of the same performer in different characters or poses like that of the Famous Polander.[43]

It remains to list a few more eighteenth-century examples of the multi-boxed prints of entertainers similar to those for Spinacuta's monkey and the Famous Polander. At the time of writing all these are on display in the Theatre Museum. One is a montage for the rope-dancer Laurence Ferzi at Sadler's Wells in 1771 or later. It shows one central figure surrounded by smaller images of the feats in floral frames, and was engraved by S. Sparrow. Another has already been mentioned earlier under 'Dogs', namely an engraving of Scaglioni's pack under their leader Moustache as they performed in *The Deserter* at Sadler's Wells in 1784. It is headed 'The Dancing Dogs, now exhibiting at Sadler's Wells, by the Sieur Scaglioni, drawn from the life'. This has eight frames, four across and two down in the usual landscape format, and was 'Published August 17th 1784 by John Wallis, Ludgate Street'. An undated print in portrait format headed 'The Surprising Venetian and his Children, Sadler's Wells' has a more complex design. A big central frame is sided by smaller ones, two each side, while ten small frames (five across and two down) appear both at the top and at the foot. A later example for another canine troupe, 'Signor Grimondi's Wonderful Dogs from Paris', is featured on a twelve-frame engraving (three across, four down, the central column of frames slightly wider than the frames at the sides). The performance announces itself as given 'before Her Majesty and the whole of the Royal Family at Windsor Castle on Tuesday November 5 1816'. Its addition 'for particulars see the bills' reinforces the idea that such pictorial prints could also be used for publicity, whether for fly-posting or as handbills.[44]

What formal degree of association there might be between multi-boxed entertainment prints of the eighteenth century and designs for decorative tiles is an intriguing question. Its pursuit must be left to anyone else who might be interested. It has still to be established whether the Famous Polander is the only one of these entertainers whose boxed engraving can be identified with a tile-series or if there are others.

NOTES

1. This essay is intended to complement, and hopefully not overmuch to duplicate, the work of playbill and poster specialists, notably Catherine Haill of the Theatre Museum (author of *Theatre Posters,* 1983) and David Gowan, formerly of the University of Oxford whose playbills thesis is in the Theatre Museum Library, and broader studies such as Jane Moody's *Illegitimate Theatre in London 1770-1840* (2000) which displays authority on playbills as on much else.

2. For 'Colour and Decoration, &c.': see Introduction.

3. Multiple sources will hereafter be suitably consolidated to save footnote-excess, space and irritation. In this paragraph: Dennis Arundell, *The Story of Sadler's Wells* (1965), 25; and Philip H. Highfill, Kalman A. Burnim and Edward A. Langhans (eds.), *A Biographical Dictionary of Actors, etc., in London 1660-1800* (15 vols, Southern Illinois University Press, Carbondale, 1984), XIV, 225. Originals of the Spinacuta illustration may be seen in the John Johnson collection of the Bodleian Library (hereafter JJC): ref. Playbills, 'London R-Z'; and also, in the two sizes, in the Sadler's Wells collection of the Finsbury Library (London Borough of Islington), hereafter FL: ref. SW box for date. Another copy of the illustration, inadequately captioned, is in Highfill *et al.*, XIV, 226, ascribed to the British Museum.

4. The bill illustrated by Bewick is in James Fowler (ed.), *Images of Show Business* (1982), f.p. 80. The Ducrow bill is in A.H. Saxon, *The Life and Art of Andrew Ducrow* (Hamden, Conn, 1976), 45. The Hull bill is reproduced from the George Speaight collection by kind permission of the owner, to whom grateful thanks are also due for drawing it to my attention. The 1795 Polander reference is in Highfill *et al.*, XII, 47.

5. Toby is currently displayed on a bill in frame 77(h) of the sliding panels in the Harry R. Beard Room at the Theatre Museum (hereafter TM). For the Aberdeen bills, see Aberdeen University Library, Morice Collection (hereafter AMC): ref. Local ff. AA Z8 Mor/5 and Mor/8. For Cooke and Bridges see JJC: ref. Bridgnorth Th. & Ents. IIIc1 (folder 1). For further playbills featuring acrobats alone see, for example, British Library Playbills (hereafter BLP): vol. 288, Warwick for 11 Feb. 1832; and vol. 274, Canterbury for 3 Sept. 1836. Be it known that at time of writing the microfilming of the British Library playbill collection at St. Pancras has mostly

been completed; once treated, the volumes themselves are placed on restricted access. The typed index to the contents of the volumes is available at the Rare Books and Music enquiry desk. Currently the box containing the microfilm register on fiche is adjacent to a fiche-reader at seat 50 of the Rare Books and Music reading-room. Accessing microfilm of playbill volumes will be via the BL's computer catalogue using the preliminary pressmark 'mic. C. 13137' for a given volume number, e.g. 'mic. C. 13137/Playbills 271'. For ordering via the online catalogue, go to 'Direct Requesting option 8', choose 'Humanities Collection (1)', press enter to move the prompt to the shelfmark box and type (e.g.) 'mic. C. 13137/Playbills 271' (or whatever volume number is needed). Facilities to photocopy from microfilm are available. In references here the volume numbers alone are given.

6. See runs of playbills for Astley's in, for example, the following collections. BLP: vol. 170. TM: Astley's microfiche set. Minet Library, London Borough of Lambeth (hereafter ML): Astley's folders. The bill featuring Ducrow as the Centaur has been reproduced on TM postcard 252.

7. For Ducrow and Cooke on tour see, for example, BLP: vol. 205 (Bristol, 1835); and AMC: ref. Local ff AA Z8 Mor/37 (Aberdeen) and Mor/58-60 (Dundee, /60 having the Gulliver cut). For racing see FL: ref. SW playbills, box for 1826. For chariots see ML: ref. RVG Coll., microfiche and Bound Vol. 2. *St George and the Dragon* at Drury Lane on Boxing Night 1833 has been reproduced on TM postcard 410. For Victoria, see account in *Queen Victoria Goes to the Theatre* by George Rowell (1978), 24. For *Dragon of Rhodes* see AMC: ref. Local ff AA Z8 Mor 66.

8. For Mrs Midnight's animals, see Alec Clunes, *The British Theatre* (Cassell, 1964), 117-8, with illustration from 'Author's collection'. I am grateful to Mrs Diana Clunes and to Messrs Cassell for leave to reproduce this illustration. It forms the central panel of a triptych-like engraving reproduced in full in Highfill *et al.,* XIV, 119, from a print published in 1753 now in the Harvard Theatre Collection. Details about Smart's 'Mrs Midnight' are from G.W. Stone (ed.), *The London Stage pt. 4, 1747-1776* (Carbondale, 1968), *q.v.* under dates. For Moustache see Arundell, 37-8, and TM flier currently in the Beard Room, sliding panel 49(b). For survey of animals on stage see Bamber Gascoigne, *World Theatre* (1968), 254-257.

9. A sheet of coloured pictures of eight scenes from *Philip and his Dog* 'forming one large one' published by Whittle and Laurie is in the BL's Percival Collection of Material Relating to Sadler's Wells, vol. IV, 60 (shelf-mark. Crach I, Tab 4b.4, I-XIV). The dog is taking the seize in the top strip, awkwardly captioned 'Rinaldo the Ruffian, discovered by Bruin the Sagacious Dog, conceal'd in the Trunk of a Tree, saves Adelaide's Life'. Sybil Rosenfeld (in *Theatre Notebook*, XV, 57-62) showed that this sheet was the same as one in the BL's Ralph Thomas Collection, vol. IX, f.6, plate 8, identified as 'Jameson's Juvenile Drama print', and went on to compare a scene on this with a design by Grieves in 'A Sadler's Wells Scene Book'; see also George Speaight's *History of the English Toy Theatre* (1969), 210. BL's Percival Coll. IV, 61 has a b/w engraving, not the same as on the music-cover, of the dog diving into water to save Adelaide, who is up to her neck. Attempts to trace the painting of Bruin by Luke Clint ('Leonidas Clint') and prints from it (for it was engraved) have failed. For the music-sheet, see FL: ref. SW, box for 1816.

10. For *Rival Indians* at Bath, see BLP: vol. 180 pt 1; and at Warwick, see BLP: vol. 288. Concerning the juvenile drama we welcome George Speaight's Union Catalogue of this important source of nineteenth-century theatrical iconography, published in 1999 by the Society for Theatre Research.

11. For *Foulah Slave* at Warwick, see BLP: vol. 288. For Bruin at Waterford, see BLP: vol. 287. For *Cherokee Chief,* see FL: box for date. For dogs at Wellington, see BLP: vol. 287. For *Cato* at Bury, see BLP: vol. 274. For Eliza Vincent as billed see J.C. Trewin, *The Pomping Folk* (1968), 137; and as 'Caesar' see account by Edwin Fagg, *The Old 'Old Vic'* (1936), 105, and *The 'Revels' History of Drama in English,* gen. eds Clifford Leech and T.W. Craik (1975), VI, 236, where the contributor confuses Eliza (Vincent) with Mary Ann (Orger? Keeley?). For a run of Bower Saloon bills, see TM: Bower microfiche series. Two doggy bills from the Bower are reproduced in *English Melodrama* by Michael Booth (1965), f.p. 80 and 81. The bill for *The French Spy* is reproduced (as are others here) from an original in a private collection, to whose owner I am much beholden.

12. For Polito, see AMC: ref. Local ff AA Z8 Mor/3. For Van Amburgh, see Astley's bills in collections named in note 6. The queen's visits are recorded in Rowell, *Queen Victoria goes to the Theatre,* 24-5,

with a reproduction of Landseer's oil painting 'Isaac Van Amburgh with his Animals' as plate 3.

13. Usher's Bristol bills are in BLP: vol. 205. For the cats and geese, see accounts in *Old Wild's* (1888), 126-8 and 143-4, as reprinted in association with *Victorian Portable Theatres* by Josephine Harrop (STR, 1989).

14. For Kellar, see JJC: ref. London misc. R-Z, end of folder for an unnamed theatre. For Gouffé at the Sans Souci, see *TN* LII/3 (1998), 173, with an illustration reproduced from the collection of Laurence Senelick. For Gouffé at Belfast, see BLP: vol. 271, three differently-illustrated bills for *Perouse* 16-21 Feb. 1828. For Gouffé at Canterbury, see BLP: vol. 274, two different composite illustrations on bills for *Jacko* 12 and 14 March 1831. Another illustration of 'Monsieur Goffe' *(sic)* as Perouse's monkey is on a bill for the Aberdeen Theatre Royal, n.d. but *c.*1838, for which see BLP: vol. 270. For Gouffé's genesis, see the account in *The Memoirs of Charles Dibdin the Younger,* ed. George Speaight (1956), 145-7. For recent correspondence about Gouffé's name and other man-monkeys, etc., see Notes in *Theatre Notebook* 52/3 (1998) and 53/2 (1999).

15. For a run of advertisements for *Tippoo Sahib* see BL, Percival Collection vol. II; see also Arundell, 47. For Chuny, see the account in William G. Knight, *A Major London 'Minor': the Surrey Theatre 1805-1865* (STR, 1997), 12-14, with reproductions of (non-pictorial) playbills (figure 3 and plate 1). See also 'Playhouse Musings' in James and Horace Smith, *Rejected Addresses* (1812, etc.), where the quote from Johnson is given in a footnote. For Astley's elephants, see BLP: vol. 170; and also TM: Astley's, microfiche 6. For freak show, see AMC: ref. Local ff AA Z8 Mor/54.

16. For Wild as Mat Meriton, see Harrop, *Victorian Portable Theatres,* plate 4, and for his lending a block see *Old Wild's,* 150. For my earlier paper 'Colour and Decoration' see Introduction. For Hallam at Ashbourne, see BLP: vol. 270. For Simpson, see ML: RVG coll., Bound vol. 2 and microfiche. For Grimaldi, see *Harlequin in his Element* by David Mayer (1969), 141; the print is sourced to the British Museum. For Crisp at Bridgnorth, see BLP: vol. 273. For 'Blind Willie' on an undated bill for the Aberdeen Exchange, c. 1825, see AMC: ref. Local ff AA Z8 Mor/24. For Aldridge at Dundee, and for Harlequin at Exmouth, see BLP: vol. 277. For *The Skeleton Hand,* see Arundell, *The Story of Sadler's Wells,* 117-8.

17. The bill for Nano in its full orange splendour, and reviews of his performance, can be seen at the City of Westminster Archives Centre: ref. Adelphi vol. III, folio 15 and Folder 3 folio 39. The *Orange Girl* quote and details first appeared (more fully) in Knight, *A Major London 'Minor'*, 302.

18. Catherine Haill on Anderson is from 'Playbills', in James Fowler (ed.), *Images of Show Business*, 80. For Franklin, see JJC: ref. Th & Ents IIIc1 (folder 2, 175). Dancer's glass-blowing bill is in Hertford Museum: ref. 6203.3, Hertford folder, early playbills box. The Trafalgar panorama print, at present uncatalogued, is from the same collection. I am obliged to Rosemary Bennett, formerly Curator of Collections, for help with these items and grateful to the museum's authorities for the generosity of their permission to reproduce. Panorama enthusiasts may like to know that Hertford Museum possesses the MS draft of H. C. Andrews's articles in *Notes and Queries* on 'The Leicester Square and Strand Panoramas: their proprietors and artists', together with supporting notes, illustrations, and cuttings.

19. The Betty copperplate is from John Doran's *Their Majesties' Servants* (1888 ed.), III, f.p. 242. For my article on the Grossmiths, see Introduction. The 1825 bill is in the Shropshire Records and Research Unit, Shrewsbury (hereafter SRRU), ref. 665/4/88. The family comment is by George Grossmith ('the Elder') in *A Society Clown: Reminiscences* (Bristol, 1888), 42.

20. For Miss Carr, see JJC: ref. Bridgnorth Th. & Ents. IIIc1, 147-9 (folder 2). For Infant Taglioni, see TM: 'Bower' microfiche 1.

21. The Artists' bill is in JJC: ref. Playbills 'London R-Z', St James's 18 May 1850. The colourful Windsor bill is reproduced in Jean Scott Rogers, *Stage by Stage: the Making of the Theatre Museum* (1985), plate 65. The 'Night Ascent' illustration has been kindly contributed by Susan Solomon, an authority on the history of ballooning; for further Cremorne Gardens bills see BLP: vol 366. For *The Eagle* and Vauxhall Gardens, see ML: ref. RVG coll., microfiche and Bound vol. 2, bills for the following dates: 15 Aug. 1831, various bills for June-Aug. 1835 and for 16 June 1837, all for ballooning; the bill of 9 Aug. 1832 for the Fancy Fair; the bill of 12 Jul. 1831 for the fête.

22. *The Guerillas* bill is an uncatalogued fragment for an unnamed theatre in the Special Collections dept. of the Templeman Library,

University of Kent at Canterbury (hereafter TL). I am grateful to Susan Crabtree for help with this and other matters.

23. Edwin's bill is in SRRU, ref. 665/4/185. I am grateful to the Unit's authorities for generous permission to reproduce this and the Grossmith bill.

24. Notably in Booth, *English Melodrama,* plate 15. The original is in the National Picture Library (Victoria and Albert Museum). I am grateful for help with getting this reproduction and other matters to Claire Hudson of TM and staff at the NPL.

25. By the unstinting generosity and kind permission of the owner, photocopies of the full catalogue have previously been deposited in the libraries of the Theatre Museum and the University of Kent as well as retained and reproduced for this study.

26. Prices and measurements correspond to new values as follows: 1s. (one shilling) equalled 5p, that is, five (new) pence, and therefore one-twentieth of £1, while 1d. (one penny) was one-twelfth of 1s. Equivalence is difficult because of inflation, but a very rough guide would be to think of a simple meal then like the 'sixpenny ordinary' being comparable in cost to a cheap fast-food snack now. One inch equals 2.54 centimetres.

27. For the work of entering brief details of each entry on a database I gratefully acknowledge the help of my wife Adrienne. By the time this book is in print, a plain-text version of the database should be available for downloading from the Society's web site, suitable for importing into almost any database program. Other versions may be provided if practicable - please visit the Society's web site at (http://www.str.org.uk) for details. Once the file has been imported into a database, the material can be sorted in several fields. Disks containing the database, in Apple Macintosh format to be read with Microsoft Works, have been made available to the depositories receiving a photocopy of the printed catalogue

28. The rider's nakedness is quoted from *Mazeppa* (the poem) and its prolegomenon. The reverent phrases come from Phyllis Hartnoll's original *Oxford Companion to the Theatre* (1951), s.v. Menken. Of the illustrations that follow, examples of the two earlier Astley's bills for the play of *Mazeppa* are in the relevant London collections, and were drawn to attention in books by Michael Booth, *English Melodrama,* 98 (the 1831 bill) and George Speaight, *Collecting Theatrical Memorabilia* (Ashbourne, 1988), 14 (the 1836 bill). The

Menken woodcut, with direction of movement reversed, is from a framed bill in the possession of the University of Kent at Canterbury and currently exhibited in TL. The review and the Tenniel are in *Punch* vol. XXI (issue for November 1851), 201; I owe knowledge of this to Gascoigne, *World Theatre*, 253.

29. The American *Mazeppa* poster is reprinted by Gascoigne, 253, in negative from *Early American Theatrical Posters* (Cherokee Press, Hollywood n.d.), being a recent republication of the Philadelphia specimen-book, *Specimens of Show Printing (c.* 1875 with updates). For transantlantic comparison see an illustration for *Notre Dame* (first performed Adelphi Theatre, 10 April 1871), firstly in BLP vol. 363 on a bill for Bradford, '28 October' (no year but c. 1871-2), and secondly in the specimen-book of the Ledger Job Printing Establishment, Philadelphia, as reprinted both in the title above, cut no. 262 (p. 16) and in Stanley Appelbaum, *Scenes from the Nineteenth-Century Stage in Advertizing Woodcuts* (New York, 1977), no. 89 (p. 51). *Notre Dame* had reached New York by 1873 and the identical images show the towered roof of the Cathedral from which Quasimodo has hurled Archdeacon Frollo, while Phoebus and Gudule on a platform in the foreground brandish a pardon for Esmerelda. The Cherokee and Appelbaum volumes draw on the same basic material from the Philadelphia press (though apparently from different editions or updates) and duplicate much of it, but there are variations in selection exemplified by cuts for *True to the Core* which appear in Appelbaum but not the Cherokee Press reprint. A copy of the Ledger specimen-book published in 1882 is in TM.

30. For Goethe, various sources including *'Revels' History* VI, 211 (n. 2), and Russell Jackson (trans. and ed.), *Shakespeare in the London Theatre, 1855-58* by Theodor Fontane (STR, 1999), 135. For the Royal Victoria in 1880, see Fagg, *The Old 'Old Vic',* 119. The first plate of Hector as 'Dragon' in *Montargis* comes from a bill originally put out by the Hartlepool press of John Proctor as reproduced in *The Victorian Provincial Printer and the Stage,* a pamphlet by the late Robert Wood (Newcastle Imprint Club, 1972). I am grateful to Graeme Cruickshank for knowledge of this study and regret that enquiries at archive services in Newcastle-on-Tyne have failed to produce either the original playbill or the present holder of the pamphlet's copyright. I am indebted to Ann Kent and her colleagues

of the Tyne and Wear Archives Service for help with this and with providing a copy of the Coxhoe bill.

31. The first reproduction of *Dick Turpin* comes thanks to help received from Susan Crabtree at TL, the second from Robert Wood's pamphlet (see n. 30). Laman Blanchard's 'Memoir of William Harrison Ainsworth' is prefaced to the 1857 edition of *Rookwood,* and reprinted with the illustrations by Cruikshank and Sir John Gilbert in the collected edition of Messrs Routledge (n.d.).

32. '*Jack Sheppard* Plays and the Influence of Cruikshank' is in *Theatre Notebook* vol. 54 no. 2 (2000), 98-123 including eight plates. The Adelphi playbill is currently on public display in the Beard Room of TM, sliding panel 93.

33. For Cruikshank and *The Bottle* etc., see '*Revels' History* VI, 236; Arundell, *Sadler's Wells,* 154; *The Life of George Cruikshank* (1882) by Blanchard Jerrold (not Laman Blanchard as given in *Revels),* II, 91 ff; and the anonymous pamphlet catalogued in BL under George Cruikshank headed *Four Rare Etchings by the Celebrated George Cruikshank.* Nicoll notes Cruikshank as director of the Surrey's *Drunkard's Children* in *A History of Early Nineteenth Century Drama* (1930), II, 383. The Surrey's playbill for *Jack Sheppard* on 21 October 1839 (copy kindly made available to me by the Southwark Local Studies Librarian) prints a message of support from Ainsworth and affirms 'the whole of the Scenery having been superintended by Mr George Cruikshank'; see also article cited in note 32, and Knight, *A Major London 'Minor',* 157.

34. Muriel St Clare Byrne analysed this woodcut of a multiple setting in *Theatre Notebook* 8/4 (1954) and illustrated it by courtesy of the British Library; it is reproduced here by kind permission of the *TN* editors. The bill for Dundee in April 1834 is in BLP vol. 277.

35. For *Walter Brand,* see *TN* IX (1954), 15, with illustration from Skelt. The published text of *The Gamblers* is in BL. Greenwood's text of his *Jack Sheppard* was published in Cumberland's play-series, vol. xv, and the five-in-one scene is discussed in my article on 'Jack Sheppard' plays already cited. The censorship-copy of *Adventures* is in BL, LCP 42964 ff 768-804b. Nicoll, *Early 19th-Century Drama* II, 334, records it as by Mark Lemon for the Olympic Theatre in October 1842. Donald Mullin's handlist of *Victorian Plays* (1987) gives the author as Bulwer-Lytton, presumably in error unless Lemon and Lord Lytton collaborated on it.

36. The handbill and quotes for *The Idiot of the Mountain* were first reproduced in Knight, *A Major London 'Minor'*, where the play and this illustration are discussed in more detail (pp. 286-8). Suter's and Lee's versions are in LCP. Neither Mullin nor Allardyce Nicoll in his *Alphabetical List of Plays* (1959) make mention of an *Idiot of the Cliff*. This means only that its existence is otherwise unrecorded, not that it did not exist, because though valuable the handlists are not infallible.

37. Framed examples of playbills on silk are not infrequently to be seen in museums and theatre foyers, and some private collections. More often than not they were prepared for commands or amateur performances, for example 'Amateur Theatricals by Officers of the 4th Dragoon Guards' in October 1859 at the Theatre Royal, Brighton. Such bills, it seems, were intended for honoured guests or patrons, both as keepsakes and to prevent the hands (or gloves) from being dirtied by the printers' ink of the period. If thin wooden rods or some margin of thicker material to facilitate rolling were provided at the top and bottom of the silk bill, it could be unscrolled and held open at top and bottom for perusal without the fingers ever getting contaminated. For most of the nineteenth century standard printers' ink was prepared in essence from soot (lampblack) and linseed oil. It dried slowly. Instantly drying rotogravure inks containing solvents such as naphtha came late on, when high-speed presses proved a need for them.

38. For *The Siege of Troy* bill see plate 2 in Catherine Haill, *Theatre Posters* (1983), 15.

39. For the cod duel see BLP 288: Warwick, 19 Sept. 1825. For the idiot boy see BLP 276: Colchester, 11 Dec. 1841. The Old Wooden House is reproduced from JJC: ref. Playbills 'London misc. R-Z'. Further illustrations may be found in specialist books, though it is not always made clear whether they come from playbills or some other source. One such book is Michael Booth's *English Melodrama,* already cited. Another is *The Victorian Theatre: a Pictorial Survey* by Richard Southern (1970), the illustrations in which include a noteworthy collation of three realisations in different media of the same scene from Charles Kean's *Merchant of Venice* in 1853 (pp. 46-7); though not incorporating a playbill illustration, the juxtaposition of old and new pictorial techniques (scene design, easel painting, photograph) epitomises the mid-century watershed of which another example is the playbill's division into poster and programme.

40. Some of the remarkable conserved items from this brick-like

nightmare of solidified paper are currently framed and on display in the Old Town Hall, Hemel Hempstead.

41. Gordon Martin, *The Playbill: the development of its typographic style* (Chicago, 1963), unnumbered 2nd and 3rd pp. of intro. This is a seeming apprentice-piece that draws conclusions from too little evidence or from thin air.

42. For sources of the Spinacuta print see note 3 above. For the 'Polander' print, see Highfill *et al.* XII, 47, ascribing the print to BL, and (currently) TM Beard Room sliding panel 49(a). For reproductions of both Polander prints see 'Prent en Tegel' by J. Pluis in *Tegel 17* (Tegelmuseum, pub. Amsterdam, 1989, ISSN 0920 4539), in which the 'Polander' print is ascribed to the BL's Percival Collection and the 'Ballance-master' to 'Part. koll. Hamburg', a private collection. At time of writing the 'Polander' print cannot be found in the first three volumes of the Percival Collection (to 1806). I owe thanks to David Withey of Finsbury Reference Library for drawing Pluis's article and its illustrations to my attention.

43. For reproductions of tiles of Moody and Mrs Ward see, for example, Hans van Lemmen, *Tiles: A Collector's Guide* (1979), 30-31, and for details about their origin see Anthony Ray, *Liverpool Printed Tiles* (1994). The George Speaight reference is to *Collecting Theatrical Memorabilia,* 124. I have received help concerning tiles from Shelley White of the Jackfield Tile Museum, Ironbridge Gorge, and Ruth Shrigley of the Manchester City Art Gallery, while Chris Blanchett, tile historian, not only provided valuable information but found two copies of *Tegel 17* for me, one of which has been passed on to TM.

44. All the bills mentioned in this paragraph are in the collection of TM. At time of writing they are on display in the Beard Room sliding panels as follows: for Ferzi see frame 48(c); for Moustache and pack see 49(b); for the Surprising Venetian see 49(c); for Signor Grimondi see 80(b). Readers may be aware that decorative tiling based on theatrical images is a feature of modern as well as past times. Any visitor to the Theatre Museum in Covent Garden (opened 1987) can and should take an opportunity to admire the stylish Shakespearean tiles that line the walls in the visitors' loos provided for Gentlemen as well (on good authority) as for Ladies.

BOOKS AND ARTICLES CITED

Appelbaum, Stanley (ed.). *Scenes from the Nineteenth-century Stage in Advertizing Woodcuts* (New York, 1977); cf. *Early American Theatrical Posters* (anon, Hollywood n.d., *circa* 1960): both being reprints of selections from *Specimens of Show Printing* (Ledger Job Printing Office, Philadelphia, *circa* 1875)

Arundell, Dennis. *The Story of Sadler's Wells* (1965)

Blanchard, Laman. 'Memoir of William Harrison Ainsworth' prefaced to *Rookwood* (1857 edition), reprinted in collected works of Harrison Ainsworth by Messrs Routledge (n.d.)

Booth, Michael. *English Melodrama* (1965)

Byrne, Muriel St Clare. 'Early Multiple Settings in England' in *Theatre Notebook VIII/4* (1954)

Byron, Lord George Gordon. *English Bards and Scotch Reviewers* and *Mazeppa* (standard works)

Clunes, Alec. *The British Theatre* (1964)

Cruikshank, George. *Four Rare Etchings* (ed. anon., n.d.)

Doran, Dr (John). *'Their Majesties' Servants'. Annals of the English Stage* ed. R.W. Lowe (3 vols, 1888)

Fagg, Edwin. *The Old 'Old Vic'* (1936)

Fontane, Theodore. *Shakespeare in the London Theatre 1855-58,* trans. and ed. Russell Jackson (STR, 1999)

Forbes, Derek. 'The Earliest Grossmiths and their Pictorial Playbills' in *Scenes from Provincial Stages,* ed. Richard Foulkes (STR, 1994), 65-87; 'Colour and Decoration on Nineteenth-century Playbills', *Theatre Notebook 51/1* (1997); 'Mons.Gouffé and man-monkeys' (note), *Theatre Notebook 53/2* (1999); *'Jack Sheppard* Plays and the Influence of Cruikshank', *Theatre Notebook 54/2* (2000)

Fowler, James (ed.). *Images of Show Business* (Theatre Museum, 1982)

Gascoigne, Bamber. *World Theatre* (1968)

Gowen, David R. *Studies in the History and Function of the British Theatre Playbill and Programme, 1564-1914* (unpub. DPhil thesis, Oxford 1998)

Grossmith, George, 'the Elder'. *A Society Clown: Reminiscences* (Bristol, 1888)

Haill, Catherine. *Theatre Posters* (Theatre Museum, 1983)

Harrop, Josephine. *Victorian Portable Theatres* (STR, 1989)

Hartnoll, Phyllis (ed.). *The Oxford Companion to the Theatre* (1951)

Highfill, Philip H; Burnim, Kalman A; and Langhans, Edward A. (eds). *A Biographical Dictionary of Actors, etc., in London 1660-1800*

(15 vols, Carbondale, 1984)

Jerrold, Blanchard. *The Life of George Cruikshank* (1882)

Knight, William G. *A Major London 'Minor': the Surrey Theatre 1805-1865* (STR, 1997)

Leech, Clifford, and Craik, T.W. (gen. eds). *The 'Revels' History of Drama in English, VI* (1975)

Lemmen, Hans van. *Tiles: a Collector's Guide* (1979)

Martin, Gordon. *The Playbill: the development of its typographic style* (Chicago, 1963)

Mayer, David. *Harlequin in his Element* (1969)

Moody, Jane. *Illegitimate Theatre in London 1770-1840* (2000)

Mullin, Donald. *Victorian Plays* (1987)

Nicoll, Allardyce. *A History of Early Nineteenth-century Drama, II* (1930); *Alphabetical List of Plays* (1959)

Pluis, J. 'Prent en Tegel' in *Tegel 17* (Tegelmuseum, Otterlo, pub. Amsterdam 1989)

Ray, Anthony. *Liverpool Printed Tiles* (1994)

Rogers, Jean Scott. *Stage by Stage: the Making of the Theatre Museum* (1985)

Rosenfeld, Sybil. 'A Sadler's Wells Scene Book' in *Theatre Notebook XV/2* (1960)

Rowell, George. *Queen Victoria goes to the Theatre* (1978)

Saxon, A.H. *The Life and Art of Andrew Ducrow* (Hamden, CT, 1978)

Senelick, Laurence. 'Monsieur Gouffé' (note), *Theatre Notebook 52/3* (1998)

Southern, Richard. *The Victorian Theatre: a Pictorial Survey* (1970)

Speaight, George. 'Early Multiple Settings in England' (note), *Theatre Notebook IX/1* (1954)
(Ed.) *The Memoirs of Charles Dibdin the Younger* (STR, 1956)
A History of the English Toy Theatre (1969)
Collecting Theatrical Memorabilia (Ashbourne, 1988)
The Juvenile Drama: a Union Catalogue (1999)

Stone, George Winchester (ed.). *The London Stage Pt 4: 1747-1776* (Carbondale, 1968)

Tenniel, Sir John. 'Backstage at *Mazeppa*' (accompanying anonymous review), *Punch XXI* (1851)

Trewin, J.C. *The Pomping Folk* ((1968)

Wild, 'Sam', ed. 'Trim' [W.B. Megson]. *'Old Wild's': a Nursery of Strolling Players and the Celebrities who appeared there* (London and Bradford, 1888); facsimile reprint with new index compiled by Josephine Harrop (STR, 1989)

Wood, Robert. *The Victorian Provincial Printer and the Stage* (Newcastle, 1972).

ARCHIVAL SOURCES OF PLAYBILLS
AND OTHER DOCUMENTS
consulted and drawn on for this study

University of Aberdeen: Special Collections Library
University of Bristol: Theatre Collection
The British Library
The British Museum
The Guildhall Library
Hertford Museum
Hertfordshire County Library: Central Resources Unit, Hatfield
London Borough of Islington: Finsbury Reference Library
University of Kent at Canterbury: Templeman Library (Special Collections)
London Borough of Lambeth: Minet Reference Library
University of Oxford: Bodleian Library (John Johnson Collection of Printed Ephemera)
Shropshire Records and Research Unit, Shrewsbury
London Borough of Southwark: Local Studies Library
The Theatre Museum, Covent Garden
Tyne and Wear Archives Service, Newcastle-upon-Tyne
Victoria and Albert Museum: the National Picture Library
City of Westminster: Archives Centre

The Graeme Cruickshank collection
The John Lambert collection
The Susan Solomon collection
The George Speaight collection
Author's and private collections.

The attention of anyone newly desirous of the rewarding experience of investigating holdings of playbills or other theatrical ephemera is drawn to the nation-wide *Directory of Performing Arts Resources,* compiled by Francesca Franchi (3rd ed., 1998) and available from the Society for Theatre Research, c/o the Theatre Museum, 1E Tavistock Street, London WC2E 7PR. This is now incorporated in the online 'Backstage' project, a developing gateway detailing holdings of major UK theatre collections (URL<www.backstage.ac.uk> at the time of going to press, or email <R.S.Holland@ukc.ac.uk>).

Illustrated Playbills

PART TWO

5

CATALOGUE.

No. 1.—FOUR SHEET ENGRAVING, 60-in. by 40-in.

Naval engagement—general fight—Men boarding, and Marines firing. Five inches room all round for a small line in type, of Title and Theatre.

No. 2.—FOUR SHEET, 40-in. by 60-in.

A Man-of-war, sailors manning the yards with flags in their hands—the officers and crew standing in the head of the vessel cheering—a sailor on the jib-boom with flag. Three boats with crew fighting, Boatswain in each, with cutlass upraised.

No. 3.—TWO SHEET, 40-in. by 30-in.

A Ship sinking, having struck upon the rocks; the Officer leaving the Vessel, being rowed away in a boat by two Seamen. Ten inches room on the paper for a line to be inserted.

No. 4.—TWO SHEET ENGRAVING, 40-in. by 30-in.

On the left-hand side, a Ship at Sea with marines in boat firing. The right-hand side, a woman standing in the attitude of prayer, with four constables. At the top are two men, the one being thrown from the rocks, and fired at by the marines in the boat. Engraved for "May Marsden."

No. 5.—TWO SHEET, 40-in. by 30-in.

The deck of a vessel, with the whole of the Crew looking at a Skeleton. In the centre is a man on one knee about to stab himself. On the left, the Captain, and on the right, an old man and a negro, who are all astonished at the appearance of the Skeleton. Engraved for the "Skeleton of the Wave."

6

No. 6.—TWO SHEET, 40-in. by 30-in.

Occupies the whole of the paper.

A Rocky Scene, with Water-mill in flames. In the centre is a smuggler fighting with a sailor, and on the right is a man killed, with a woman kneeling over him. Engraved for "May Marsden."

No. 7.—SINGLE SHEET, 30-in. by 20-in.

On the right hand a Man-of-war firing a salute. On the left is a boat, an Officer and two Sailors with flag; over which is Fame, with a trumpet, from which is issuing the word "Success." Four inches blank on the paper for a line.

No. 8.—SINGLE SHEET, 30-in. by 20-in.

Occupies the whole of the paper.

A Ship on Fire, with Crew, Passengers, &c., escaping.

No. 9.—SINGLE SHEET, 30-in. by 20-in.

A Ship in flames. This Engraving occupies the whole sheet of paper.

No. 10.—SINGLE SHEET. 30-in. by 20-in.

Occupies the whole of the paper.

Representing two vessels in action, a man floating on a hen-coop, and two others clinging to a portion of a mast. Engraved for 'Afloat and Ashore."

No. 11.—(Destroyed.)

No. 12.—FOUR SHEET ENGRAVING. 60-in. by 40-in.

Scene—a Coral Cave, with Figure of Britannia, and a group of Fairies on each side.

No. 13.—FOUR SHEET, 60-in. by 40-in.

Originally engraved for a Pantomime. The whole of the left-hand side occupied by the full figure of Harlequin, and the right-hand by different Pantomimic Figures.

7

No. 14.—TWO SHEET ENGRAVING, 40-in. by 30-in.

The Scene—on the left hand is a pavilion, with lords and ladies viewing the Tournament, the back is a castle, and the left the entrance. Engraved for the Pantomime of "Johnny Horner.'

No. 15.—SINGLE SHEET, 30-in. by 20-in.

A Mystic Cavern. Nondescript Figure with wand and large serpent on the same, with group of Fiends dancing around him. Engraved for the Pantomime of "The Sea Serpent."

No. 16.—SINGLE SHEET, 20-in. by 30-in.

Nondescript figure of a Clown—very large head and eyes.

No. 17.—SMALL ENGRAVING, 20-in. by 15-in.

Clown, with poker in his hand, and Pantaloon, both on horseback.

No. 18.—FOUR SHEET, 60-in. by 40-in.

A Tournament. Tents at back with spectators; left hand, tent, with King, Queen, and Attendants; centre, two Knights in combat—one vanquished, the other standing over him.

No. 19.—(Destroyed.)

No. 20.—FOUR SHEET, 40-in. by 60-in.

With room for a line of 4-in. all round.

A Full-size figure of an Egyptian Mummy, with the words—"Roman Models ! Living Pictures ! ! Egyptian Mummy ! ! !

No. 21.—SINGLE SHEET ENGRAVING, 30-in. by 20-in.

Virginia Minstrels—containing five figures, Bones, Concertina, Violin, Banjo, and Tambourine. About 4-in. room top and bottom.

No. 22.—SINGLE SHEET, 20-in. by 30-in.

Different views of the Gold Diggings, with the following words engraved on the blocks,—"Monstre Panorama from England to the Gold Regions of Australia." A round blank in centre for letter-press.

No. 23.—SINGLE SHEET, 20-in. by 30-in.

Balloon, with three persons seated in the car. Aperture for the name; 6-in. room top and bottom, and 4-in. at sides.

No. 24.—SINGLE SHEET, 30-in. by 20-in.

Occupies the whole of the paper.

Interior of a Temple—large figure of an Elephant, with man on his back, and various figures prostrating themselves to him.

No. 25.—SMALL ENGRAVING, 10-in. by 20-in.

Wrestlers.

No. 26.—FOUR SHEET, 60-in. by 40-in.

Or can be used the long way, 30-in. by 80-in—First sheet, "GIN," Second, "WATER," Third, two Tableaux, Fire Scene, and Quarrel in the Balcony; Fourth, two Tableaux, Gin Palace, and Outside Institution.

No. 27.—TWO SHEET, 60-in. by 20-in., or 30-in. by 40-in.

First Sheet, "GIN ;" Second Sheet, "WATER;" with room for a line at the top and bottom.

No. 28.—TWO SHEET, 60-in. by 20-in., or 30-in. by 40-in.

First sheet, two Tableaux, "The Fire," and "Quarrel in the Balcony;" Second Sheet, Two Tableaux, "Gin Palace," and "Outside of Institution."

No. 29.—SINGLE SHEET, 30-in. by 20-in.

With room for line top and bottom. The Tableau "GIN."

No. 30.—SINGLE SHEET, 30-in. by 20-in.

With room for line at top and bottom. The Tableau "WATER"

No. 31.—SINGLE SHEET ENGRAVING, 30-in. by 20-in.

With room for line at top and bottom. Two tableaux "The Fire," and "Quarrel in the Balcony."

No. 32.—SINGLE SHEET, 30-in. by 20-in.

With room for line at top and bottom. Two tableaux, "Gin Palace," and "Outside of Institution."

☞ From No. 26 to No. 32, engraved for "GIN and WATER."
The above Engravings will form Single Sheets or Four Sheet Engravings.

Nos. 33 & 34.—(Destroyed.)

No. 35.—SINGLE SHEET, 30-in. by 20-in.
Occupies the whole of the paper.

This Scene represents Red Ralph having shot the Colonel, and Joe Beans entering with a Lighted Candle. Engraved for "**The Will and the Way.**"

No. 36.—BOARD BILL ENGRAVING, 17-in. by 24-in.

A border with small figures, which work in two colors with names in border underneath each, of Ellen, the Khan, the Ayah, Old Martin, Meeran Hafiz, and Joe Beans. Engraved for "**The Will and the Way.**"

No. 37.—FOUR SHEET, 60-in. by 40-in.

Five inches' room all round for line in type. On the right-hand side a farmhouse and orchard with water-butt, at the side a broom and pail. A ladder against the window, with full-sized figure of a man with his foot on the bottom rail, escaping with bag of money in his hand. On the left is two compartments—the top a sleeping-room, with bed, and a man lying in front, having been stabbed, with upright figure of the murderer bewildered against the doorway. The bottom part of the kitchen, with dresser; cloth laid for supper; female sitting at the table, an old man on the right standing in horror at the other female on the left showing one of the plates on the table stained with blood.

No. 38.—FOUR SHEET ENGRAVING, 60-in. by 40-in.
Occupies the whole of the paper.

Large figure of the Drunkard, seated in a chair, with bottle to his lips, and wife and children in imploring attitudes. Engraved for "**The Bottle.**"

10

No. 39.—TWO SHEET, 40-in. by 30-in.

A very large country inn, with gateway—a cab standing partly under it. Centre, toll-house and gate, with sign-post. On the right-hand are a number of villagers with torches. On the left, various people who have come from the Inn with lights; also the cabman in custody of two men. In the centre is the figure of a man who has been shot, supported by a female, and a man pointing to the cabman as his murderer. Engraved for "**The Murder at the Old Cross Roads.**" Room for line at top.

No. 40.—(Destroyed.)

No. 41.—SINGLE SHEET, 30-in. by 20-in.
(TURKISH.)
Occupies the whole of the paper.

Scene—a Castle, in the centre is the Sultan standing with uplifted sword over the prostrate body of a Soldier. On the right is a Turk about to run a man through whom he has just knocked down. Also the figure of a woman praying. On the left is a Turk waving a banner with the three crescents, in token of the Victory of the Turks.

No. 42.—SINGLE SHEET, 30-in. by 20-in.
Occupies the whole of the paper.

Castle at side, Guerillas and Troops engaged, Women praying on the right, two Ships in action at the back. Engraved for "**Guerillas, or the Storming of St. Sebastian.**"

Also a crown Border and five small Engravings.

No 43.—SINGLE SHEET, 30-in by 20-in.
Occupies the whole of the paper.

Gipsies' Tent, with two children; in the centre, a large figure of a gipsy, a Woman on the right, the hanger and pot, and a man sitting down, smoking, and a gipsy-woman with long staff in the distance.

No. 44.—TWO SHEET ENGRAVING, 30-in. by 40-in.

Full-size figure of a Woman dressed as a Vivandiere, with keg over her shoulders, also a child in her arms. Room for line at top.

11

No. 45.—SINGLE SHEET, 20-in. by 30-in.

A Donkey and panniers, with Man singing—Dick Turpin on horseback.—Engraved for "**Turpin's Ride to York.**"

No. 46.—SMALL ENGRAVING, 10-in. by 20-in.
Engraved for "**The Cricket on the Hearth.**"

No. 47.—SMALL ENGRAVING, 8-in. by 6½-in.

Figure of a General on horseback, with Officer carrying colours, and Soldiers on the left side. On the right hand are two Soldiers, one delivering the colours and the other offering sword. Engraved for "**The Will and the Way.**"

No. 48.—SINGLE SHEET, 30-in. by 20-in.
Occupies the whole sheet, the broad way of the paper.

In the centre of the engraving is the figure of the Carpenter standing between a man and woman, kneeling, a man lying dead on the right, and soldiers in the act of firing on the left.

No. 49.—SINGLE SHEET, 30-in. by 20-in.

With room for line top and bottom. The Sea crowded with ice, a child on a portion of it, praying, and three figures of men struggling among the ice. Engraved for "**The Sea of Ice.**"

No. 50.—SINGLE SHEET, 20-in. by 30-in.

View of a Duel Scene, with several figures in the back ground; the wounded man lying on the ground attended by his seconds, and his victorious antagonist wiping the blood from his sword. In the foreground, the apparition of the murdered man appearing to two figures. Engraved for "**The Corsican Brothers.**"

No. 51.—SINGLE SHEET, 30-in. by 20-in.

Represents a garden with a female lying on the ground, and a cup labelled "Colde Pizen," by her side; also the figure of a man supposed to be her lover) standing quite horror-stricken at the sight of the body of the unfortunate female. Engraved for "**Villikins and his Dinah.**"

No. 52.—SINGLE SHEET ENGRAVING, 30-in. by 20-in.

Representing a View of a Street in Boston with the dwelling of Nan Grant. The figure of Uncle True, with a Ladder on his Shoulder and a Torch in his hand, in the act of presenting Gerty with a Kitten, which she is receiving with astonishment, also figures of men at the end of the street in conversation.

No. 53.—(Destroyed.)

No. 54.—BOARD BILL ENGRAVING, 17-in. by 24-in.

Border, with four engravings, viz.:—Death of Meeran Hafiz; death of Colonel Mowbray by Red Ralph; Will Sideler on the Calais Pier recognised by Henry Ashton and his companion; and Old Martin denouncing Will Sideler as a murderer. Engraved for "**The Will and the Way.**"

No. 55.—TWO SHEET, 30-in. by 40-in.

Can be used singly if required. The top sheet represents the exterior of the Inn, at Lieursant, with cellar beneath; woody country with winding mail road; Dubosc in the act of shooting Jerome Lesurges, the innkeeper, while his companions are robbing the Mail. The second sheet represents the Place de Greve, with the apprehension and recognition of Dubosc the assassin. Engraved for the "**Courier of Lyons.**" Room for name of Theatre and date.

No. 56.—SINGLE SHEET, 30-in. by 20-in.
"Battle of the Alma."

No. 57.—SINGLE SHEET, 30-in. by 20-in.
One side represents "Gin," and the other "Water."

No. 58.—A BORDER, 17-in. by 24-in.

With five small Engravings, which work in two colours. Engraved for "**The Skeleton of the Wave.**"

No. 59.—FOUR SHEET, 60-in. by 40-in.

Represents a garden in the centre; in a car is the Fairy Queen and her attendant, the former waving her wand to the right, from which appears a female; the attendant is waving another wand to a fountain on the left, from which a man appears; fairies on either side. Engraved for a Pantomime.

No. 60.—FOUR SHEET, 40-in. by 60-in.

Represents the Garden of Freedom. In the centre is a circle, with Britannia in the middle, and her name around it, over which is a ship; the Fairy Freedom attended by the Messenger, Young Liberty; on the right stands Uncle Tom and the slave driver; and on the left Dandy Jim and other slave drivers.   Engraved for the Pantomime of **"Uncle Tom and Lucy Neal."**

No. 61.—SMALL ENGRAVING, 30-in. by 10-in.

On the right is seen a clown on a donkey, followed by three men, also on donkeys; on the left the Pantaloon is striking his donkey with a ladle to make him go.   Engraved for a pantomime.

No. 62.—BOARD BILL ENGRAVING, 17-in. by 24-in.

Figures, with ornamental frame, that work in two colors, viz:— Two Clowns, Harlequin, Columbine, Pantaloon, and Sprite.

No. 63.—SINGLE SHEET, 30-in. by 20-in.

Sylvan retreat of the Fairy Queen, surrounded by her Elfin Court; on the right, a youth seeking protection from her, on the left, a grotesque figure dancing.   Occupies the whole of the paper.

No. 64.—SINGLE SHEET, 30-in. by 20-in.

A coral cave, with rocks on each side; on the right are two sailors with large comical heads and swords in their hands; on the left, a figure representing Nicholas, with clenched fist and sword in hand; on the ground are two grotesque figures, with fairies on each side.   Room in centre for name and date.

No. 65.—SINGLE SHEET, 30-in. by 20-in.

An emblematical transformation scene; on the right, Clown and Pantaloon; on the left, Harlequin and Columbine; in the back ground, a group of fairies.   Room for name of Theatre and date.   Engraved for a Pantomime.

No. 66.—TWO SHEET, 60-in. by 20-in.

Representing a double street. Buyers and spectators, numerous people travelling in different directions; in the front, on one side are two clowns on geese, followed by pantaloon on the other; harlequin and columbine dancing.

14

No. 67.—(Destroyed.)

No. 68.—SINGLE SHEET, 30-in. by 20-in.

Representing a Hall; a male and female (lovers) alarmed at the sudden appearance of two persons, with large heads; one a negro, holding up a ring between his fingers, which both the lovers seem anxious to obtain. Engraved for " **The Fish and the Ring.**"

Nos. 69 & 70.—(Destroyed.)

No. 71.—FOUR SHEET, 60-in. by 40-in.

In the centre is a lad holding a scroll, saying, "he knows;" on the right, a boy is laughing: and another, on the left, who says, "I know and you know," pointing to the other two.   Engraved for a Pantomime.

No. 72.—FOUR SHEET, 40-in. by 60-in.

The Fairy Queen in the centre drawn in her car by 4 swans; on the right and left, her attendant fays are welcoming her appearance.   Engraved for a Pantomime.

No. 73.—SINGLE SHEET, 30-in. by 20-in.

A man in the act of firing a pistol, when he is seized by a dog, which has caused him to fall to the ground.

No. 74.— (Destroyed.)

75.—TWO SHEET, 40-in. by 30-in.

Representing a yard with shed at the side, houses seen at the back. Two ruffians, who have entered the yard, have caused the inmates to rise; villagers seen climbing the wall to the rescue; a man lying on the ground, thrown down by one of the ruffians; on one side a dog has seized another by the throat, on the other side a dog has seized another by the throat, on the other side his companion is seen escaping into a shed by a ladder, closely pursued by another dog.

No. 76—FOUR SHEET, 60-in. by 40-in.

On the right is a dog with a lantern in his mouth, on the left, Dame Gertrude is looking amazed.   Engraved for the "**Dog of Montargis.**"

15

No. 77.—TWO SHEET, 30-in. by 40-in

Representing a forest.   In the centre is a dog seizing a man by the throat, in the tree above a monkey in the act of throwing a cocoa-nut.

No. 78.—FOUR SHEET, 60-in. by 40-in.

In the centre is a man lying down as if dead, and another weeping over him at whose back is the murderer leaving the room, when he is seized by the throat by a dog.

No. 79.—FOUR SHEET, 60-in. by 40-in.

Plantation: in the distance is seen a cottage, and on the right a tree; on one side is a man in the act of firing a gun, on the other an Indian, with an axe in his hand ready to strike; on the left is an Indian with two dogs, one caressing him while the other is standing at his feet.

[No. 80.—FOUR SHEET, 60-in. by 40-in.

Forest; in front a man is seen lying on the ground, in contact with a lion that he is about to strike with a broken sword; at the back, five men are coming to his rescue.

No. 81.—(Destroyed.)

No. 82.—TWO SHEET, 30-in. by 40-in:

Figure of a demon, with a blank scroll in his hand, which can be filled up with type.   Engraved for "**Faust,**"

No. 83.—TWO SHEET, 40-in. by 30-in.

On the right are Turks, and on the left the French, both engaged in battle.

No. 84.—FOUR SHEET, 40-in. by 60-in.

Virginius embracing his daughter.

No. 85.—FOUR SHEET, 60-in. by 40-in.

Marguerite in the centre placing a bracelet on her arm, on the right hand Faust is approaching her; on the left hand, at a distance, is the demon looking on.   Engraved for "**Faust and Marguerite.**"

No. 86.—SMALL ENGRAVING, 15-in. by 20-in.

Figure of a man in rags, holding in his right hand a lamp, and in his left a dagger.

No. 87.—SMALL ENGRAVING, 20-in. by 15-in.

Representing in the centre the stern of a ship, on which are the words "Gallant Tom, or the Perils of a Sailor Ashore and Afloat;" on the right, a sailor holding a flag; on the left a negro with a torch.

No. 88.—SINGLE SHEET, 30-in. by 20-in.

Sea shore in the centre, with three men, one with a cutlass and about to strike a sailor who is lying on the ground exhausted, on the right is a sailor embracing a female.

No. 89.—SINGLE SHEET, 30-in. by 20-in.

A room. Two men quarrelling, one has struck the other, on the head; a man with a child kneeling at his feet is seen in the centre endeavouring to separate them.

No. 90.—SINGLE SHEET, 30-in. by 20-in.

A man descending a ladder, supporting a female, who has fainted. Engraved for the "**Fire of London.**"

Nos. 91 & 92.—(Destroyed.)

No. 93.—FOUR SHEET, 40-in. by 60-in.
Sampson carrying the gates of Gaza.

No. 94.—SINGLE SHEET, 20-in. by 30-in.
Tom Thumb in his Highland dress.

No. 95.—SINGLE SHEET, 20-in. by 30-in.
Tom Thumb as Field Marshal.

No. 96.—SINGLE SHEET, 20-in. by 30-in.
Tom Thumb executing his Jockey Dance.

No. 97.—SINGLE SHEET, 30-in. by 20-in.
Masquerade.

No. 98.—SINGLE SHEET BORDER, 30-in. by 20-in.
Half-figure of an African, holding a scroll, with the words "All should see."

No. 99.—THREE SINGLE SHEETS, each 30-in. by 20-in.
Horsemanship.

Nos. 100 & 101.—(Destroyed.)

No. 102.—TWO SHEET, 40-in. by 30-in.
A man chained to a rock, in which position he is attacked by an eagle.

No. 103.—TWO SHEET, 30-in. by 40-in.
Figure of a monkey.

No. 104.—SINGLE SHEET, 30-in. by 20-in.
In the centre is a bridge, on which the military force are engaged in battle ; an officer is overcome by one of the guerillas, who is defending a female ; on the right hand is another of the guerillas, followed by an officer with his standard ; on the left, reinforcements of the military are soon advancing.

No. 105.—SINGLE SHEET, 20-in. by 30-in.
Three-legged dancer.

No. 106.—SINGLE SHEET, 20-in. by 30-in.
Guy Faux.

No. 107.—SINGLE SHEET, 30-in. by 20-in.
In the centre is a man on horseback, leaping a gate ; on the right, a man running, trying to keep time with the horse.

No. 108.—SINGLE SHEET, 30-in. by 20-in.
A man in the act of seizing a gun, and is prevented by a female.

No. 109.—SINGLE SHEET, 30-in. by 20-in.
Represents at the back, a house on fire, with a man lying on a rafter as though dead ; on the right, a sailor, with sword in hand, has defeated two ruffians ; a woman standing behind in the attitude of prayer ; on the left, a highwayman and a groom pointing to the man on the rafter.

No. 110.—FOUR SHEET, 40-in. by 60-in.
Horsemanship. In the centre there is a tournament ; at the back, a clown conjuring ; on the right, a horse, with his fore legs on the back of a chair ; on the left is a horse, with his fore legs on a chest.

18

No. 111.—SMALL ENGRAVING, 20-in. by 15-in.
Walking match.

No. 112.—THREE SMALL ENGRAVINGS, 20-in. by 15-in. each.
Horse-riding.

No. 113.—(Destroyed.)

No. 114.—SMALL ENGRAVING, 15-in. by 20-in.
Balloon.

No. 115.—SMALL ENGRAVING, 15-in. by 20-in.
Sparring.

No. 116.—SMALL ENGRAVING, 15-in. by 20-in.
Full size figure of a Clown.

No. 117.—BOARD BILL ENGRAVING, 17-in. by 24-in.
Full size figure of a Clown.

No. 118.—SMALL ENGRAVING, 15-in. by 20-in.
A man executing a summersault in the air from a tight rope, while firing two pistols.

No. 119.—FOUR SHEET, 60-in. by 40-in.
Æriel flight of a female on a tight rope, surrounded by fire-works. Printed in two colours, if required.

No. 120.—FOUR SHEET, 40-in. by 60-in.
Top of the bill represents the launch of a Ship, surrounded by boats, gaily decorated with flags. The centre of the engraving, the storm at sea, crew cutting away the masts, sailor hauled up the side with female on his arm. Bottom, the break-up of the Ship, crowds of persons looking on. Engraved for "The Life of a Ship from Cradle to Grave."

19

No. 121.—FOUR SHEET, 40-in. by 60-in.
Top part represents the hold of the Tender off the Tower, sailor seizing man who is about to stab a youth, the youth, defending himself from a ruffian, black man in livery behind assisting him, the scene filled up by a crowd of persons. Bottom part, a vault with chests, swords, pistols, and guns hanging up, figure of sailor with axe in hand, emerging from an aperture in the centre.—Engraved for "Frank Heartwell."

No. 122.—FOUR SHEET, 60-in. by 40-in.
In the centre, large shilling with crown and one shilling engraved on it. L. H., chamber, man seated on chair, female standing by his side, the gamester's despair, over his head, cards, deeds, pistol, dagger, dice box, dice, goblet of poison. R. H., sailor relieving the wife and children of his dead messmate, flag over his head, anchor and cable, large purse with guineas falling from it, the sailor's prize.—Engraved for "The Last Shilling."

No. 123.—FOUR SHEET, 60-in. by 40-in.
L. H., the sea in a violent storm, forked lightning, Ship in centre (foundering,) man lashed to the mast, boat with three men in it leaving the ship and doomed man to his fate. R. H., the storm stone beacon rock, sailors and female on top looking down upon man who has been hurled from it, men rushing up with lighted torches, beacon light on rock. Engraved for "The Lost Ship."

No. 124.—FOUR SHEET, 60-in. by 40-in.
In the centre, space for Letter-Press, round the centre representing large cable coiled, with anchor hanging from it, L. H., figure of water-man standing with oar in hand, back ground representing a rowing match. R. H., figure of a British tar wielding cutlass, action between two ships in the back ground. Engraved for "Tom Trim."

No 125.—FOUR SHEET, 60-in. by 40-in.
Men-of-war assembled at Spithead, boats filled with sailors and marines, vessels and boats out, boat in centre, man with cat-o'-nine tails, man overboard, the whole shewing the preparations for flogging a man round the fleet. Engraved for "Armstrong the Shipwright."

No. 126.—FOUR SHEET, 60-in. by 40-in.
In the centre, the open sea, rising of the moon. Boat in the centre landing crew, officer standing up in the bows with flag, man-of-war sailing. On L. H. soldiers headed by officer firing upon men in boat. R. H., high and rugged rock, female standing on it with dagger in hand, another on her knees behind her, sailor falling from it into the sea beneath, winding road, with hut upon it, leading to the top of rock, groups of men armed with guns, standing in picturesque attitudes. Engraved for "Raby Rattler."

No. 127.—TWO SHEET, 40-in. by 30-in.
Hold of a ship, hatchway open, sailor descending by rope, another firing a pistol, a man falling, flames rising from the lower deck. Engraved for "Ben the Boatswain."

No. 128.—TWO SHEET, 40-in. by 30-in.
Ship on fire and running on shore, man at the wheel, a man and woman about to jump overboard, soldiers on shore firing at them, villagers, &c., exhibiting great alarm.

No. 129.—TWO SHEET, 40-in. by 30-in.
Ship foundering, man and woman escaping on raft. Engraved for the "Life Raft."

No. 130.—TWO SHEET, 30-in. by 40-in.
The phantom ship in full sail, off the Cape. Engraved for the "Flying Dutchman."

No. 131.—TWO SHEET, 40-in. by 30-in.
The "Flying Dutchman" boarding the Cape trader, crew and passengers in attitudes of dismay and horror—Engraved for the "Flying Dutchman."

No. 132.—TWO SHEET, 40-in. by 30-in.
Deck of a ship, crew in a state of mutiny, captain firing pistol, his arm arrested by a sailor—Engraved for the "White Squall."

No. 133.—SINGLE SHEET, 30-in. by 20-in.
Ship on fire, boat's crew with captain leaving her, drowning sailors, exhibiting a fearful picture of the vicissitudes of a seaman's life.

No. 134.—SINGLE SHEET, 20-in. by 30-in.
Represents a seaman lowering himself from the bowsprit of a ship, rescuing a woman and child from the raging waves beneath. Engraved for "**The Sea, the Sea.**"

No. 135.—SINGLE SHEET, 30-in. by 20-in.
Represents the cabin of a ship, sailor springing thro' cabin window firing pistol at man, L. H. Figure of female with hands uplifted, R. H.

No. 136.—SINGLE SHEET, 20-in. by 30-in.
British sailor pointing to the flag of victory.

No. 137.—SINGLE SHEET, 15-in. by 20-in.
Five tableaux in frame work, with colored ink and black pictures. L. H. top, ship on fire, crew and passengers escaping from it by bowsprit, vessel bearing down in distance. R. H. top, desperate combat between smugglers and preventive men, sailor on ground, man about to fire, female on her knees interceding, centre rocky ravine with cataract of water, men with torches, smugglers firing at man on rock, who is falling from it, sailor and girl on their knees. L. H. bottom, middle deck of a ship, fire rushing from the hold, man with torch escaping up ladder, men and women in a state of agony and despair. R. H. bottom, deck of a ship, man supported by two sailors, female in the arms of a sailor, general picture. Engraved for a *Nautical Drama.*

No. 138.—SIX SHEET, 60-in. by 60-in.
In the centre is a splendid pavilion in which her Majesty and the late Prince Albert are discovered, unique vase of flowers, the whole surmounted by the crown of England surrounded by portraits of Lord Palmerston, Lord John Russell, Lord Brougham, B. D'Israeli, the late Duke of Wellington, the Prince of Wales and Princess Royal.—Engraved for the Pantomime of "**Harlequin Ice Queen.**"

No. 139.—FOUR SHEET, 30-in. by 80-in.
Full-length figure of a clown, with placard on his breast, "hilloa! how are you? Come and see me!"

22

No. 140.—(Destroyed.)

No. 141.—FOUR SHEET, 60-in. by 40-in.
Exterior of Hardiknute's castle. R. H., Hardiknute seated with goblet in hand, twelve females dancing and representing the twelve months of the year, an old man representing Winter, three females representing Summer, Spring, and Autumn, grotesque figures L. H., with large knife and fork, banners with inscriptions. Back ground filled up with army of soldiers. Engraved for "**Hardiknute or the Wood Demon.**"

No. 142.—FOUR SHEET, 60-in. by 40-in.
Representing the exterior of Hasting's Castle, combat between Harold and William the Conqueror, Normans and Saxons in grotesque costumes fighting, banners with quaint inscriptions upon them. Engraved for the Pantomime of "**William the Conqueror.**"

No. 143.—FOUR SHEET, 60-in. by 40-in.
Engraving of grotesque heads round border. Engraved for the Pantomime of "**Riddle me Ree.**"

No. 144.—FOUR SHEET, 60-in. by 40-in.
Six tableaux top. Centre represents the Queen seated, Prince Albert by her side, the Princess Royal handing her a rose. L. H. corner demon with lighted torch rising out of the ground, females holding lights. R. H. corner, interior of room, bedstead, shelf over door with culinary utensils on it, man's head in saucepan on floor, man knocking it in with a poker, boys in the back ground shouting. R. H. bottom woman in centre holding up wand, females with garlands, Saint Paul's in the distance. Bottom, three comic figures. L. H. corner, interior of a room, select vestry up over the door, beadle with staff, vestrymen, &c. Engraved for the Pantomime of "**Old Bogle.**"

No. 145.—FOUR SHEET, 60-in. by 40-in.
Ten comic figures of boys with large figures over them, ranging from 1 to 10; beneath, figures representing reduction, substraction, long and short division, multiplication, Dame Interest, and Young Practice, comic head looking down upon them. Engraved for the Pantomime of "**Harlequin and Old Cocker.**"

23

No. 146.—FOUR SHEET, 60-in. by 40-in.
Represents a number of comic letters, forming the words, "The knight and the sprite," monstrous fish swimming about, two knights and the enchanted lady, figure of hydropathy in the centre. Engraved for "**The Knight and the Sprite.**"

No. 146½.—FOUR SHEET, 40-in. by 60-in.
Represents St. Paul's in the distance, Whittington seated in a disconsolate attitude by a mile-stone, bundle and stick at his feet, large cat standing on hind legs pawing him on the shoulder. Engraved for the Pantomime of "**Whittington and Cat.**"

No. 147.—THREE SHEET, 60-in. by 30-in.
Represents the three magic letters "L. S. D." clown entwining himself round the letter S., with bottle in one hand and goose in the other harlequin and columbine dancing behind the letter L., pantaloon leaning upon stick, looking out of letter D.—Engraved for the Pantomime of L. S. D.

No. 148.—THREE SHEET, 60-in. by 30-in.
Magnificent Hall, grotesque figures seated in the centre, surrounded by golden peacocks of the sun. R. H., band of grotesque yeomen of the guard, led by tiny trumpeters. L. H., the same, four nymphs dancing in the centre, peacocks of golden hues standing on pillars of gold, harlequin and columbine on the one side, clown and pantaloon on the other. Engraved for the Pantomime of "**King of the Castle, or Harlequin in the Land of Dreams.**"

No. 149.—THREE SHEET, 60-in. by 30-in.
Magic car led by fairies with golden wands tipped with brilliant stars, bands of fairies above and below, bestowing a hearty welcome upon their queen. Engraved for "**Cinderella.**"

No. 150.—THREE SHEET, 60-in. by 30-in.
Represents on each side medallion portraits of the principal persons in the drama of "Cinderella," Cinderella blowing the fire, Cinderella and the fairy, the transformation, the ball-room scene, dancing with the prince, trying on the glass slipper. Engraved for "**Cinderella.**"

No. 151.—TWO SHEET, 60-in. by 20-in.
Represents a clock in the centre, harlequin and columbine, clown and pantaloon, supporting it on either side. Engraved for the Pantomime of "One o'clock or Harlequin Wood Demon."

No. 152.—TWO SHEET, 30-in. by 40-in.
Comic figure with crown on head—knife and fork in hand seated on plum pudding.

No. 153.—TWO SHEET, 30-in. by 40-in.
Comic figure with cap on head and skates on feet, sliding down a globe.

No. 154.—TWO SHEET, 30-in. by 40-in.
The old dame dancing with her cat. Engraved for Pantomime of "Dame Trot and her Comical Cat."

No. 155.—TWO SHEET, 30-in. by 40-in.
The Cock that crowed in the early morn,—
  "Cock-a-doodle doo, dame has lost her shoe,
  "Master's lost his fiddlestick, and don't know what to do."
Engraved for Pantomime of "Goody Two Shoes."

No. 156.—TWO SHEET, 30-in. by 40-in.
Georgy Barnwell with large blunderbuss, figure on gibbet hanging in chains, mile-stone with imp upon it, other imps surrounding it. Engraved for the Pantomime of "Harlequin Georgy Barnwell."

No. 157.—TWO SHEET, 30-in. by 40-in.
Coral cave with sprite suspended in the air, nymphs of the coral cave dancing around the rescued knight and lady, showers of golden fire. Engraved for the Pantomime of the "Spirit of the Snow Drift, or the Frozen Charm."

No. 158.—TWO SHEET, 30-in. by 40-in.
Figure of a magician, and large magic te-to-tum. Engraved for the Pantomime of "Fe-fo-fum, or Harlequin te-to-tum."

25

No. 159.—TWO SHEET, 40-in. by 30-in.

In centre, brilliant revolving star, fairies floating in the air surrounded by sportive cupids, magic car of peacocks, harlequin, columbine, clown and pantaloon. Engraved for the Pantomime of "**Saint Monday, or Harlequin Crispin and the Demon Dwarf.**"

No. 160.—TWO SHEET, 30-in. by 40-in.

Lion and clown, lion springing on the clown's back, who exhibits great horror and dismay.

No. 161.—TWO SHEET, 40-in. by 30-in.

Robin De Bord in the centre with large club spiked, surrounded by his attendants, platters on their heads, ye Town of Lud in the distance. Engraved for the Pantomime of "**Harlequin King Arthur or Merlin and the Queen of Fayre Land.**"

No. 162.—TWO SHEET, 40-in. by 30-in.

In the centre, the demon dwarf standing over the body of his victim, serpents, imps, owls, bats, &c., flying in the air, knights, ladies and attendants in attitudes of horror and dismay. Engraved for the "**Demon Dwarf.**"

No. 163.—TWO SHEET, 40-in. by 30-in.

Splendid tableau of last scene, fairies, sprites, harlequin, columbine, clown and pantaloon in the grove of a thousand palms. Engraved for a Pantomime.

No. 164.—TWO SHEET, 30-in. by 40-in.

Large clown's head, head of all the clowns.

No. 165.—TWO SHEET, 40-in. by 30-in.

A baronial hall in the palace of King Lud, King Lud with uplifted mace in the centre surrounded by his attendants, revolving star at the back, lady kneeling to demon, the whole lighted up with brilliant fires. Engraved for "**Harlequin King Lud.**'

No. 166.—TWO SHEET, 30-in. by 40-in.

Tower in centre, a little yellow man springing from it, king an queen of the golden mountains gazing with astonishment. Engrave for the Pantomime of "**The Little Yellow Man.**'

26

No. 167.—SINGLE SHEET, 30-in. by 20-in.

Gigantic cavern, rocky steps in centre descending from an enormous height, figures, male and female, entering cave. R. & L., demons in different attitudes, on each side colossal pillars, wreathed with serpents.—"**Earth.**"

No. 168.—SINGLE SHEET, 30-in. by 20-in.

The interior of a vine-covered villa, fairy figures ascending with lovely female. R. H., two figures in expressive attitudes pointing to the ascending group.—"**Air.**"

No. 169.—SINGLE SHEET, 30-in. by 20-in.

Represents in the centre a car rising with figures rejoicing at their escape from the fiery regions below, pillars on each side entwined with blazing serpents, a sea of fire at the bottom with frantic demons. "**Fire.**"

No. 170.—SINGLE SHEET, 30-in. by 20-in.

Represents the ascent of the "Storm King" and his bride from the fathomless waters of the mighty deep. R. H., figure of a knight about to plunge in. L. H., man gazing with fear and astonishment.—"**Water.**"

No. 171.—SINGLE SHEET, 20-in. by 30-in.

Full length figure of a clown.

No. 172.—SINGLE SHEET, 30-in. by 20 in.

Old dame with the shoes in a circle, on each side harlequin and columbine, clown, and pantaloon. Engraved for the Pantomime of "Goody Two Shoes."

No. 173.—SINGLE SHEET, 30-in. by 20-in.

Old dame with broom in hand standing by large shoe. Engraved for the Pantomime of "Goody Two Shoes."

No. 174.—SINGLE SHEET, 20-in. by 30-in.

Large cat's head. Engraved for the Pantomime of "Old Dame Trot."

No. 175.—(Destroyed.)

27

No. 176.—FOUR SHEET, 60-in. by 40-in.

Exterior of a gothic mansion. This engraving represents four scenes in one. R.H., upper chamber, a man seated at table, writing. R.H., lower chamber, staircase leading to upper room, man going up with dark lantern in one hand and pistol in the other, man entering at window. In the centre, a door at which a man is knocking, overhead a female ringing a bell in turret. L.H., upper chamber, bed with children asleep, window with the moon's rays beaming through underneath, part of a forest, woman rushing to the door. Engraved for "**The Dream of Life.**"

No. 177.—FOUR SHEET, 60-in. by 40-in.

Interior of a gothic hall. Man in the centre, with dagger in his uplifted hand; man resisting his attack, another standing on chair, R. H., escaping at winding; table with goblets upon it, L. H., man and female looking on with wonder and affright. Engraved for "**Crichton of Clunie.**"

No. 178.—FOUR SHEET, 60-in. by 40-in.

Represents the destruction of the Bastile. Immense concourse of persons looking from the walls upon the populace beneath. Man standing towards L. H., with pike and human head upon it; man waving flag in centre over the head of a man and female. Priest standing, L. H., over the body of a dead officer; groups of the dead, dying, and wounded on the ground. Engraved for "**The Destruction of the Bastile.**"

No. 179.—FOUR SHEET, 60-in. by 40-in.

View in a forest. In the back ground, rude rustic bridge; spire of village church in the distance; numerous figures of dead and dying soldiers stretched upon the ground; female upon her knees anxiously looking in the face of a soldier extended dead upon the hearth. Engraved for "**Poor Susan.**"

No. 180.—FOUR SHEET, 60-in. by 40-in.

Exterior of an old Mansion on the banks of the river Thames. Extreme end of the building, Mervyn leaping through the window into the water; man looking out of window above him with dagger; boat with two men in it, looking on with astonishment and dread. In chamber, R. H., a man about to fire pistol at Mervyn, when his arm is arrested by Claude Duval. Chamber, L. H., figure on the ground, man standing over him with uplifted dagger; man rushing in at the back. Medallion portrait of Old Elkanah, R. H. Ditto of Claude Duval, L. H. Engraved for "**Whitefriars.**"

No. 181.—FOUR SHEET, 60-in. by 40-in.

Full length figure of Guy Faux, seated in dungeon, dead body of a man at his feet. Engraved for "**Guy Faux.**"

No. 182.—FOUR SHEET, 40-in. by 60-in.

The upper part of the Engraving represents the ill-fated lovers on the rock of Bourbon; men descending from rock with torches, the wild waves dashing against the rocks; the lower chambers represent the dungeons in the Bastile, R. H., surrounded by flames; woman standing at window; man standing with cap of liberty on pole. Beneath in a dungeon, a man supporting another. In the centre, men armed with battle axes, preparing to break through. Three figures, L. H., in picturesque attitudes. Engraved for "**The Black Doctor.**"

No. 183.—FOUR SHEET, 40-in. by 60-in.

In the centre, a large Bottle; woman lying on the floor with child on her lap; girl standing up, clasping her hand, and pointing to the bottle. Man, L. H., seated on chair, with bottle in one hand, and glass in the other; a youth in rags gazing upon him; Gin Demons in wreaths pointing with exultation and joy at the bottle. Engraved for "**The Bottle.**"

No. 184.—FOUR SHEET, 40-in. by 60-in.

Represents Jolly Christmas, giving a welcome to Scrooge, the miser; barrel of double X with punch-bowl on it, surrounded by bottles, on the floor pies, tarts, puddings, beef, game, &c.; large fire on hearth; holly, mistletoe, &c., wreathed round the ceiling. Engraved for "**Christmas Carol.**"

No. 185.—FOUR SHEET, 60-in. by 40-in.

Scene, wild forest scenery; ruins of abbey. Man, R. H., armed with pistols, on horse leaping over gate; another restraining horse by the old tree; winding road, with coach and horses. Old wall, L. H.; man on horseback, armed with blunderbuss; behind, another man, armed, on foot, watching, and ready for action. Engraved for "**Paul Clifford.**"

No. 186.—FOUR SHEET, 60-in. by 40-in.

Represents scene in cottage; man entering door; blind girl seated at fire; female standing, her hands uplifted in astonishment; man and two females seated round a table; girl with child. Engraved for "**Cricket on the Hearth.**"

29

No. 187.—FOUR SHEET, 40-in. by 60-in.

The upper part represents a number of men dressed in singular costumes, representing the Bohemians of Paris ; beneath, the river Seine, with bridge over it, crowds of persons looking down at two figures, male and female, in a boat. A chamber, L H., with numerous figures in the back ground ; man standing in centre ; two men rising another from cellar, one with uplifted arm, about to strike. Forest, R. H. ; old man about to stab a female who is kneeling. Bottom picture, R H , file of soldiers in centre ; struggle between two men ; female on her knees ; figures behind gazing on them. Engraved for **"The Bohemians of Paris."**

No. 188.—FOUR SHEET, 60-in. by 40-in.

Gothic stone bridge, supported by massive pillars, with chambers top and bottom ; crowds of warriors defending the bridge on either side ; a terrific melée in the foreground ; Turkish warrior waving his scimitar ; large bodies of Turks rushing on R. and L. ; Turks and Christian warriors engaged in fearful conflict. Engraved for **"The Silver Crescent."**

No 189.—FOUR SHEET, 60-in by 40-in.

Represents, L H., a mountain torrent, surrounded by rocks ; bridge broken in half, from which a man is falling into gulf of water below ; woman on rock gazing on with horror and dismay. Represents, R. H., a vaulted chamber, table, bed, man about to stab himself, but is prevented by a female. Engraved for **"The Capture of Silesia."**

No. 190.—FOUR SHEET, 40-in. by 60-in.

The progress and fall of a drunkard's children, illustrated in six tableaux ; boy smoking, playing at cards ; doctor closing the transport's eyes ; girl dressed in finery, dancing at a casino ; jumping from bridge, meeting a fearful death. Engraved for **"The Drunkard's Children."**

No. 191.—FOUR SHEET, 60-in. by 40-in.

The alchymist's hall ; in the centre, large cauldron, from which the Evil One is rising. Right hand, large telescope on stand ; knights and ladies gazing on with fear and wonder. Left hand, knights and ladies, tables on both sides, with globes, bottles, &c., on them ; skeletons, birds, and reptiles hanging up. Engraved for **"The Devil's Opera."**

30

No. 192.—THREE SHEET, 60-in. by 30-in.

Magnificent hall with lofty pillars ; in the distance the city and lake by moonlight, groups of ladies and cavaliers ascending marble steps, in the centre of the hall a couch. R. H., table with splendid vases and flowers, chamberlain with wand, announcing a visitor. L. H., a table with writing implements upon it, Don Cæsar starting up in chair with a paper in his hand. Duenna and lady looking on with astonishment, on either side the figure of Don Cæsar seated. Engraved for **"Don Cæsar de Bazan."**

No. 193.—THREE SHEET, 60-in. by 30-in.

Represents R H., the exterior of a prison, woman letting herself down by rope, people rushing from house gazing upon her, mob of people with lighted torches looking down upon her from the walls, ladder raised against window. L. H., outside of the jail, crowds of people assembled gazing upon a figure kneeling, having just alighted from a horse, man rushing forward with paper, the whole exhibiting a scene of excitement and wonder. Engraved for **"Margaret Catchpole."**

No. 194.—TWO SHEET, 30-in. by 40-in.

In the centre, a female clinging to a man, soldiers firing and rushing down upon the brigands, figures in foreground in a state of anxiety and fear. Engraved for **"The Profligate."**

No. 195.—TWO SHEET, 30-in. by 40-in.

Head of a Turkish chief. Engraved for **"Blue Beard."**

No. 196.—TWO SHEET, 40-in. by 30-in.

Woman on tower looking out with telescope, large clock in the centre, female on her knees, a man about to strike off her head with a scimitar, a black man alarmed in the back ground. Engraved for the burlesque of **"Blue Beard."**

No. 197.—TWO SHEET, 40-in. by 30-in.

Coach on Hounslow Heath, surrounded by footpads in masks, figures descending from coach, figure in centre levelling pistol at them. Engraved for **"Paul Clifford."**

31

No. 198.—TWO SHEET, 40-in. by 30-in.

Temple in the centre surrounded by populace, Abelard and Heloise in the temple, figure on the ground, man supporting female, people kneeling. Engraved for **"Abelard and Heloise."**

No. 199.—TWO SHEET, 40-in. by 30-in.

Magnificent temple and tournament. R.H., cottage and mill. L.H., warrior contending for the prize of victory, King upon the throne surrounded by his court, knights with banners. Engraved for the **"Mountain Cataract"**

No. 200.—TWO SHEET, 30-in. by 40-in.

Precipitous rock with figure of a man partly kneeling, female falling from the top into the waves beneath. Engraved for **"Simon's Yat."**

No. 201.—TWO SHEET, 30-in. by 40-in.

Scene in the Highlands, highlanders assembled on the mountains at the firing of the beacons, vessels on the lake, warrior crossing a bridge. Engraved for **"The Gathering of the Clans."**

No. 202.—TWO SHEET, 30-in. by 40-in.

Antique houses closed, old street and place in London. Engraved for **"The Earl of Poverty."**

No. 203.—TWO SHEET, 30-in. by 40-in.

Female clinging to a bell in the belfry of Old Chertsey Church. Engraved for **"Blanche Herriot."**

No. 204.—TWO SHEET, 30-in. by 40-in.

Portrait of Hogarth and his Dog. Engraved for **"Marriage-a-la-mode."**

No. 205.—TWO SHEET, 30-in. by 40-in.

A negro lady in full costume. Engraved for the Drama of **"The Black Swan."**

No. 206.—TWO SHEET, 40-in. by 30-in.

The Lone Hut, man appearing at window, in the centre, female on her knees, man with dagger approaching to kill her. Engraved for **"The Lone Hut."**

No. 207.—TWO SHEET, 40-in. by 30-in.

Battersea Bridge, cutter with four women in it and coxswain. Engraved for **"The Water Witches,"**

No. 208.—TWO SHEET, 30-in. by 40-in.

Barnaby Rudge, full length. Engraved for **"Barnaby Rudge,"**

No 209.—TWO SHEET, 40-in. by 30-in.

"Mazeppa" bound to the Wild Horse.

No. 210.—TWO SHEET, 30-in. by 40-in.

Shadow appearing to man in the foreground. Engraved for the Drama of **"The Shadow, or the Mother's Dream."**

No. 211.—TWO SHEET, 30-in. by 40-in.

Engraving of Guy Fawkes, from Ainsworth's **"Tower of London."**

No. 212.—TWO SHEET, 30-in. by 40-in.

Richard the Third in full costume, with "Richard's himself again." Engraved for the burlesque of **"Richard the Third."**

No. 213.—TWO SHEET, 30-in. by 40-in.

Richard the Third in full costume. Engraved for the Burlesque of **"Richard the Third."**

No. 214.—TWO SHEET, 40-in. by 30-in.

Man standing on a piece of rock in the centre of a stream, two men extended from R. to L., girl rushing over them. Engraved for " **The Bridge of Life.**"

No. 215.—TWO SHEET, 40-in. by 30-in.

"Gin and Water."—Immense goblets, R. and L.; the spirit of gin rising from a goblet, water ascending, the whole forming a splendid tableau. Engraved for "**Gin and Water**'

No. 216.—TWO SHEET, 40-in. by 30-in.

"Gin and Water"—The brutal husband and misery; the happy husband, children, and friends. Engraved for "**Gin & Water.**"

No. 217.—(Destroyed.)

No. 218.—TWO SHEET, 40-in. by 30-in.

A raft floating down the river with two females upon it, boats and men sinking; huts being destroyed by the flood of waters, the whole representing a fearful inundation. Engraved for "**The Inundation.**"

No. 219.—TWO SHEET, 40-in. by 30-in.

"Tyburn Tree."—Jack Sheppard cut down, crowds of soldiers, mobs surrounding the death cart. Engraved for "**Jack Sheppard.**"
☞ Various other Engravings connected with this Drama can also be had.

No. 220.—TWO SHEET, 30-in by 40-in.

Satan dressed in the fashion of the present day. Engraved for "**Asmodeus.**"

No. 221.—SINGLE SHEET, 30-in. by 20-in.

View of the "George Inn," shewing. L.H., a sleeping apartment, Mr. Hayes asleep in chair, Dan Macraisy entering window. R. H., apartment, bed, table, and chair, Mr. Hayes dead on the floor. Beneath, bar of the innkeeper. Jonathan Bradford, Bradford on his knees, Ann Bradford clasping her hands with grief, man shewing bloody knife, soldiers with muskets. R. and L. sign up, "the George Inn." Engraved for "**Jonathan Bradford.**"

34

No. 222.—SINGLE SHEET, 30-in. by 20-in.

The vault beneath the church. In the centre, the tomb of Mr. Hayes. R.H., Caleb Scrimmage. L.H., Dan Macraisy, forming tableau. Engraved for "**Jonathan Bradford.**"

No. 223.—SINGLE SHEET, 20-in. by 30-in.

Represents the figure of a man asleep in a chair, female kneeling protecting him from the Dream Spectre who is hovering over him as if about to depart from his victim. Engraved for the "**Dream Spectre.**"

No. 224.—SINGLE SHEET, 30-in. by 20-in.

Represents in the back ground a road side cottage, winding road and waggon. In the foreground, a man dressed as a vagrant, child crying by his side, woman carrying a dead youth, a child clinging to her back. Engraved for the "**Vagrant and his Family.**"

No. 225.—SINGLE SHEET, 30-in. by 20-in.

The interior of Perrybingle's cottage. R.H., man with his head on table asleep, gun by his side. In the back ground, a vision, female kneeling with infant in her arms, other figures surrounding her; L.H., the fairy with wand. Engraved for "**The Cricket on the Hearth.**"

No. 226.—SINGLE SHEET, 30-in. by 20-in.

Forest scene, representing a road in forest with cave beneath, general conflict between soldiers and brigands. Beneath, in the cave, man and female escaping, man with drawn sword assisting their escape.

No. 227.—(Destroyed.)

No. 228.—SINGLE SHEET, 30-in. by 20-in.

Clouds dispersing. Female with child surrounded by guardian angels ascending to Heaven. L.H., female supporting a dying youth in centre, man on the earth dead, figure kneeling over him. R.H., woman falling on her knees, man raising his hands in prayer.

No. 229.—SINGLE SHEET, 30-in. by 20-in.

Represents a snow drift, female figure standing centre, one hand uplifted, the other supporting child. R.H., man in suppliant attitude, L. H., girl extended dead on the bank, mother kneeling shielding her from the snow storm.

35

No. 230.—SINGLE SHEET, 20-in. by 30-in.

In the back ground a bridge extending from side to side, conflict between soldiers and brigands. Centre foreground, man embracing female and youth, girl kneeling to them, figures exhibiting joy and happiness behind.

No. 231.—SINGLE SHEET, 30-in. by 20-in.

Mazeppa fastened to the back of the "Wild Steed" of the forest, figures restraining the horse, rocky mountains in distance. Engraved for "**Mazeppa.**"

No. 232.—SINGLE SHEET, 30-in. by 20-in.

Man on horseback, riding in the air, pointing upward. Engraved for the "**The Bronze Horse.**"

No. 233.—SINGLE SHEET, 30-in. by 20-in.

Represents a bridge, back ground. Centre, a dog seizing man who is escaping from him. R.H., man stabbing another who has fallen on the ground.

No. 234.—SINGLE SHEET, 30-in. by 20-in.

In the back ground, village church and village. In the centre, man standing with uplifted torch, officer giving the word of command, R.H., soldiers in the act of firing. L.H., deserter kneeling, keeping off the dog, who has broken away and is vainly struggling to leap upon his master. Engraved for the "**Deserter and his Dog.**"

No. 235.—FOUR SHEET, 40-in. by 30-in.

Full length figure of Joan of Arc. Engraved for the Burlesque of "**Joan of Arc.**"

No. 236.—FOUR SHEET, 40-in. by 60-in.

Female figure in the centre, youth kneeling to her. Man dressed as African Chief with club, looking out of window in the back ground, fountains and a swing bridge. Engraved for "**Davis and ...**"

No. 237.—FOUR SHEET, 60-in. by 40-in.

View of Waterloo Bridge by moonlight. Toll gate. Jack in the water talking to fireman. Waterman smoking pipe; R.H., the toll collector standing by. Engraved for "**Jack in the Water.**"

No. 238.—FOUR SHEET, 60-in. by 40-in.

Temple Bar. Man driving a cab, with gentleman inside; lady and gentleman walking, umbrella up, waterman holding out hand for a copper, old man and swell, man with basket of sandwiches. Engraved for "**The Road of Life.**"

No. 239.—FOUR SHEET, 80-in. by 30-in.

The cabman, the swell, the excavator, and the father. Engraved for "**The Road of Life.**"

No. 240.—FOUR SHEET, 60-in. by 40-in.

The Temple of Antigone. Priests, warriors, &c., Creon, Antigone, band, audience, and conductor. Engraved for the Burlesque of "**Antigone.**"

No. 241.—FOUR SHEET, 60-in. by 40-in.

Represents an extensive landscape. Gods and goddesses, Cupid, male and female figures. R. & L., clusters of rich grapes hanging about. Engraved for the "**Boyhood of Bacchus.**"

No. 242.—FOUR SHEET, 80-in. by 30-in.

Four comic heads, Norma, Adalgisa, Pollio, and Flavio. Engraved for the Burlesque of "**Norma.**"

No. 243.—FOUR SHEET, 60-in. by 40-in.

Interior of a kitchen. Female coming down stairs and looking with astonishment upon a man dressed very fashionably, man dressed as costermonger touching his hat to him, old woman looking on with wonder. Engraved for "**The Railway King.**"

No. 244.—FOUR SHEET, 40-in. by 60-in.

Figure of a lad seated on a mile stone, with bundle at his foot, large cat standing up by his side. Engraved for "**Whittington and his Cat.**"

No. 245.—THREE SHEET, 60-in. by 30-in.

A street with houses on each side, old-fashioned house at the back. In the centre, man standing with a ladder, link in his hand surrounded by mob. R.H., woman with a barrow of cherries, behind her, man at stall, bawling out saloop ! L. H., costermonger and donkey laden with vegetables. In the corner, black brushing shoes, woman looking over balcony. Engraved for "**Life's a Lottery.**"

No. 246.—THREE SHEET, 60-in. by 30-in.

A wood, man in chaise handing out purse, man on horseback levelling pistol at him ; sign post, London, Hounslow. Centre, figure of man with purse in one hand, boot in the other, man bound to a tree, boy pulling his boot off. Engraved for "**Sixteen String Jack.**"

No. 247.—TWO SHEET, 30-in. by 40-in.

Figure of an opera dancer standing in an imposing attitude. Engraved for "**The Pet of the Ballet.**"

No. 248.—TWO SHEET, 30-in. by 40-in.

Man seated on stile, with hat on side of his head ; country village in the distance. Engraved for "**The Artful Dodger.**"

No. 249.—TWO SHEET, 30-in. by 40-in.

In the centre a sailor and his lass dancing, the medallion formed of a knotted cable over their heads, sailor hanging on yard cheering them on, beneath them the wreck of a ship, two flags each side of them. L. H. top, Tom Tulloch the ostler. Bottom, Tom Tulloch the seaman. R. H. top, Polly Marygold the country lass. Bottom Polly Marygold the ballad singer and seller. Engraved for "**Our Village.**"

No. 250.—TWO SHEET, 40-in. by 30-in.

In the centre, a man dressed as a robber brandishing a long knife, pistols in belt, long cap and feather, looking fiercely at a girl on her knees, dressed in long pinafore and frilled trousers ; doll on ground R. H., great overgrown lubberly boy crying, handkerchief to his eyes, frill around his neck, hoop and stick in his hand. In the back ground a wood by moonlight ; each side the engraving is a large dagger and pistol. Engraved for the Burlesque of "**The Babes in the Wood.**"

38

No. 251.—TWO SHEET, 30-in. by 40-in.

Cupid, with another, dancing the mock Tarantella. The border composed of serpents, grotesque faces looking up and upon the dancers, flowers lying at their feet. Engraved for "**The Olympic Tarantella.**"

No. 252.—TWO SHEET, 30-in. by 40-in.

Effigy of "Robinson Crusoe ;" parrot on stick.

No. 253.—TWO SHEET, 40-in. by 30-in.

Trial scene in "The Merchant of Venice." Engraved for the Burlesque of "**The Merchant of Venice.**"

No. 254.—TWO SHEET, 40-in. by 30-in.

Section of a house open to the audience. Upper chamber, L. H., man kneeling to clergyman. Upper chamber, R. H., female lying on bed ; rooms beneath filled with company. Engraved for "**The Adventures of a Gentleman.**"

No. 255.—SINGLE SHEET, 20-in. by 30-in.

The interior of a mill : In the upper part female fainting in the arms of a soldier ; figure of a man hanging by one leg from the rafter ; two soldiers advancing with fixed bayonets ; large mill stones. Engraved for "**The Deserted Mill.**"

No. 256.—SINGLE SHEET, 20-in. by 30-in.

Figure of an opera dancer burlesquely attired as Cupid ; wreath of carrots and turnips ; wings at his back. Engraved for "**Black Cupid,**"

No. 257.—SINGLE SHEET, 20-in. by 30-in.

Figure of a man with tray in front, with boxes of lucifer matches, holding one in his left hand ; angel's head on the one side, Lucifer's on the other. Engraved for "**Angels & Lucifers.**"

No. 258.—SINGLE SHEET, 20-in. by 30-in.

Young Norval with bow and quiver full of arrows, leaning on a spear, sword by his side, buckler on his arm, plaid scarf over his shoulder, cap and feather. Engraved for "**Norval.**"

39

No. 259.—SINGLE SHEET, 30-in. by 20-in.

Interior of a room, the fire burning brightly ; man seated on a chair with his head on a table fast asleep ; a bottle and plate, with knife and fork ; window open, looking on the roof next house ; moon shining ; man entering with dark lantern and bag in hand. Round the border, chops and knife and fork. Engraved for "**Pork Chops.**"

No. 260.—SINGLE SHEET, 20-in. by 30-in.

Tinkering Joe, with box of implements, old saucepans and pan of fire. Engraved for "**Tinker Joe.**"

No. 261.—SINGLE SHEET, 20-in. by 30-in.

The Little Gipsy, fancifully attired, telling a fortune. Engraved for Miss Fanny Williams.

No. 262.—SIXTEEN SHEET, 120-in. by 80-in.

The Golden Temple of Guadina at Rangoon, lighted by candlesticks of virgin gold ; canopies of golden stars ; myriads of rockets ascending in honour of the great idol Dagon ; giving a very lively portraiture of the Burmese manners and customs.

No. 263.—TWELVE SHEET, 90-in. by 80-in.

Pedestal with bust of Shakespeare placed on the top of a gigantic wreath ; cupids soaring in the air with small wreaths, about to crown the poet for all ages. Melpomene, L. H., standing with dagger and bowl. Thalia, R. H., with mask in hand ; emblems of art and science at their feet. In the centre, large space for letter-press. This engraving can be printed in two colored inks.

No. 264.—NINE SHEET, 90-in. by 60-in.

The town and forts of Cronstadt, by moonlight ; men-of-war and shipping cruising about. This beautiful engraving is supported, L. H., by a British tar bearing the Union Jack ; on the R. H., by a French soldier, with red, white, and blue flag, surmounted by an eagle ; the munitions of war lying at their feet. The Balkan Pass in the distance. This engraving can be printed in three colored inks.

No. 265.—EIGHT SHEET, 60-in. by 80-in.

Paul Bedford as Adelgisa in the Burlesque of "**Norma.**"

No. 266.—EIGHT SHEET, 60-in. by 80-in.

The great Nassau balloon, piloted by the veteran Green, with ladies and gentlemen seated in the car, rising from the Royal Gardens upon its perilous night ascent.

No. 267.—FOUR SHEET, 60-in. by 40-in.

The Piaza de Toros at Madrid ; temple at the back reflected on the lake, surrounded by admiring crowds ; the magnificent buildings around thrown out in strong relief by showers of gold and red fires ; the whole forming a grand tableau of the most brilliant spectacle ever witnessed in the city of Madrid.

This engraving can be printed in two colored inks.

No. 268.—FOUR SHEET, 60-in. by 40-in.

A night with Punch. A variety of eccentric characters, with Punch in the centre ; Toby on drum with pipe in his mouth ; Shallabala on the opposite side gazing upon him.

No. 269.—FOUR SHEET, 60-in. by 40-in.

Man on the fan of a windmill, with flag in his hand, surrounded by a blaze of fireworks. Engraved for "**The Fire Mill.**"

No. 270.—FOUR SHEET, 40-in. by 60-in.

Splendid full length figure of Taglioni, in her celebrated *pas.*

No. 271.—FOUR SHEET, 40-in. by 60-in.

Full length figure of "Jem Crow," in the attitude of singing the celebrated song of "Wheel about, and turn about."

No. 272.—FOUR SHEET, 60-in. by 40-in.

Celebrated characters at a Judge and Jury Club. Judge, counsel, jury, and spectators assembled. Suitable for a *Judge and Jury Club.*

No. 273.—FOUR SHEET, 60-in. by 40-in.

Grand coronation scene in Westminster Abbey in the olden time ; king and queen on throne ; knights in armour seated under their respective banners ; peeresses seated under theirs ; entrée of the champion.

41

No. 274.—FOUR SHEET, 60-in. by 40-in.
The Golden Temple of the great Pagoda Guadina of Dagon at Rangoon, the capital of the Burmese empire. The Burmese king, surrounded by his court, seated in regal magnificence amidst a blaze of fireworks, in eastern splendour.
Can be printed in two colored inks.

275.—TWO SHEET, 30-in. by 40-in.
Splendid tent. Figure of a youth standing up blind-folded; figures in oriental costume around him; man exhibiting ring; another handing up letter. Engraved for a *Wizard*.

No. 276.—TWO SHEET, 40-in. by 30-in.
Male in deep sleep suspended in the air, representing the second-sighted boy. Engraved for a *Wizard*.

No. 277.—SINGLE SHEET, 30-in. by 20-in.
Represents in the back-ground the battlements of a castle, with trench in front; figures on the battlements; figure leaping from them over the trench, firing pistol at a man with drawn scimitar and child on his shoulder, R. H. A man, L. H., in an attitude of alarm. Engraved for **"The Bedouin Arabs."**

No. 278.—TWO SHEET, 40-in. by 30-in.
Men standing on each other's shoulders in fantastic attitudes. Engraved for **"The Bedouin Arabs,"**
(See Nos. 287 & 332).

No. 279.—TWO SHEET, 40-in. by 30-in.
Black dressed in Spanish costume, firing pistol at a man.

No 280.—TWO SHEET, 40-in. by 30-in.
Holly tree, for Christmas.

No. 281.—TWO SHEET, 40-in. by 30-in.
Portraits of the celebrated judge and jury club. Engraved for **"Giles Scroggins."**

42

No. 282.—TWO SHEET, 40-in. by 30-in.
Van Amburgh defying the lions.

No. 283.—TWO SHEET, 30-in. by 40-in.
"PUNCH."

No. 284.—TWO SHEET, 40-in. by 30-in.
"Zulu Kaffirs." The meal song, the death song, and combat. Engraved for **"The Zulu Kaffirs."**

No. 285.—SINGLE SHEET, 15-in. by 20-in.
Represents five tableaux, in frame work, with colored ink and black pictures. L. H. top, cottage, rocks and sea by moonlight, figure of sailor in the centre with pistol in hand, man in the centre, female by his side. Smugglers and preventive men in the back ground. R. H. top, female kneeling to smuggler with uplifted sword, man on the ground by the side of rock. Centre, mill in flames, &c. L. H. bottom, ruined abbey by moonlight, man in rags on ground. R. H., sailor in centre, with boy on his arm. R. H. bottom prison, sailor escaping by rope to building opposite, soldiers rushing from building, opposed by sailor with pistol, female opposite, man pointing pistol to her head. Engraved for "May Marsden."

No. 286.—SINGLE SHEET, 30-in. by 20-in.
In the back ground, the explosion of a mill. In the centre, two sailors waving their hats, female kneeling, clasping her hands, man dead on the ground. R. H., man dressed as smuggler, looking on, two soldiers behind him. L. H., female standing in a disconsolate attitude, soldiers guarding her at the back, the mill stream. Engraved for "May Marsden."

No. 287.—SINGLE SHEET, 20-in. by 30-in.
Represents three Arabs dancing; the second and third standing on one foot upon the head of the undermost figure; R. H., man turning a summersault with a drawn sword in each hand; L. H., another firing off gun, leaping over the heads of soldiers with uplifted swords. Engraved for **"The Bedouin Arabs."**

No. 288.—SINGLE SHEET, 30-in. by 20-in.
Burmese state carriage inlaid with precious gems, drawn by two elephants. Peacocks of enchanting plumage, attendants bearing splendid banners.

43

No. 289.—SINGLE SHEET, 20-in. by 30-in.
Female figure on lion's back with flowing drapery.

No. 290.—SINGLE SHEET, 20-in. by 30-in.
Large horse shoe. Engraved for **"The Lucky Horse Shoe."**

No. 291.—SINGLE SHEET, 30-in. by 20-in.
Represents a cave. Woman standing in centre exhibiting great fear; man firing pistol at hat on stick; man, R. H., on ground. Engraved for **"The Deserted Mill."**

No. 292.—SINGLE SHEET, 20-in. by 30-in.
Balloon; male and female in car.

No. 293.—SINGLE SHEET, 20-in. by 30-in.
Head of a judge. Suitable for a Judge and Jury Society.

No. 294.—SINGLE SHEET, 20-in. by 30-in.
Figure of a tall man.

No. 295.—SINGLE SHEET, 20-in. by 30-in.
Figure of a boy with stick and bundle on his shoulder. Engraved for **"Oliver Twist."**

No. 296.—SINGLE SHEET, 20-in. by 30-in.
Mr. Punch, attired in the costume of the present day.

(297) No. 927.—SINGLE SHEET, 20-in. by 30-in.
Man on tub; cask vaulter.

No. 298.—SINGLE SHEET, 20-in. by 30-in.
Female figure. Engraved for **"The Little Devil."**

No. 299.—SINGLE SHEET, 20-in. by 30-in.
Statue of Don Guzman on horseback. Engraved for **"Don Juan."**

No. 300.—SINGLE SHEET, 30-in. by 20-in.
A Flag.

No. 301.—SINGLE SHEET, 30-in. by 20-in.
Roman gladiators on pedestals; L. H., herculean figure holding boy by the foot and the hair of his head, about to hurl him to a distance; R. H., gladiator holding man's head up, sword in hand.

No. 302.—SINGLE SHEET, 30-in. by 20-in.
Roman gladiators about to enter into mortal conflict.

No. 303.—(Destroyed.)

No. 304.—SINGLE SHEET, 30-in. by 20-in.
Full size figure of a man standing in a disconsolate attitude with bare feet. Engraved for **"Jacob Faithful."**

No. 305.—SINGLE SHEET, 30-in. by 20-in.
Medallion portrait of Shakespeare, supported by the tragic and comic muses.

No. 306.—SINGLE SHEET, 30-in. by 20-in.
Figure of a youth fancifully attired; hat adorned with peacock's feathers, a basket at his back with a raven looking out. Engraved for **"Barnaby Rudge."**

No. 307.—SINGLE SHEET, 20-in. by 30-in.
Represents splendid fountains of water, supported by Neptune and his sea horses; knights and demons in fierce conflict; sprites with lighted flambeaux floating in the air. Engraved for **"The Mountain Cataract."**

No. 308.—SINGLE SHEET, 30-in. by 20-in.

Grand march of Turkish and Tartar warriors ; warrior in the centre raising sacred banner of the port in the cause of freedom ; troops of soldiers marching over bridge ; minarets and domes of the capital in the distance.

No. 309.—SINGLE SHEET, 30-in. by 20-in.

Band of Ethiopian minstrels, four figures, one standing with the banjo, the rest seated playing bones, accordeon, tambourine.

No. 310.—SINGLE SHEET, 30-in. by 20-in.

Ethiopian Serenaders, four figures, seated playing on the banjo, the bones, accordeon, and tambourine.

No. 311.—SINGLE SHEET, 20-in. by 30-in.

Figure of a Kaffir chief, dressed in picturesque costume of his country. Suitable for an exhibition.

No. 312.—SINGLE SHEET, 20-in. by 30-in.

Figure of a Kaffir queen, with spear in her hand.

No. 313.—SINGLE SHEET, 30-in. by 20-in.

Represents a forest. Man with boxing gloves in an attitude of defence, lion opposite on hind legs with boxing gloves on fore paws opposing him.

No. 314.—SINGLE SHEET, 20-in. by 30-in.

Jim Crow singing "Sich-a-gitting-up-stairs."

No. 315.—SINGLE SHEET, 20-in. by 30-in.

Man with "Times" newspaper in his hand.

No. 316.—SINGLE SHEET, 30-in. by 20-in.

Interior of a Roman temple. In the centre, emperor looking on two warriors defying each other to combat ; warriors and women in picturesque attitudes filling up the back ground

46

No. 317.—SINGLE SHEET. 20-in. by 30-in.

The death of Abel. Herculean figure with upraised club standing over a prostrate man.

No. 318.—FOUR SHEET, 60-in. by 40-in.

Represents Old London Bridge on the night of a great storm ; R. H., Sir Rowland and two of his companions in a boat ; Sir Rowland firing at Thames Darrel's father, who is struggling in the water ; L. H., a boat upset. Owen Wood receiving Thames Darrel from his father. Engraved for "**Jack Sheppard.**" Room for a line.

No. 319.—TWO SHEET, 30-in. by 40-in.

Full-length portrait of Jack Sheppard, with a brace of pistols in his belt, his cap under his left arm, and in his right hand a whip ; on the ground is a lantern and a mask. Engraved for "**Jack Sheppard.**"

No. 320.—ONE SHEET, 30-in. by 20-in.

Jack Sheppard's interview with his mother in Bedlam. Engraved for "**Jack Sheppard.**"

No. 321.—ONE SHEET, 20-in. by 30-in.

Death of Sir Rowland Trenchard in the well-hole ; Mendez with a lighted torch, and Jonathan Wild with an uplifted bludgeon on the secret staircase, the latter striking Sir Rowland, who is clinging to the rails. Engraved for "**Jack Sheppard.**"

No. 322.—DEMY SHEET, 18-in. by 22-in.

Constitutes five small engravings, representing the principal incidents connected with the great drama of Jack Sheppard. First, Jack carving his name on the beam. Second, Jack's escape from Willesden cage after the robbery at the village church. Third, Jack's interview with Jonathan Wild in the stone-hall. Fourth, death of Sir Rowland Trenchard in the well-hole. Fifth, Jack and Edgeworth Bess escaping from Clerkenwell. Engraved for "**Jack Sheppard.**"

47

No. 323.—TWO SHEET, 30-in. by 40-in.

Full-length portrait of Bill Sikes, with a very shabby hat and band, sporting coat, figured waistcoat, knee breeches and Blucher boots ; on his right hand is his celebrated bull-dog. Engraved for "**Oliver Twist.**" Room for line.

No. 324.—TWO SHEET, 30-in. by 40-in.

Represents Jacob's Well, with view of the Thames (by moonlight ;) the burglar's house ; Sikes haunted by Oliver Twist ; the officers of justice gains the roof of the house ; Sikes having tied one end of a rope firmly round himself, and with the other end made a strong running noose round a stack of chimneys, is about to lower himself down to effect his escape, when, from the other side of the ditch, he is shot by the avenging hand of Oliver Twist. Engraved for "**Oliver Twist.**" Room for line.

No. 325.—SINGLE SHEET, 20-in. by 30-in.

Represents a sleeping apartment in Holly-tree Inn. On the left hand is a bed, upon which Isaac Scatchard, or Unlucky Isaac, as he is so called, is lying, looking amazed at Rachael (who is on the opposite side of the bed), with an uplifted dagger. On the right hand is a table with a candlestick and candle upon it, a stick and bundle, also a pair of boots. Engraved for "**The Holly-tree Inn.**"

No. 326.—TWO SHEET, 30-in. by 40-in.

Represents three of the principal incidents connected with the great American drama of "Dred." First, the wreck ; old Uncle Tiff rescuing his master's children, Teddy and Fanny, from a watery grave. Second, Uncle Tiff's hut ; R. H., is a cradle with a child in it. Third, the great dismal swamp (by moonlight) ; the escape of Harry, his wife, and child, headed by Dred, followed by old Uncle Tiff with the two children. On the left hand is Milly, the mulatto. On the right hand of the tableau, is Tom Gordon whipping a slave ; on the left hand, is Dred, the gallant son of the wilderness, armed with revolvers, rifle, bowie-knife, hatchet, and dagger. Engraved for "**Dred.**" Room for a line.

No. 327.—(Destroyed.)

No. 328.—ONE SHEET, 20-in. by 30-in.

Represents the wild waste of waters. Tableau—The treble vision of James Lindsay, Willie, and the little Golden Lucy. Engraved for the "Wreck of the Golen Mary." Room for a line.

No. 329.—ONE SHEET, 30-in. by 20-in.

Represents a ship struck by the icebergs, passengers and crew escaping in boats. Engraved for the "Wreck of the Golden Mary."

No. 330.—FOUR SHEET, 60-in. by 40-in.

In the centre is the Spirit of Peace, with trumpet, and wreath of laurels. On her right hand is an English officer ; on her left hand is a French officer ; at the back of which is a star, surrounded on each side by soldiers, with hats on their bayonets, forming a splendid tableau. Engraved for "**The Battles of the East.**" Room for a line.

No. 331.—FOUR SHEET, 40-in. by 60-in.

A large hand holding five cards, viz.: ace of spades, jack of spades, four of diamonds, three of clubs, and two of hearts. Engraved for "**The Hand of Cards.**" Room for line.

No. 332.—TWO SHEET, 20-in. by 60-in.

A man bearing three men on his shoulders ; on the centre one is another man standing upon his head. Engraved for "**The Bedouin Arabs.**"

No. 333.—TWO SHEET, 30-in. by 40-in.

A full-length figure of a female in armour, with a hatchet in her hand. Engraved for "**Jane of the Hatchet.**" Room for a line.

No. 334.—TWO SHEET, 40-in. by 30-in.

A youth in deep sleep, suspended in the air by a stick under his right arm. Suitable for a *Wizard.*

No. 335.—TWO SHEET, 30-in. by 40-in.

On the right hand, is an Irishman with a patched coat, smoking a pipe, and looking at a placard, (type to be inserted). On the left hand, is a flag, sword, gun, kettle-drum, soldier's cap, &c.; in the centre, is a grotesque figure beating a drum. Engraved for "**Charles O'Malley, the Irish Dragoon.**" Room for line.

No. 336.—DOUBLE CROWN SHEET, 20-in. by 30-in.

Six small engravings, representing the principal incidents connected with "**The Fire of London.**" Room for line top & bottom.

No. 337.—SINGLE SHEET, 30-in. by 20-in.

Represents the sally-port of Calais. On the right hand is D'Artagnan in a boat, firing at Le Tour, who is bound to a flag-staff, an officer directing the soldiers, L. H., to fire upon D'Artagnan, who is showing the stolen pass. Engraved for "**The Three Musketeers.**"

No. 338.—DOUBLE FOOLSCAP SHEET, 17-in. by 24-in.

Five small Engravings in border, representing the principal incidents in "**The Lucky Horse-shoe.**" Room for line.
Printed in two colored inks.

No. 339.—DEMY SHEET, 18-in. by 24-in.

Five small Engravings in border, representing the principal incidents in "**The Sealed Sentence.**" Room for line.
Printed in two colored inks.

No. 340.—DEMY SHEET, 18-in. by 24-in.

Six small Engravings in border representing the principal incidents in "**Marco Sciarra.**" Room for line.

Nos. 341, 342, & 343.—(Destroyed.)

No. 344.—SINGLE SHEET, 20-in. by 30-in.

Is a grotesque figure of Nicholas lying on the ground in a fright, with very long spurs on his boots, at the side of which is a shell about to explode; over him is standing the Spirit of Freedom with a wand in her right hand. Engraved for a Pantomime. Room for line.

50

No. 345.—SMALL ENGRAVING, 15-in. by 20-in.

Full-size figure of a Cat. Engraved for "**The White Cat.**" Room for line.

No. 346.—SMALL ENGRAVING, 20-in. by 15-in.

Grand standard combat between a pirate and a sailor. Room for a line.

No. 347.—SMALL ENGRAVING, 30-in. by 20-in.
SPARRING.

No. 348.—SMALL ENGRAVING, 15-in. by 20-in.

Engraved for the popular game of Puff and Dart. Room for line.

No. 349.—SMALL ENGRAVING.
A HAT.

No. 350.—SMALL ENGRAVING, 20-in. by 15-in.

Large Eye. Engraved for "**The Evil Eye.**" Occupies the whole of the paper.

No. 351.—SMALL ENGRAVING, 20-in. by 15-in.

Engraved for **The Evil Eye.** Room for type all round.

No. 352.—SMALL ENGRAVING, 20-in. by 15-in.

Engraved for **The Evil Eye.**

No. 353.—SMALL ENGRAVING, 15-in. by 20-in.

Full-length figure of a Female. Engraved for "**Eliza Fenning.**"

No. 354.—SMALL ENGRAVING, 20-in. by 15-in.
A man firing at a target.

No. 355.—SMALL ENGRAVING, 15-in. by 20-in.
Full-length figure of a sailor.

51

No. 355½.—THREE SHEET, 60-in. by 30-in.

The field of Waterloo. English and French soldiers engaged in battle; on the left hand the Duke of Wellington and staff on horse-back; in the centre, men and horses lying dead and wounded; on the right hand Napoleon and staff retreating, the whole forming a grand picture of "**The Battle of Waterloo.**"

No. 356.—SMALL ENGRAVING, 20-in. by 15-in.

Three Scotchmen, the centre one playing the bagpipes, the other two dancing.

No. 357.—FOUR SHEET, 60-in. by 40-in.

Represents a Gallery in Macbeth's House. Comic figure of Macbeth (dressed as a soldier, with spurs in boots,) holding up a dagger in each hand. Lady Macbeth smiling at him. Engraved for "**Macbeth,**" somewhat removed from the Text of Shakespeare.

No. 358.—FOUR SHEET, 60-in. by 40-in.

Represents a Fairy Grotto, with water in the back ground, in which numerous nymphs are sporting, King Neptune in his car attended by a Nymph, above which is the Fairy Queen, in her car drawn by two doves, in the shape of a Hansom, on which are the following words: "Handsomer than Hansom," out of which is a comical figure showing his head, and the Queen's Attendant flying before. Engraved for a Pantomime.

No. 359.—TWO SHEET, 40-in. by 30-in.

Represents the interior of a Court House. In the centre is a female in the disguise of a lawyer; comical figure of Shylock with a large pair of scales and a knife; at the side of which is another comical figure with a large round box; on the opposite are two men, one with a hand truck and bag, on which is engraved "6,000," the other dressed as a butcher, both smoking; in the back ground is the judge, seated on the bench, also various other figures. Engraved for "**Shylock; or, the Merchant of Venice Preserved.**"

No. 360.—TWO SHEET, 30-in. by 40-in.

Full length figure of a tall man, at which a male, female, and a boy are looking. Engraved originally for Mr. T. Goode, the American Colossus.

No. 361.—SINGLE SHEET, 20-in. by 30-in.

Full length figure of a tall man, at which three children and a man are looking. Engraved originally for Smith's Giant Barman.

No. 362.—SINGLE SHEET, 20-in. by 30-in.

Head of a Judge. Suitable for a Judge and Jury Society.

No. 363.—SINGLE SHEET, 30-in. by 20-in.

Represents the interior of a Cottage. In the centre is a table upon which is a man clothed in rags, with a pistol in each hand, keeping at bay two ruffians; at one side of the engraving is the full length figure of a sailor dancing, on the other side is the man in rags, with ballads on his arm and in the band of his hat.

No. 364.—(Destroyed.)

No. 365.—SINGLE SHEET, 30-in. by 20-in.

Represents the interior of a Pleasure Garden, tastefully arranged; in the centre is a light building, of which the upper part is an orchestra, and the lower part for refreshments, at which various groups are standing; a balloon ascent, several promenading about; at the back is a view of the river.

No. 266.—SINGLE SHEET, 30-in. by 20-in.

Interior of a Casino, brilliantly illuminated by countless jets of gas, and Chinese lanterns in the centre; at the back, is the orchestra, various groups dancing.

No. 367.—SINGLE SHEET (Double Demy), 35-in. by 22-in.

The Grove Farm at Farnborough. The DEPARTURE. At the back is George Fielding crossing a stile, bidding adieu to Susan Merton; Isaac Levi waving his hat at him, wishing him success; in front is Mr. Meadows, standing with his arms folded, Tom Robinson by his side, with a pair of handcuffs on. Engraved for "**It's never too late to mend.**"

No. 368.—SINGLE SHEET (Double Demy), 35-in. by 22-in.

The Model Prison at Farnborough. Tom Robinson attacking the turnkeys, having stuck Hawes to the Ground with a blow from his fist; Mr. Eden supporting poor Josephs, who is dead, in his arms. Engraved for "**It's never too late to mend.**"

No. 369.—SINGLE SHEET (Double Demy), 35-in. by 22-in.

Australia. At the back, on a rude bridge thrown from rock to rock, is Isaac Levi, about to strike Peter Crawley with his stick; George Fielding defending himself from the bushrangers; a man falling from the bridge into the water beneath; in front is Jackey, struggling with a bushranger; a bushranger lying dead on the ground. Engraved for **"It's never too late to mend."**

No. 370.—SINGLE SHEET (Double Demy), 35-in. by 22-in.

The Grove Farm at Farnborough. The RETURN. At the back is Isaac Levy accusing Mr. Meadows of robbery; Peter Crawley standing by his side; Mr. Wood with a warrant for his apprehension; in front is George Fielding, Tom Robinson, and Susan Merton. Engraved for **"It's never too late to mend."**

The above four Engravings can be used singly, or printed to form a four sheet bill.

55

No. 374—Four Engravings for the drama of **Guy Faux.**

1st, 4-in. by 3-in., Guy Faux, with long sword, in conversation with two of the conspirators, one of which has a paper in his hand showing him. 2nd, 4½-in. by 3-in., vaults beneath the House of Parliament, filled with barrels of gunpowder and bundles of faggots; Guy Faux with cloak around him and lantern in his hand laying the train. 3rd, 3½-in. by 3-in., two men bound by chains to a post, with a quantity of wood around them; two men with lighted torches waiting for the word of command from a man smartly dressed. 4th, 4-in. by 3-in., vaults beneath the House of Parliament; Guy Faux with cloak around him, large sword and hat, brimstone match, and lantern in his hand (comic).

No. 375—Two Engravings for the drama of **Gin and Water.** 3½-in. by 3-in. each.

1st, Gin; the drunkard seated on a chair catching hold of his son by the hair of his head, the children around him in imploring attitudes; 2nd, Water; the happy husband playing with his children, the wife looking fondly at them, forming a complete tableau of happiness.

No. 376—One Engraving for the drama of **The Guerillas.** 7-in. by 5-in.

Storming of a fort in the centre, on the ruins is a guerilla supported by a female in her arms; terrific conflict of soldiers and guerillas; several figures dead on the ground; reinforcement of military seen advancing.

No. 377—Five Engravings for the drama of **The Guerillas.** To work in two colours, forming a sheet of crown, 15-in. by 20-in.

1st, Terrific standard fight between two soldiers, one of whom has fallen to the ground on his knees; general fight in the distance. 2nd, a mountainous pass; a guerilla standing over a female who is lying on the ground, protecting her with his sword from an officer. 3rd, two of the guerillas keeping at bay a body of soldiers; at the back is a wooden bridge, upon which is a general fight. 4th, the battle-field by moonlight; numerous dead and dying soldiers stretched upon the ground; a female upon her knees anxiously looking in the face of a guerilla and sprinkling it with water. A mountainous pass with a bridge in the centre, on which the military are engaged in battle; an officer is overcome by one of the guerillas, who is defending a female; soldiers coming to the rescue.

No. 371—Four Engravings for the drama of **The Will and the Way.** To work with border in two colours, for a sheet of double foolscap, 17-in. by 27-in.

1st, the pier at Calais and sea view; Henry Ashton accompanied by his friend, recognises Will Sideler, the warrener. 2nd, chamber in Carrow Abbey; lawyer Elsworthy and friends seated round a table; old Martin standing up denouncing Will Sideler as the murderer of Sir William Mowbray. 3rd, the belfry tower, Meeran Hafiz lying extended dead upon a bed of straw, the Ayah kneeling by his side with her hand raised; Joe Beans, Red Ralph, and a villager entering a door. 4th, the Picture Gallery; Red Ralph standing over Colonel Mowbray, whom he has shot with a pistol; Joe Beans entering with a lighted candle; a pistol, hat, and cash-box, lying upon the floor.

No. 372—Six Engravings for the drama of **The Will and the Way.** To work with border in two colours, forming a sheet of double foolscap, 17-in. by 27-in.

1st, the full length figure of Joe Beans. 2nd, ditto Ayah. 3rd, ditto Ellen. 4th, ditto Meeran Hafiz. 5th, ditto old Martin. 6th, ditto the Khan.

No. 373—One Engraving of **The Triumph of the Jews,** 6-in. by 7½-in.

Interior of a temple, large pillars each side falling down in pieces; in the centre, on a raised platform, are also three men, one in a coat of mail with sword in hand, over which is a seraph placing a wreath of laurels on his head; a terrific conflict.

No. 378—Four Engravings for a drama (name not known), 6½-in. by 6-in. each.

1st, exterior of a cottage; a man supporting a female, who has fainted, on his knee; a man behind them looking on in attitude of astonishment. 2nd, a country fair; in the centre is a man with a thimble-rig table, at which a female is playing; a man dressed as a jockey, by his side, looking astonished; a set of cockshies and booths; at back also various figures. 3rd, a marshy swamp by moonlight; the body of a man extended dead on the ground; two countrymen, one with a lantern, and three men standing by, having discovered him. 4th, showing three compartments at one time; first compartment a solitary garret with a bed on the floor; second compartment, a man having entered a room, with a pistol, by means of a ladder through the roof, also another man outside, standing on the ladder; third compartment, a room, in the centre is a man discharging a pistol, which has shot his assailant; at the side is a man shaking hands with another who is wrapped in a mantle; various figures looking on in attitudes of astonishment.

No. 379—Six Engravings for the drama of **The Fire of London** forming a demy sheet, 17½-in. by 22½-in.

1st, a tavern and a baker's shop; two men in close conversation, one in a smock frock. 2nd, barn in the baker's shop, sacks of flour, loaves on the shelves, and stacks of wood on the floor; a female extended on the ground dead; a ruffian, with a dagger, looks with horror at the deed he has committed. 3rd, a large wall, houses seen above it; a ladder placed against the wall, a female at the top escaping with a man who is on the wall ready to receive her; a conflict between two men, one of which has beaten the other to the ground with his sword. 4th, the great fire of London; a man supporting a female who has fainted, down a ladder from the window, persons waiting to receive her; various groups are throwing things out of windows; mob, &c., &c. 5th, a wretched garret, with a bed; a man in the garb of a pirate protecting a female from the insult of a ruffian, whom he has felled to the ground with his fist. 6th, showing three compartments at one time; at the top, persons entering a door, one with a lighted torch, who is proceeding in the second compartment, a solitary chamber, with a round table in it; a man descending a ladder into the third compartment, a vault, with a lighted torch; one man leaning on an axe looking at a skeleton he has just dug up; a ruffian with dagger in hand seized by the throat by the man in the garb of a pirate; various figures in the background.

No. 380—One Engraving for the drama of **The Cross Roads**, 5-in. by 7-in.

Embracing three of the principal tableaux. 1st, two men fighting with daggers, various figures looking at them. 2nd, a sailing boat in a storm, in which is a male and a female who are terrified at the lightning. 3rd, highwayman on horseback, striking at a man with the butt-end of his whip; one is lying on the ground; in the centre is a cross, with the following words around it,—"The Cross Roads;" the whole on one engraving.

No. 381—Three Engravings for the drama of **The Christmas Carol.** The first two 10-in. by 6-in. each.

1st, a scantily furnished apartment, with table in the centre, upon which is a bason with a spoon in it, and a candle with a long flare to it; old Scrooge, the miser, seated in an easy chair, holding his hand towards the fire-place, in which there is no fire, with his head half turned towards a spectral figure (Marley's ghost), which has entered the apartment; his head bound round, frill shirt, and tassels to his boots, chains bound round his waist, to which is attached keys, padlocks, and boxes, also a pocket-book in his hand. 2nd, a church-yard; a figure mysteriously wrapped in a mantle pointing to a grave, at which an old man is kneeling, his face covered with his hand as if weeping; upon the grave-stone are engraved the following words,—"Ebenezer Scrooge." 3rd, 11¼-in. by 6¼-in., a room decorated with holly and mistletoe; in the centre is a stout male and female dancing, various groups looking on; at the back is a man elevated, playing a fiddle, with a pot by him; at the side is an old dame seated in an arm-chair, with two children by her side.

No. 382—Four Engravings for the drama of **The Blind Child of Africa,** 4¼-in. by 3¼-in. each.

1st, a plantation; in the centre is a pirate vowing vengeance on the blind child, who has fainted in the arms of a sailor, at the side of whom is the blind child's mother, also fainted in the arms of a slave; various figures looking on in the attitude of astonishment. 2nd, the deck of a pirate ship; the blind child saving his mother from the vengeance of the pirate, by firing a pistol at him; a man coming up the hatchway. 3rd, interior of a prison, with a bed of straw; the blind child and his mother, with her hand pointing upwards, at the side of whom is the jailor. 4th, interior of a prison; the blind child asleep on a bed of straw, at the side of which is the mother, lying on the ground; a fairy at each end with their wands, displaying a vision of a temple and figure of an elephant, with the blind child on his back; various figures with spears and banners.

58

No. 383—Three Engravings for the drama of **The Abbot of Saint Paul's; or, Blanche Herriot.** The first two, 4-in. by 4-in.

1st, the prison of Sybil Merton the orphan; Walter Lisle protecting Sybil, who has fainted in his arms, from the insult of the Abbot of St. Paul's. 2nd, interior of the Cathedral of Old St. Paul's and clock tower. Despair of the abbot, on beholding Sybil in the act of making the bell strike the thirteenth chime. 3rd, 5½-in. by 3½-in., a vault beneath St. Paul's, the prison of Sybil Merton; her cries for help bring Walter Lisle, sword in hand, who seizes the abbot by the wrist.

No. 384—One Engraving for the drama of **Azael,** 5½-in. by 7½-in.

The Spirit of the Desert appearing to Azael, beckoning him to return to his father.

No. 385—Four Engravings for the Drama of **The Assyrian Spy,** 4½-in. by 3½-in each.

1st, interior of a temple; a youth, with a spear and shield, keeping at bay a body of soldiers; various figures standing by looking amazed. 2nd, a corridor; an old man, dressed as a Turk, attended by his daughter, having an interview with the Assyrian spy, who is disguised as a Jew. 3rd, a forest; a youth protecting a female from two ruffians, one of whom he has slain, and the other he is in the act of striking down with his dagger. 4th, a temple; in the centre, on a raised platform, is a man in the act of placing a crown on a youth's head, at the side of which is a female; various groups standing in an attitude of astonishment.

No. 386—One Engraving for the drama of **The Bloomers,** 7-in. by 4-in.

Two females dressed as Bloomers, in conversation with another female, very stout, with her hair in paper.

No. 387—One Engraving for the drama of **The Surgeon of Paris,** 7-in. by 5-in.

Grand apartment in the Palace of the Louvre; Madelon saved by the Surgeon of Paris; the queen and her page; guards with muskets each side.

59

No. 388—Two Engravings for the drama of **The Deserter.**

1st, 3½-in. by 3-in., a file of soldiers with their muskets presented to a soldier blindfolded, standing by a coffin; an officer on horseback giving the word of command. 3rd, 4-in. by 3-in., a file of soldiers standing around a soldier who is kneeling on a coffin blindfolded; a female running in at the back.

No. 389—One Engraving of **The Soldier's Dream,** 6-in. by 4-in.

The battle-field by moonlight; a soldier in a Scotch dress lying on the ground with his knapsack under his head; a vision appearing before him, representing a country farm; men ploughing, his wife and children meeting him and clinging affectionately around him.

No. 390—Six Engravings for the drama of **The Soldier's Progress.** Forming a sheet of double foolscap, 17-in. by 27-in.

1st, the enlistment; a country fair; villagers, both male and female, dancing to a piper; the sergeant placing the colours upon the hat of a man who is tipsy; a child clinging to his leg; countrymen seated on a form smiling at him; a sergeant in the midst of them. 2nd, the departure; interior of a cottage; the husband taking leave of his wife, who is weeping upon his shoulder; a child catching hold of his hand; the sergeant with his hand upon his shoulder, pointing to the door with his cane; an old lady seated in a chair weeping; a recruiting sergeant in conversation with two countrymen at the back, the door of the cottage being partly open. 3rd, the desertion; street densely crowded; a countryman with handcuffs on in the custody of three soldiers; a female and child walking by the side endeavouring to catch a glimpse of his face. 4th, the battle; in the centre is an officer encouraging his men, who are pressing forward amidst the dying and the dead. 5th, the field after the battle; a man with a bundle at his back and sword by his side, about to strike a wounded soldier with a hammer, whom a female is protecting; the dead and dying scattered about in all directions. 6th, the return; country road with distant view; a poor wounded soldier, with his head bound round with a handkerchief, his arm in a sling, and a crutch by his side, seated on the trunk of a tree; a female standing by his side looking mournfully towards the village.

No. 391—One Engraving for the title of **Dred,** 16-in. by 4-in.

Slave-owners examining slaves, also lashing them; slave in chains; a slave battling with dogs; all of which are in between the letters.

No. 392—One Engraving of the drama of **Captain Hawk,** 6-in. by 7-in.

Full length figure of a highwayman, with a riding-whip in one hand, and taking a pistol out of his belt with the other.

No. 393—Eight tableaus of the principal incidents connected with the **Drunkard's Children.** To work in two colours, forming a sheet of demy, 17½-in. 22½-in.

Interior of a low tap-room; various figures seated at a table, also the drunkard's children; the boy playing at cards with a man; the girl with a pot in her hand; a man lying on the floor with a bonnet on, and a woman seated on a form with the man's hat on, both drunk; a body of men bonneting an old gentleman who is entering. 2nd, interior of a low casino; various figures dancing, also the drunkard's children; a youth with a cigar in his mouth standing at a bar, where a woman is serving him with drink. 3rd, the bar of a tavern crowded with people; the landlord serving drink to a beggar; at the side is a woman in the act of giving a baby some drink out of a glass; the drunkard's children are in conversation with some of the bystanders. 4th, interior of a model lodging-house, with beds around the room in which people are sleeping; two policemen capturing the drunkard's son in bed, the landlord and landlady entering with a candle. 5th, interview of the sister with her brother in newgate; at the side is the jailor beckoning her out. 6th, the trial of the drunkard's son; his sister standing by his side weeping. 7th, an apartment in the dock-yard; the doctor closing the transport's eyes; two men putting a screen around his bed. 8th, the sister hearing of her brother's death, throws herself off a bridge, and is drowned.

No. 394—Four Engravings for the drama of **Eliza Holmes,** 5-in. by 3-in. each.

1st, grand dance of garlands, by the reapers, male and female. 2nd, a country dance by the peasantry, male and female, with flags. 3rd, Earl Mowbray extended on the ground dead; Black Walter gazing at a spectre which is crossing a bridge; groups of gipsies each side. 4th, the marriage by torchlight; Black Walter and gang witnessing the marriage between Frederick Viscount Mowbray and Eliza Holmes.

No. 395—One Engraving for the drama of **The Dumb Man of Manchester,** 4-in. by 5-in.

An apartment in Mrs. Wilton's house; Mrs. Wilton seated in a chair, having been stabbed by her nephew, Edward Wilton, and whose cries have brought the dumb man, who is sliding down a rope, to her assistance.

No. 396—Six Engravings for the drama of **Marco Sciarra**.
Forming a sheet of demy, 17½-in. by 22½-in.

1st, a country village; a dance by villagers, male and female. 2nd, interior of a room; a man in the act of stabbing a female with a dagger, who is kneeling on the ground, but is prevented by a man holding his arm. 3rd, showing two cells in a prison; in the first, is a female kneeling in an imploring attitude to a man with his arms folded, smartly dressed; in the second, is a man turning his head away from a figure enveloped in a long cloak and mask over his face. 4th, a wild retreat; a brigand leaning on his gun, looking at a grave with a cross at the head of it. 5th, the place of execution; the executioner shot by a man, at whom three soldiers are firing at, from a building opposite; a female kneeling by the block with her hands clasped, and hold upwards; two men at the side pointing to the executioner. 6th, in the centre is the brigand chief lying on the ground wounded, his wife leaning over him; general conflict between brigands and soldiers:

No. 397—One Engraving for the drama of **The Earl of Poverty**, 2-in. by 2½-in.
Two antique houses closed; old street in London; an old man leaning on a stick with a bag at his back.

No. 398—One Engraving for the drama of **Emigration**, 7-in. by 5½-in.
A wild mountainous pass; a man lying on the ground before the fire, with three sticks across, gipsey fashion; another man with a gun in his hand, standing by his side.

No. 399—One Engraving for the drama of **Minnigrey**, 8-in. by 6½-in.
Figure of a general on horseback, with officers carrying colours; Gus and Peter kneeling, presenting the sword and eagle to the general.

No. 400—One Engraving for the drama **Mary Clifford**, 4-in. by 3-in.
Interior of a prison; a female with chains on her arms, waist, and feet; a man standing on a chair trying to force one of the bars from the window.

No. 401—One Engraving for the drama of **Mary Clifford**, 4-in. by 7-in.
Embracing three incidents. 1st, Mary Clifford chained to the wall; Mother Brownrigg lashing her with a cat-o'-nine-tails. 2nd, Mary Clifford making her escape from a window by a sheet. 3rd, interior of Newgate, the doors of which are open; the hangman is seen in a cart waiting for Mother Brownrigg, who is kneeling down with her hands clasped together, pointing upwards; the chaplain by her side; various figures in the background.

No. 402—Five Engravings for the drama of **Mary Clifford**.
Forming a sheet of crown, 15-in. by 20-in.

1st, Mother Brownrigg in the act of inflicting the lash upon Mary Clifford, but is prevented by a female holding her arm. 2nd, interior of a room; Mary Clifford lying in bed, a female weeping by her side; her father and the doctor raising her up in the bed, to speak to a man who is standing at the other side of the room. 3rd, a wretched garret; Mary Clifford bound round her wrists with chains fixed into the ground; a man looking through the skylight at her. 4th, interior of a prison; the chaplain supporting Mother Brownrigg, who has fainted in his arms; her son standing with his arms folded in an attitude of defiance; at the back is a crowd of people, also the hangman's cart, with a coffin inside it. 5th, full length figure of Mary Clifford in rags, bound round the waist and wrists with large chains fixed in the ground.

No. 403—One Engraving for the spectacle of **The Battle of the Alma**, 15-in. by 14-in.
English soldiers opposed by Russians in all directions; an officer protecting a female, whom he holds firmly round the waist; in the centre is a sailor with the Russian flag beneath his foot, waiving the union jack; the dying and the dead scattered in all directions.

No. 404—Five Engravings for the drama of **The Rye House Plot**. Forming a sheet of crown, 15-in. by 20-in.

1st, a chamber; a female with her hair hanging down, and her hand up to her head, in conversation with a man pointing towards the window. 2nd, a wall; a man upon a ladder looking over the wall, another falling from it; a man lying in the centre wounded, and a female kneeling over him, and various groups standing round rejoicing. 3rd, the battle field; desperate conflict; two soldiers bearing a dead body from the field; soldiers with banners; the dead and dying scattered about in all directions. 4th, the place of execution; a block in the centre; a female lying extended before it on the ground; a man pointing upwards, child by his side; a priest with a book in his hand; the exe-

cutioner with a mask on, kneeling down with an axe in his hand; a soldier holding a scroll; body of guards at the back. 5th, a terrace overlooking the river, with distant view; a throne, with a body of soldiers standing by it; two males and a female kneeling before the king; a large ship entering at the side.

No. 405—Two Engravings for the drama of **Uncle Tom's Cabin**.
1st, 7½-in. by 5½-in., balcony of Mr. Selby's house; Haley lying on the ground, having fallen from his horse, which is running away at a rapid pace; negroes with sticks and mangolia leaf trying to stop him; Mr. and Mrs. Selby looking from balcony. 2nd, 4-in. by 4-in., interior of Uncle Tom's cabin; George Selby seated by the fire, looking at Uncle Tom, who has a child on his shoulder; two children on the floor pointing at him; Aunt Chloe at the table gazing at him.

No. 406—Five Engravings for the drama of **May Marsden**.
To work in two colours, forming a sheet of crown, 15-in. by 20-in.

1st, exterior of May Marsden's house, with sea-shore, by moonlight; a sailor and the village reprobate quarrelling; a female wringing her hands in despair; various figures looking on. 2nd, a female kneeling before a smuggler, imploring him to spare the life of a man he has beaten to the ground with his sword. 3rd, a building each side, with a rope reaching from one window to the other, and a sailor sliding along it; two men, one presenting a pistol at a female, the other presenting a pistol at a party of men. 4th, the ruins of an old abbey, by moonlight; a sailor protecting a disguised female from the insults of a ruffian whom he has felled to the earth. 5th, fearful destruction of the mill, flames bursting forth from every side; a water-mill at work; a figure extended dead upon the ground; a sailor waving his hat; female kneeling with her hands clasped, looking upwards; villagers, soldiers, &c., &c., at back.

No. 407—Eleven Engravings for the drama of **My Poll and my Partner Joe**. Forming a crown sheet, to work in two colours, 15-in. by 20-in.

1st, exterior of the "Crown and Crozier" public house; Harry Halyard standing over Black Brandon, whom he has felled to the earth, Sam Snatcher standing by him with his hat over his eyes; Watchful Waxend upon a table with a pipe and pot in his hand, Old Sam Sculler

and watermen looking on. 2nd, exterior of Dame Halyard's cottage; two of the press-gang pressing Harry Halyard in the king's name; Mary Maybud clinging round his neck, his mother standing by his side; Joe Tiller and watermen looking on. 3rd, quarter-deck of the "Polyphemus;" Captain Oakheart reprimanding Harry Halyard; officers on each side. 4th, between decks of a slaver; Watchful Waxend firing a pistol out of a cask at Black Brandon, who is in the act of stabbing Harry Halyard in the back with a dagger. 5th, exterior of a fort; general fight between sailors and pirates; a sailor, with sword in hand, waving the standard on the top of the fort. 6th, a mail-coach drawn by four horses, crowded with sailors; one on the top with a purse in his hand, dancing; another with the union jack. 7th, exterior of Mary's cottage, with distant view; Harry Halyard in conversation with Mary; she having read an account of his supposed death, has married his friend Joe Tiller, the knowledge of which she endeavours to keep from him. 8th, a room; Joe Tiller lying dead in the centre; Harry Halyard and Mary kneeling hand-in-hand; watermen and villagers looking on. 9th, full length figure of a sailor, with sword in hand. 10th, full length figure of a waterman. Full length figure of a sailor, with a purse in his hand.

408—Six Engravings for the drama of **Nicholas Nickleby**.
Forming a crown sheet, 15-in. by 20-in.

1st, a street; Squeers seizing poor Smike, who has caught hold of a lamp-post with the hooked handle of his umbrella; a woman sitting at a stall, smoking a pipe; bricklayers, schoolboys, &c., looking on. 2nd, interior of Ralph Nickleby's counting-house; Ralph Nickleby seated on a high stool; Squeers seated on a chair talking to him, with his hat on the floor; Newman Noggs opening a door with a bottle in his hand. 3rd, interior of Madame Mantilini's mangling shop; Mons. Mantilini turning a mangle, his wife with basket in her hand, both quarrelling; Nicholas Nickleby entering. 4th, interior of Ralph Nickleby's office; Mr. Nickleby seated in a chair, in conversation with Ralph, who is standing with his hands behind him; a man seated, smartly dressed, with a handkerchief in his hand; Newman Noggs peeping through a glass door at the back. 5th, a garden; poor Smike lying upon a bed; a man in conversation with him; a three-legged stool with bottle and glass upon it; an old man leaning on a stick seen through the trees; in the distance is a female sitting at a door. 6th, interior of a room; an old man reading a paper; an old woman listening and warming her hands at the fire; behind the chair of the old man are two men listening, one with a pair of bellows in his hand.

No. 409—Ten Engravings for the drama of **Oliver Twist.** To work in two colours. Forming a demy sheet, 17¼-in. by 29¼-in.

1st, Parlour in the house of Mrs. Corney; Bumble the beadle and Mrs. Corney at tea. 2nd, Oliver on the door-step of Mrs. Maylie's house, the door open, servants looking at him amazed. 3rd, Coffin-maker's kitchen; Oliver knocking Noah Claypole down; female striking Oliver; undertaker's wife entering. 4th, Fagin's den; the Dodger introducing Oliver to Fagin; thieves seated at a table at the back. 5th, Bookseller's stall; the Dodger picking Mr. Brownlow's pocket; Charley Bates standing by his side; Oliver Twist looking on in affright. 6th, Parlour in the house of Mr. Brownlow; Oliver supported by pillows in an arm-chair; Mrs. Bedwin and Mr. Brownlow in conversation. 7th, Exterior of a public-house; Bill Sykes re-capturing Oliver, who has a parcel in his hand; Nancy and others looking on. 8th, Back of a house; Sykes having forced Oliver through a window, is watching him; the inmates aroused; one firing a pistol at Oliver. 9th, Southwark side of London Bridge; steps leading down to the river; Nancy disclosing her secrets of Fagin to Rose Maylie and Mr. Brownlow; Noah Claypole listening. 10th, Thieves' retreat overlooking the river; Sykes pursued by the officers; gains the roof; he is about escaping by means of a rope fastened round a stack of chimnies, when he is shot by Oliver Twist.

No. 410—Three Engravings for the drama of **Phœbe Hessel,** 4-in. by 4½-in. each.

1st, Phœbe Hessel with gipsy hat and cloak. 2nd, Phœbe Hessel as the female soldier. 3rd, Phœbe Hessel, leaning on stick, with basket on her arm, as nurse to the lunatic asylum.

No. 411—One Engraving for the drama of **Paul Clifford,** 11-in. by 7-in.

Ruins of an old abbey in the forest; man armed with pistols on horse leaping over gate; another restraining horse by the old tree; winding road with coach and horses; man on horse-back armed with a blunderbuss, and another on foot, armed, watching behind an old wall.

No. 412—Three Engravings for the drama of **The Old Fleet,** 4½-in. by 3-in. each.

1st, Exterior of the debtors' prison; a box attached to the wall, on which are the words, ".pray remember poor debtors;" a man striking another on the ground with a stick, who is pointing to a window, through which a man is looking. 2nd, Interior of a room; two men struggling, one on the floor; a third with a pipe, shaking his fist at the downmost one. 3rd, Bank of the river by moonlight; two females in a boat; man support one, at whom another man on shore has fired a pistol.

No. 413—Six Engravings for the drama of **The Road to Transportation.** Forming a sheet of double foolscap, 17-in. by 27-in.

1st, Road; wooden railings round a square; the idle apprentice playing, his master catching hold of his jacket collar, and pointing to the work-shop; boys laughing. 2nd, A room; the brutal husband about to strike his wife, with a child in her lap; girl seated in a chair; a hat upon the ground, with cards falling out. 3rd, Exterior of a pawnbroker's shop; the wife inside pawning some clothes; the husband leaning against the wall smoking a pipe, a child standing by his side. 4th, A room; a man with his boots off, handing a watch through the window to his companion, who is on a ladder; a female asleep in bed; Room in great disorder. 5th, Interior of a gaming-house; two men quarrelling, one with a bottle in his hand; man whispering to him behind; the other with a cue in his hand; his wife holding him back; broken bottles about the floor. 6th, The hulks; the idle apprentice at last a convict, working in chains; various figures about the ship.

No. 414—One Engraving for the drama of **The Holly-tree Inn,** 5½-in by 4-in.

A bed-chamber in the Holly-tree Inn; Wilfred preventing Rachel from murdering Unlucky Isaac, who is lying on the bed, by holding her hand, which has a dagger in it.

No. 415—Five Engravings for the drama of **Tic-doloreux.** To work in two colours. Forming a quarto double crown sheet, 10-in. by 15-in.

Four figures of different females, supposed to be personated by one female; the centre engraving represents the interior of a room, a sofa in the middle, with a pistol and hat upon it; a man in conversation with a female in man's attire, leaning against the sofa.

No. 416—Two Engravings for the drama of **Lucy Woodbine,** 5-in. by 3-in. each.

1st, Interior of a court of justice; Lucy Woodbine fainting in the arms of her lover, Leonard Graham, on hearing him accused of murder; jailor at the side with a bunch of keys in his hand; judges seated at

the back. 2nd, Dead Man's Hollow; Sir John Eastlake captured by two countrymen; a judge standing by him; villagers supporting a man who is dying; Leonard Graham and Lucy Woodbine embracing; various groups at back, some with torches.

No. 417—Seven Engravings for **The Ice Fiend.** Forming a sheet of crown, 15-in. by 20-in.

1st, A room; the ice fiend dancing in the centre; a comic figure kneeling down in an attitude of fear; a vision of a female is seen at the back, in a brilliant glare of light. 2nd, A room; the ice fiend seated on a blazing fire; a comic figure looking at him with astonishment. 3rd, The sea shore; the ice fiend dancing; two men looking at him, one rather comical. 4th, A female kneeling to a man smartly dressed; at the side is a man with his fist clenched; various figures at back. 5th, A wood, with a coral cave in the distance; a man with his sword drawn, making towards another man who has a female clinging to him. 6th, A cave; fairies displaying to a man a vision; in the centre, a corn field; a male and female embracing. 7th, A fairy retreat; in the centre is a splendid tableau formed with fairies, above which is a figure standing, behind it a brilliant star; various groups of figures in all directions.

No. 418—Five Engravings for the drama of **Jolly Dick, the Lamplighter.** Forming a demy sheet, 17½-in. by 22½-in.

1st, Exterior of a prison; the jailor standing at the door with a bunch of keys in his hand, in conversation with a man, who is standing outside with a loaf under his arm. 2nd, interior of a casino, brilliantly illuminated with chandeliers, with a distant view by moonlight; persons of high rank, both male and female, seeming amazed at the entrance of a country girl wheeling a barrow with fruit. 3rd, A square; two persons fighting a duel; Jolly Dick running between them with his ladder, in order to separate them; various figures in the balcony in attitudes of fear. 4th, The forest; a pic-nic party; in the centre is a female with a donkey, who is eating from a man's hand; a country lass upon her lover's knee, who is drinking to her; various groups are seated on the ground with eatables before them. 5th, Full length figure of Jolly Dick, with ladder and lantern.

No. 419—Five Engravings for the drama of **Jane Paul.** Forming a demy sheet, 17½-in. by 22½-in.

1st, Exterior of Necker's lace shop; Philip Necker accusing Jane Paul of stealing a lace veil, which a servant is holding up to the by-standers. 2nd, Interior of a room; Jane Paul's husband drawing the likeness of his wife at a table; his child asleep upon a sofa, dreaming; a circle of clouds at the back, with the vision of his mother in prison, over which is the figure of Hope in a brilliant star. 3rd, The forest, by moonlight; Jane Paul encircled in the arms of her husband, who presents a pistol to Philip Necker and two constables; the gipsy queen, at the back, warning him. 4th, Showing three compartments; at the top, a garret, selected for Jane Paul, to keep her from the persecution of her enemy, Philip Necker, through the window of which she is escaping on to the house-tops; the bottom, a room, with a ladder reaching to the above, upon which is Necker, opening a trap, having discovered her abode; a man, dressed as a smuggler, with a pistol in his hand, stopping below; in the third compartment, is a man climbing up the chimney. 5th, The house-tops; smoke issuing from chimney; tops of houses in the distance; Jane Paul seeking refuge from her persecutors.

No. 420—Five Engravings for the drama of **Jack Sheppard;** Forming a crown sheet, 15-in. by 20-in.

1st, Interior of Wood's workshop; a bench in the centre with some tools upon it; Jack standing upon a three-legged stool in order to reach the beam upon which he is cutting his name. 2nd, Exterior of Willesden Cage; Jonathan Wild and Blueskin standing in attitudes of astonishment on beholding Jack placing his cap on a finger post making his escape through the roof. 3rd, Exterior of Clerkenwell prison; Jack aiding the escape of Edgeworth Bess, by means of a blanket, which he has fastened to the iron railing of the window. 4th, The well-hole; Jonathan Wild in the act of striking Sir Rowland on the head with his bludgeon; Mendez, with a lighted torch, behind him. 5th, Interior of the Stone Hall; Charcum striking the chains off Jack's ancles, and Jonathan Wild in conversation with him; the chaplain, jailor, sheriffs, &c., at the back.

No. 421—One Engraving for the drama of **Jack Sheppard,** 4-in. by 6-in.

Interior of Wood's workshop; a bench in the centre, with planes, a glue-pot, an oil-stone, &c., upon it: Jack standing upon a three-legged stool to reach the beam, upon which he is carving his name; Owen Wood behind a plank watching him; some saws, squares, compasses, &c., hanging against the wall, also various placards stuck about.

No. 422—One Engraving for the title of **Jack Sheppard,** 14-in. by 3½-in.

This Engraving represents the beam with the name upon, and Jack in the centre, standing upon a stool with a knife in his hand.

No. 423—One Engraving for the drama of **Jack Sheppard,** 6-in. by 5-in.

Jonathan Wild's interview with Jack Sheppard whilst in prison.

No. 424—Two Engravings for the title of **Jack Sheppard.**

1st, 16-in. by 22-in. The words "Jack Sheppard," engraved in letters, as generally seen in the engraving of Jack cutting his name on the beam. 2nd, 11-in. by 2-in., a smaller ditto.

No. 425—One Engraving for the drama of **The Lamplighter,** 6-in. by 4½-in.

A gigantic ship on fire; Emily Graham clinging to the side; Mick Milligan on the paddle-box, about to jump off to save her from a watery grave; various figures looking on; one lying lifeless on the ground.

No. 426—One Engraving for the drama of **The Lucky Horse-shoe,** 7-in. by 8-in.

Interior of a room; a female with a child presenting a pistol to a ruffian in a Spanish dress, who is standing over the dead body of a man; a border round the whole, forming a horse-shoe, with the following words: "The Lucky-Horse-shoe."

No. 427—Six Engravings for the drama of **The Lucky Horse-shoe.** To work in two colours. Forming a double foolscap sheet, 27-in. by 17-in.

N.B.—One of the last two must be omitted, there being only room for five in the frame-work.

1st, Interior of a room; a duel between two men, one with a cloak on; a female looking on, with her hands clasped, in an attitude of despair. 2nd, Interior of a room; a female with a child in her arms, discharging a pistol at a man in rags; dead body of a man lying on the floor. 3rd, Interior of a kitchen, with chairs and a table; a man in livery in conversation with the man in rags. 4th, A view in Rome; a man in livery standing over a man with his fist clenched; also a struggle between two men, one dressed as a brigand. 5th, Various figures on pedestals; brigands, both male and female, kneeling; one at the side, standing up with his arms raised, representing mass in Rome. 6th, Exterior of the Golden Horse-shoe, with distant view by moonlight; a man with lantern in his hand, at whose side is standing the landlord and a man in long livery, who are being watched by a man at the back.

No. 428—One Engraving for the drama of **The Knights of St. John,** 6-in. by 4-in.

A knight in full armour, with a cross upon his breast, holding a banner, also with a cross upon it; a Saracen with his sword drawn, also holding a banner, with a crescent upon it; a shield belonging to each lying in the centre.

No. 429—One Engraving for the play of **Rolla,** 3½-in. by 3½-in. Rolla with sword in hand, holding a child over his shoulder.

No. 430—Three Engravings for the drama of **The Sailor's Wife.**

1st, 4½-in. by 3-in., The churchyard; Hugh Pierce in the act of striking a roué who is pursuing Nancy Bluebell; a man with a donkey, throwing turnips. 2nd, 4½-in. by 3-in., Main-deck of the "Flyfish;" in the centre is Spritsail Jack jumping out of a chest, firing a pair of pistols at Luke Walton, the skipper; a comic figure firing a pair of pistols from a tub at one of the pirates; general fight in the back-ground. 3rd, 6-in. by 4½-in., Showing three compartments; in the first, houses and a bridge with the river beneath; a plank across reaching to a window, upon which Hugh Pierce has fallen, the roué holding a dagger over him; Spritsail Jack sliding along a rope reaching to the second compartment, where two ruffians with daggers are standing over a female who is lying on the ground; an old man with a lamp, in the third compartment, listening at the noise from the adjoining chamber.

No. 431—Two Engravings for the drama of **The Ocean Monarch,** 4½-in. by 3-in. each.

1st, Between decks of a ship; Wildfire Dick ascending a ladder with a lighted torch in his hand, having set fire to the ship; flames issuing from the hold; crew and passengers in attitudes of excitement. 2nd, Ship in flames; passengers and crew escaping into boats.

No. 432—(Destroyed.)

No. 433—Three Engravings, **Nautical.**

1st, 4½-in. by 3-in., Sea shore; a female kneeling to a smuggler, who is holding a pistol to a sailor lying on the ground; general conflict. 2nd, 4½-in. by 3-in., Deck of a ship; two sailors supporting a man who appears dead; a man also supporting a female, who has fainted; crew looking on in bewilderment. 3rd, 3-in. by 4½-in., A rocky defile by moonlight; soldiers firing at a man, who is falling from the rocks; a sailor and female kneeling side by side, with their hands clasped, looking upwards; villagers with torches, &c., at back.

No. 434—Four Engravings for the drama of **The Flying Dutchman.**

1st, 4½-in. by 3-in., The Flying Dutchman, with flag in his hand, boarding the Cape trader; crew and passengers in dismay and horror; the phantom ship in the distance. 2nd, 4½-in. by 2-in., The Flying Dutchman, with flag in his hand, on the deck; a man sinking down in a flame of fire; two others standing in attitude of bewilderment; the phantom ship in the back ground. 3rd, 4½-in. by 3-in., In the centre is the phantom ship, the Flying Dutchman standing on the bow with flag in his hand; a male and female kneeling down; various figures waving their hats and hands. 4th, 3-in. by 4½-in., Full length figure of the Flying Dutchman, with knee breeches, top boots, large belt, gloves, and feather in hat; a cloud behind him, in which is seen the phantom ship.

No. 435—Five Engravings for the drama of **The Skeleton of the Wave.** To work in two colours. Forming a sheet of double foolscap, 17-in. by 27-in.

1st, Interior of a room; a sailor standing over a man who is lying on the ground, presenting two pistols at his assailants; a negro kneeling, also presenting a pistol; soldiers with guns at the back. 2nd, A sea shore, with a long cross in the ground; a sailor stepping out of a boat rowed by a negro; a man upon the rocks. 3rd, A wild retreat; a sailor combating with four pirates, two of whom are beaten to the ground. 4th, The sea shore; a smuggler presenting a pair of pistols to a negro in chains kneeling before him; at the back is a man cutting a rope that is attached to a buoy, with the skeleton of the wave upon it, at which four smugglers are firing; a man extended dead on the ground. 5th, A monster ship, showing the three decks at one time; on the bottom are slaves in chains; two smugglers capturing a man, at which, a man standing upon the ladder, is presenting a pistol; on the middle deck, smugglers charging guns and ascending ladders to the main-deck, upon which there is a general fight; a sailor upon the rigging waving the union-jack; a gun-boat manned with sailors and officer alongside.

No. 436—One Engraving for the drama of **The Wreck of the Royal George,** 7-in. by 5-in.

The open sea; the Royal George sunk, all but the rigging and sails, to which seven seamen and an officer are clinging, some waving their hats for signals of distress; a boat with a female and two men inside, saving some of the crew from a watery grave; also a boat the other side, with two men in it, one throwing out a rope.

No. 437—One Engraving for the drama of **The Smuggler King,** 4-in. by 3½-in.

A cave; two men in cloaks; one with a sword about to strike the smuggler, who is blowing a whistle.

No. 438—One Engraving, 5-in. by 7-in. Full length figure of a sailor.

No. 439—Five Engravings for the drama of **Gallant Tom.**

1st, 4½-in. by 3-in., In the centre is a pirate about to stab an officer, whom he has beaten to the ground, on his hand and knee, but is preserved by a youth who is holding his arm; at the side is a sailor holding his sword over a pirate who is lying on the ground. 2nd, 4½-in. by 3-in., In the centre is a sailor with a drawn sword, protecting youth who is standing at his back; various figures threatening; at the side is an old man in a long dress, nearly touching the ground, with a long stick in his hand, warning them. 3rd, 4½-in. by 3-in., A sailor holding a man by the throat, who has fallen on his knee; the old man pointing to a spectre-looking female with a cross hanging from her waist, who is on the rocks; various figures looking on in amazement. 4th, 4½-in. by 3-in., Two figures lying dead on the ground, over which is a sailor and a soldier; in the centre is the old man embracing the spectre-looking female that was on the rocks; a youth kneeling by her side; soldiers seen at the back. 5th, 5½-in. by 3-in., Room in a splendid mansion; Gallant Tom seated in a chair; a man standing with a chair before him in conversation; a negro at the other side of the table looking at Tom in an attitude of astonishment.

No. 440—One Engraving of a boat in a storm, 6-in. by 4-in.

Representing the sea; a boat in a storm, in which is a male kneeling with his hands clasped looking upwards, and a female terrified at the lightning.

No. 441—Two Engravings for the drama of **The Chesapeake and Shannon,** 5½-in. by 3½-in. each.

1st, Interior of a cottage; in the centre are two sailors kneeling before two females, protecting them from ruffians, which has caused the inmates to appear, who are looking on in an attitude of astonishment. 2nd, A ship during an engagement at sea; in the centre is an officer cutting down a man with his sword, who is falling into the water; a sailor waving his hat; a man on the rigging putting up the colours; men boarding, and marines firing; forming a grand tableau.

No. 442—Six Engravings for the drama of **Afloat & Ashore.**
Forming a sheet of double foolscap, 17-in. by 27-in. Room for line top and bottom.

1st, A country road ; a man dressed in a pilot jacket with a stick in his hand, in the act of striking a man on the ground, with two small barrels attached to a cord on his arm. 2nd, A villa residence ; a female and youth welcoming the return of the old veteran, who is seen at the back advancing towards, them delighted. 3rd, A mountain pass during a snow storm ; a man lying on the ground exhausted before a fire, another man assisting to raise him up ; at the back is a man driving a sleigh drawn by two horses, with a man inside. 4th, At the back, a view of the river, with shipping ; in the centre is a youth dressed as a sailor, waving his hat, at whose side is an officer also waving his hat ; at the other side is a sailor with the union jack ; various groups of sailors with flags, and their lasses. 5th, Represents two ships in action ; three men clinging to a portion of the mast. 6th, Represents the wild waste of waters ; various figures clinging to a portion of the mast ; also a man rescuing a female from a watery grave.

No. 443—One Engraving for the drama of **The Anchor's Weighed,** 16-in. by 4½-in.
Figure of an anchor with the words, "The Anchor's Weighed." Suitable for a title in a board bill.

No. 444—One Engraving of a ship at sea, 7-in. by 5-in.
Rocks each side ; a ship going steadily along.

No. 445—One Engraving for the drama of **Admiral Sam ; or, the Old Mint of Southwark,** 7-in. by 5-in.
Representing the exterior of the fort by moonlight ; at the side is a sentinel asleep ; Admiral Sam firing a pistol from the fort at the sentinel, whilst Frank is making his escape by a rope attached to the window.

No. 446—One Engraving for the serio-comic pantomime of **Don Juan,** 7-in. by 9½-in.
Full length figure of Scaramouch, with ladder and lantern.

No. 447—Two Engravings for the pantomime of **Jack and Jill,** 6-in. by 5-in. each.

1st, A pattern, or Irish fair ; Jack protecting Jill from the insult of Sir Harkaway Breakneck, an Irish fox-hunting baronet, who has placed himself behind the beadle ; a grotesque figure with a large head lying on the ground ; an Irishman dancing before a booth with a fiddle and bow in his hand, and a general row at the back. 2nd, The Devil's Pond, situated amidst the hills, with a pathway leading to the Elfin Haunt ; Jack and Jill falling down the hill, and various groups of demons in attitudes of triumph.

No. 448—Four Engravings for the pantomime of **Ladye Birde.**
Forming a double foolscap sheet, 17-in. by 27-in. To work in two colours.

1st, A beautiful view of the river Rhine and the Castle of Rosenberg, with distant country, (sunrise). The count about to seize Lady Heron's daughter, whom she is protecting, a child kneeling by their side ; the count's creature holding his sword over a comic figure lying on the ground, during which D'Orsenpang, the Gold Fiend, appears above, them, mounted on a fiery dragon ; a terrific conflict between the count's and Lady Heron's party. 2nd, The gorgeous Valley of Flowers, the home of the fairy Ladye Birde queen ; group of ladye birdes (fairies) in various parts, in the the centre of which is a magnificent appearance of the ladye birde queen, who rises, seated in a splendid car of glittering shells and flowers. 3rd, Giant's Hall in the castle of the count ; Lady Heron and Albert attired as two knights ; Puck, the Ladye Birde Queen's attendant, making the count's creature and retainers stand motionless, whilst they release the lady's daughter. 4th, Exterior of the Gold Gnome's castle, and gigantic golden stone with a light burning upon it ; desperate battle-axe and shield fight between the gold fiend's agent and Lady Heron ; Albert in possession of the magic key ; terrific combat betwixt the dwarf gnomes and fairy knights, forming a grand tableau.

No. 449—Five Engravings for the pantomime of **A. E. I. O. U.**

1st, 2-in. by 3½-in., A female with the letter A on the skirt of her dress. 2nd, 2½-in. by 4-in., A youth with the letter E on his breast. 3rd, 1-in. by 3½-in., A comical figure, very thin, with the letter I before him. 4th, 2½-in. by 3½-in., a comical figure with the letter O in the centre of him. 5th, 2½-in. by 3-in., a comical figure with his head looking through the letter U.

No. 450—One Engraving, Clown's Head, 7½-in. by 7½-in., in a border.
At each corner is a clown in grotesque attitudes ; in the centre, a clown's head, at the top of which are the following words : " Lots of fun !" at the bottom, "Come !"

No. 451—Six Engravings of Clowns.
1st, 3½-in. by 4½-in., Full length figure of a clown. 2nd, 2½-in. by 3½-in., Full length figure of a clown. 3rd, 1½-in. by 2½-in., Full length figure of a clown, with goose and sausages hanging out of his pockets. 4th, 2-in. by 3-in., Full length figure of a clown dancing. 5th, 2½-in. by 4-in., Full length figure of a clown, with a gun in one hand and a dead cat in the other. 6th, 2½-in. by 2½-in., Clown's head.

No. 452—One Engraving, a grand Transformation Scene for a Pantomime, 12½-in. by 8-in.
Large piece of water ; in the centre are water nymphs sporting about ; massive pillars each side with wreaths of roses around them ; at the back is a brilliant star, with various groups of fairies with wreaths of flowers, surrounded by clouds ; fairies sporting about.

No. 453—Six Engravings of Pantomimic Figures. Forming a double foolscap sheet, 17-in. by 27-in. To work in two colours.
1st, Sprite standing on one leg, with six tumblers on his forehead. 2nd, Columbine dancing. 3rd, Harlequin dancing. 4th, Clown with his hand behind him. 5th, Pantaloon on stick. 6th, Clown playing a trumpet.

No. 454—One Engraving for the drama of **The Idiot of the Cliff,** 5-in. by 6-in.
A cottage in flames ; in the centre is a man supporting a female who has fainted ; villagers with pitch forks, rakes, &c., securing a ruffian, all of whom are looking in an attitude of excitement at a man falling headlong from the ruins ; also a man in a Scotch dress, who is seized at the back of the neck by a dog, whilst he is holding on by a rafter.

No. 455—One Engraving for the drama of **The Dogs of Saint Bernard,** 4-in. by 3-in.
A mountainous pass, with a convent in the distance ; a youth lying exhausted on the back of a dog, who has a small keg round his neck.

No. 456—One Engraving for the drama of **Cato ; or, the Dogs of the Plantation,** 6-in. by 4½-in.
A mulatto about to strike a youth with a dagger, who is kneeling before him, but is prevented by two dogs springing upon him.

No. 457—Three Engravings of Dog Pieces, 3-in. by 2½-in. each.
1st, A female with a trunk in her hand, keeping at bay a robber with a pistol ; a dog closely pursuing his companion, who has a dagger in his hand. Engraved for the drama of **The Mountain Guide.** 2nd, Deck of a pirate ship ; the pirate chief, with his flag in his hand, firing a pistol at a mulatto who is lying on the deck, when he is seized at the throat by a dog. Engraved for the drama of **The Phantom Barque.** 3rd, A room ; a large box in the centre with lid partly open, from which an Indian, with beads round his neck, and a large dog, are looking out of. Engraved for the drama of **Wonga.**

No. 458—One Engraving of the Learned Dog, 4-in. by 12-in.
A variety of cards scattered about the floor, with letters on them ; a dog with one in his mouth.

No. 459—Eight Engravings, 6-in. by 3½-in. each, suitable for a troupe of Dogs and Monkeys.
1st, A monkey dancing on the tight-rope ; two French dogs walking on their fore-legs. 2nd, Three monkeys seated at a table drinking ; a monkey with a candlestick, drinking out of a bottle. 3rd, A monkey riding a horse ; also another monkey dressed in livery, whipping the horse ; a dog walking on one of his fore and hind legs. 4th, A monkey dressed as a lady ; a small monkey, with a lantern, holding up her train ; three dogs walking on their hind legs. 5th, Two monkeys dressed as soldiers, one with a gun, and the other playing a fiddle. 6th, Two monkeys dressed as soldiers, one firing a gun at the other, who is seated, blindfold, on a coffin. 7th, A monkey driving a chaise, which has upset, drawn by two dogs, with two monkeys inside. 8th, Two monkeys, dressed as females, at work at spinning-wheels.

No. 460—Two Engravings of Monkeys.
1st, 3½-in. by 2½-in., Monkey catching a butterfly. 2nd, 1½-in. by 2½-in., Monkey climbing a tree.

No. 461—Seven Engravings of Monkeys.

1st, 7½-in. by 4½-in., Monkey dressed as a lady, with parasol and fan; another monkey dressed as her footman, holding her train, also a lantern. 2nd, 4-in. by 4½-in., A monkey drawing a cart with fruit. 3rd, 6-in. by 4½-in., Monkey with night-cap on, candle and candlestick in each paw. 4th, 4-in. by 4½-in., Monkey smartly dressed, with a music-book in his paw. 5th, 4-in. by 4½-in., Monkey carrying a wine-basket, with bottles, drinking. 6th, 4-in. by 4½-in., Monkey capering about with sword in paw. 7th, 6-in. by 4-in., Two monkeys, one dressed as a male, playing a fiddle, the other dancing and playing a tambourine.

No. 462—Three Engravings for the drama of **Mazeppa**.

1st, 6-in. by 4½-in., A forest with large trunk of a tree lying across, over which a horse is madly plunging onwards, bearing on his back a man bound with cords, exhausted; wolves right and left, ready to spring upon their prey. 2nd, 5½-in. by 4-in., A forest; horse partly in a pool of water, madly plunging onwards, bearing on his back a man bound with cords; two wolves following him; an eagle hovering above him; lightning. 3rd, 2-in. by 1½-in., Ditto.

No. 463—Eight Engravings for the drama of **Dick Turpin**.

1st, 8-in. by 6-in., Exterior of the toll-house; Dick Turpin mounted on his mare, Black Bess, who is leaping the gate; toll-keeper looking at him in an attitude of astonishment; two officers pursuing him in the distance. 2nd, 7-in. by 5-in., Ditto; Dick Turpin firing a brace of pistols. 3rd, 11-in. by 6-in., Dick Turpin mounted on his mare, Black Bess, riding at full speed. 4th, 5-in. by 4-in., Exterior of an inn; Dick Turpin mounting his mare, Black Bess; ostler holding his head. 5th, 6-in. by 4-in., Dick Turpin mounted on his mare, Black Bess, leaping the gate. 6th, 5-in. by 4-in., Exterior of an inn; Dick Turpin tying the steak to his horse's bridle; ostler rubbing her down. 7th, 6-in. by 4-in., The forest; death of Black Bess; Turpin leaning over her; Luke Rookwood calling his attention to the officers in the distance. 8th, 7½-in. by 2½-in., Three officers in the distance, mounted on horse-back, pursuing Turpin.

N.B.—The last six Engravings can be used singly, or worked together, forming a crown sheet, 20-in. by 15-in.

No. 464—One Engraving of Horsemanship, 7½-in. by 5½-in.

Man with helmet on, shield and spear in his hand, on a horse, going down a precipice.

No. 465—Two Engravings of Horsemanship.

1st, 8-in. by 5-in., A man leaping over nine horses, and discharging a pair of pistols whilst throwing a somersault; a clown looking at him in a grotesque attitude. 2nd, 9½-in. by 6-in., A man leaping over twelve horses, also through a balloon, whilst discharging a pair of pistols.

No. 466—One Engraving of Horsemanship, 7-in. by 5½-in.

Four men in armour, with swords and shields, seated upon one horse.

No. 467—Nine Engravings of Horsemanship.

1st, 5-in. by 7½-in., A man riding two horses, bearing two children on his shoulders. 2nd, 8-in. by 5-in., Figure of a sailor on a bare-backed steed. 3rd, 3-in. by 3-in., A youth on the back of a horse, leaping through a balloon. 4th, 3-in. by 3-in., A female dancing on a horse. 5th, 3-in. by 3-in., A man and horse dancing. 6th, 3-in. by 3-in., Othello, with dagger and lamp in his hand, on a horse. 7th, 8-in. by 3-in., A man on a horse playing with balls. 8th, 3-in. by 3-in., a female leaping on and off a horse in full gallop. 9th, 3-in. by 3-in., Sir John Falstaff, with a goblet in his hand, on a horse.

No. 468—One Engraving of Horsemanship, 6-in. by 3-in.

A man leaping over twelve horses, through a hoop, surrounded with pipes.

No. 469—Eleven Engravings of Horsemanship.

1st, 12-in. by 7-in., A chariot drawn by four horses, two seraphs holding the reins; in the centre is a female with a crown on her head, wings extended, and a wreath of laurel in each hand. The remaining Engravings are 5-in. by 4-in. each. 2nd, Punch on horseback. 3rd, The Flying Dutchman on horseback. 4th, Fame blowing a trumpet, with wings, also a shield with wreath of laurel round it, and a portrait in the centre. 5th, a horse jumping through a hoop. 6th, Harlequin on horseback. 7th, Dusty Bob on horseback. 8th, Paul Pry, with umbrella turned inside out, on horseback. 9th, Dutch girl with brooms, on horseback. 10th, Sailor on horseback. 11th, A horse with wings, dancing.

No. 470—One Engraving, 9½-in. by 9-in. Equestrian Border.

On the top are three horses prancing about; a horse's head each side, holding up a curtain (type to be inserted); at the bottom, at each end, is a horse galloping.

No. 471—One Engraving, 6-in. by 5-in. Interior of an Amphitheatre.

Three tiers of boxes, pit, and amphitheatre, stage, orchestra with musicians, also an arena, in which are various figures holding banners. some on horses; three men on horses, with banners, riding before a chariot with a man inside, driving three horses; the place splendidly illuminated with chandeliers round the boxes; also a large one suspended in the centre from the ceiling.

No. 472—One Engraving, 5-in. by 3-in. Equestrian Border.

A man on horseback each side, type to be inserted in the centre.

No. 473—One Engraving, 12-in. by 8½-in. Equestrian.

One of the Furies, with snakes in her hand, seated on a gigantic horse with winged hoofs.

No. 474—One Engraving, suitable for a Procession. When put together, in rotation, will form a length of 73-in. by 4-in.

Officers on horseback, yeomen guards with spears, grooms leading horses; trumpeters on horseback; a grand carriage drawn by eight horses, with grooms at the side of each, &c., &c.

No. 475—One Engraving, 15-in. by 13-in. Ornamental Border.

Splendid ornamental border; at the top is the coat-of-arms, under which are the following words: "Victoria Regina," with a medallion portrait of the Queen and Prince Albert; on the sides are various seraphs, with wreaths of roses reaching from one to the other; various flags, cannons, anchor, sword, &c.; at the bottom, two figures seated, one with a book and the other with a sceptre, in their hands; a wreath of laurel, with crossed spears each side. Room for letter-press in the centre and each side of the coat-of-arms. Suitable for an announce-bill or military spectacle.

No. 476—Four Engravings of Niggers.

1st, 7½-in. by 3½-in., In front are five males and three females; at the back of whom are six females, playing banjo, bones, fiddle, triangle, tambourine, and cymbals. 2nd, 6½-in. by 4½-in., Stage drapery, with banjo in the centre, round the top; five males playing tambourine, flutina, fiddle, banjo, and bones. 3rd, 8-in. by 4-in., Youth in the centre playing the fiddle; four men playing banjo, bones, tambourine, and fiddle. 4th, 1½-in. by 2½-in., A negro seated on a stool, playing a tambourine.

No. 477—One Engraving, 5-in. by 8½-in. Suitable for Acrobats.

Man with a flag in each hand, bearing two men upon his shoulders, with flags in their hands; another man above, with a hand on each of their heads; at the bottom are the following words: "The Quatre Wonders."

No. 478—One Engraving, 17-in. by 9-in. The Golden Temple of Guadma.

Representing the great Pagoda of Dagon Rangoon, lighted by candle-sticks of virgin gold; canopies of golden stars; myriads of rockets ascending, in honour of the great idol Dagon; giving a very lively portraiture of the Burmese manners and customs.

No. 479—One Engraving, 4-in. by 3½-in. The War with China.

General conflict with Chinese and English soldiers; the dying and the dead scattered around in all directions; a view of the city in the distance.

No. 480—One Engraving, 9-in. by 7½-in. For an Opera.

Interior of a grand hall, with distant view; a coat-of-arms over the entrance; two males and a female in the centre; various figures standing by; the hall densely crowded with spectators.

No. 481—One Engraving, 9-in. by 7-in.

The Queen, Prince Albert, two of the children, and female attendant, seated in the royal box at the theatre.

No. 482—One Engraving, 7-in. by 10-in. The Rat-catcher's Daughter.

Full length figure of a man with a black eye, having a stick in his pocket; distant view of St. Paul's and London Bridge; the rat-catcher's daughter going down head-foremost into the water; Lilly Vite with his donkey and cart; a border round the whole, upon which are rats and fish baskets; at the top, in the centre, is a rat in a trap; at the bottom, a donkey's head.

No. 483—One Engraving of the Burlesque of **Richard the III**, 11-in. by 8-in.

Lady Anne dressed in widow's weeds, with a weather-cock upon her head, pointing a long sword at Richard, who is upon his knees, large hat by his side.

No. 484—One Engraving of the opera of **Robert le Diable,** 3½-in. by 3-in.

In the centre is a man kneeling, catching hold of another man, who is standing by his side; a figure enveloped in a cloak behind them; demons, snakes, coffins, with bodies, lying on the top of them.

No. 485—One Engraving for a Battle Scene, 6½-in. by 5½-in.

Terrific engagement between the French and Turks; in the centre is a Turk, slain, also his horse, both of which are falling.

No. 486—Three Engravings of Balloons, 1½-in. by 3-in.

No. 487—Several Engravings of Slight-of-hand Tricks, suitable for Wizards.

This set of Engravings comprise some of the most astounding tricks performed by the first wizards of the day, amongst which will be found the following.—The great gun trick, the inexhaustible bottle, firing a watch from the barrel of a gun, the enchanted lady, &c., &c.

No. 488—One Engraving of a Grand Professional Car, 7½-in. by 6½-in.

Beautifully ornamented, with a band of music; at the back of which is a man with drums, drawn by twelve horses.

No. 489—Two Engravings of the Flags of England and France.

1st, 5½-in. by 4½-in., The flags of England and France, with a hand-in-hand, and the word "welcome" at the bottom. To work in two colours. 2nd, 4½-in. by 3½-in. A smaller ditto, to work in one colour only.

No. 490—One Engraving, 1½-in. by 1½-in. for General Notes of the Season.

No. 491—One Engraving of Mr. & Mrs. Caudle, in bed, 5½-in. by 3½-in.

No. 492—One Engraving of a Man in Rags, 3-in. by 4½-in. With patched cloak, and arms folded across his breast.

No. 493—One Engraving, 5½-in. by 4-in., Skating.

At the side is a building with balcony, from which various groups are witnessing people skating on the ice; splendid distant view.

No. 494—One Engraving, 4½-in. by 2½-in., the Bust of Shakespeare.

No. 495—Nine Engravings for Grecian Statues.

1st, 9½-in. by 7-in., A man with helmet on his head, with uplifted club, striking at a monster half man and half horse, representing Theseus and Centaur. 2nd, 3-in. by 3-in., Ditto. 3rd, 9½-in. by 7-in., A man supporting a female who has fallen on her knees; various figures on a rock; a man rescuing a female who has two children, from a watery grave; representing the Deluge. 4th, 9½-in. by 7-in., Three figures, one fallen on his knees, another holding his shield before him, protecting him from his assailant; representing Socrates saving Alcibiades at the Battle of Potedia. 5th, 9½-in. by 7-in., Two figures wrestling; representing Lucta-Tores. 6th, 5-in. by 3-in., Full length figure of a man with helmet, in the act of drawing his sword; representing Ajax. 7th, 5-in. by 8-in., A figure sticking a long spear into a monster, half man and half serpent; representing Michael and Satan. 8th, 5-in. by 8-in., Full length figure of a man with helmet, dagger in hand, and scarf over his shoulders; representing Hector. 9th, 5-in. by 4-in., Figure of a man with long spear in his hand embracing a female; representing Mars and Venus.

No. 496—Four Engravings of Van Amburgh, 6-in. by 4-in. each.

1st, Van Amburgh seated by the side of a lion and lioness; a tiger licking his face. 2nd, Van Amburgh kneeling; a youth with one foot on his thigh, the other upon a lion's head, holding a lamb in his arms, also a lamb between his paws; a tiger, a leopard, and a lioness, around them. 3rd, Van Amburgh thrusting his head down a lion's mouth; a tiger behind him with his paws on his back; a lioness and leopard seated by his side. 4th, Van Amburgh catching hold of a lion and tiger; a leopard climbing up his back, with one paw upon his head; leopards each side.

No. 497—Two Engravings, Sparring.

1st, 4½-in. by 5½-in., Two men with gloves on. 2nd, 2½-in, 2½-in Two men without gloves.

No. 498—One Engraving of a train, 13-in. by 4-in.

Engine with tender and two carriages, with people inside them.

No. 499—One Engraving, 2½-in. by 4-in.

Full length figure of Thalia, with mask in her hand.

No. 500—One Engraving, 4-in. by 4-in.

A man in a temple, surrounded by fireworks.

No. 501—Eight Engravings suitable for a Chinese Collection, 4½-in. by 4-in. each.

1st, A Chinese workshop; two Chinese seated, with their implements scattered about the floor. 2nd, A mansion illuminated with Chinese lanterns; two Chinese in conversation, attended by a servant with an ornament in his hand. 3rd, A Chinese temple, with three figures seated inside. 4th, A street in China; two servants bearing a palanquin, in which a female is seated; also another servant walking by the side fanning her. 5th, 2½-in. by 4½-in., A Chinese mandarin gorgeously attired. 6th, 1½-in. by 5-in., A Chinese lady also gorgeously attired. 7th, 6-in. by 4-in., A Chinese family; in the centre is two children; on the right, two males, one of whom is playing an instrument; on the left, two females, one also playing an instrument. 8th, A garden; a Chinese mandarin smoking a pipe with his lady, who is fanning herself; both seated in large arm chairs before a table, upon which are cups and saucers; a servant at the back, holding a parasol over the lady.

No. 502—One Engraving, 4-in. by 5½-in.

Door of a mansion with iron railings, at which a servant in full livery is standing outside.

No. 503—Several Engravings, suitable for Acrobats.

1st, 6-in. by 7-in., A man firing a gun whilst throwing a somersault over some railings; a man stretched full length on the back of two chairs, bearing three men on his chest; a man bending over a chair, holding a half-cwt. in his hands; a man taking two eggs out of cups whilst throwing a somersault; a man stretched out on the top of a pole; a man attached by his feet at the side, hanging out full length with a man seated on him, and holding another man by the waist; a man as described before, holding up a horse; all these incidents are on one engraving. 2nd, 8-in. by 7-in., a man on a globe catching bottles

from one hand to the other; ditto, with daggers, as described. 3rd, A border, 6-in. by 4-in., with the following around it: at the top a tableau vivant of Cain and Abel; at one side is a man bearing another man (with his head downwards) on his head; at the other is a man bearing two men on his shoulders; at the bottom is a little view with a cottage; a man looking out of the window; a man on the top of a ladder jumping towards him. Room for a line of type to be inserted in the centre. 4th, 4-in. by 7-in., A man leaping through a balloon, discharging a pair of pistols. 5th, 3½-in. by 4½-in., A man on a slack wire, performing with three sticks. 6th, 1½-in. by 2½-in., A man on a pyramid made with basons and decanters, with ten basons about him on sticks.

No. 504—Several Engravings, representing Mythological Figures.

Diana with bow and arrow in hand, at the side of whom is a dog. Apollo with a wreath round his head, a bow and arrow in his hand, and harp by his side. Aurora in her chariot with a burning torch in her hand, drawn by two horses with wings. Venus with two seraphs by her side, above which is a seraph playing on the harp. Cybele in her car drawn by two lions, with a key and a shepherd's crook in her hand. Minerva in a suit of armour, with a spear and shield, at whose side is an owl and a cock. Saturn with scythe and snake in his hand. Mercury with wings on his head and feet. Jupiter seated on his throne, with a sceptre in his hand; a man underneath his feet, and at the side of whom is an eagle. Bacchus in his car drawn by two leopards, upon which is seated Pan blowing his horn. Esculapius leaning on a stick, around which is a snake; at the side is a man naked, with a babe in his arms. King Neptune seated in his car drawn by two sea horses.

No. 505—One Engraving of the Ball of All Nations, 4½-in. by 4½-in.

With a beautiful wreath of grapes around it; at the top of which is a rose; a figure dressed as a count; a female in man's attire; also two other females.

No. 506—Two Engravings for Wrestling.

1st, 8-in. by 6½-in., Two men wrestling. 2nd, 7-in. by 9-in., Ditto; one having caught his opponent in his arms, is about to throw him forward.

No. 507—Three Engravings for the pantomime of £ s. d., 2½-in. by 4-in. each.

1st, The queen with ball and sceptre in hand, the £ entwined around her. 2nd, John Bull with his hand in his waistcoat pocket, the S entwined around him. 3rd, A man smoking a pipe, seated on a basket, with a stall before him, the D entwined round him.

No. 508—One Engraving of the Pressgang, 4-in. by 2½-in.

Sea shore, with public-house at the side; pressgang seizing a young waterman.

No. 509—One Engraving of the Death of Nelson, 5½-in. by 5½-in.

Dock of the "Victory;" Nelson supported in the arms of two sailors; Captain Hardy on his right; at the back are three sailors, one pointing to the direction from which the shot proceeded, the other two with fire-arms; various groups of sailors and officers about the deck.

No. 510—Three Engravings of Naval Engagements, 7-in. by 4-in. each.

1st, Grand naval engagement; sailors clinging to part of a wreck; officers and sailors in boat. 2nd, Storming of Algiers; several ships bombarding a fort; town in the distance. 3rd, Naval engagement; several ships and a steam-boat bombarding a fort, which is blown up; rockets flying in all directions.

No. 511—One Engraving, Naval Engagement, 4-in. by 2½-in.

Deck of a vessel; sailors giving a double-shotted broadside to their enemy in the distance.

No. 512—Two Engravings, Nautical, 2-in. by 3-in. each.

1st, A full-rigged ship in harbour. 2nd, Ditto, in stay.

No. 513—One Engraving, Ship on Fire, 9-in. by 5-in.

The open sea; a ship in flames, passengers and crew escaping in boats, some clinging to part of a mast; various other vessels coming to their assistance.

No. 514—One Engraving of the Artic Regions, 2½-in. by 1½-in.

Icebergs in various parts; men in a boat; ship in the distance.

No. 515—One Engraving of Crossing the Line, 4-in. by 3-in.

Deck of a ship; in front is a man blindfolded, on his knees; a sailor by his side with pot and brush, another with a razor; various groups looking on; at the back is Neptune and Amphitrite, with their attendant Tritons.

No. 516—One Engraving, Exterior of Exeter Hall, 2½-in. by 3-in.

No. 517—Eight Engravings of Horsemanship.

1st, 2½-in. by 1½-in., Two knights tilting with lances; a barrier between them. 2nd, 2-in. by 1-in., Knight in armour, on horseback, with lance. 3rd, 2½-in. by 1½-in., A man in a chariot, drawn by two horses. 4th, 1½-in. by 1½-in., Soldier on horseback, with lance. 5th, 1½-in. by 1½-in., Gladiator standing on a horse, with sword and shield. 6th, 1½-in. by 1½-in., A youth jumping through hoop on the back of a horse. 7th, 1½-in. by 1½-in., Knight in full armour, on mailed horse. 8th, 1½-in. by 1-in., Soldier on horseback, with lance.

No. 518—Five Engravings of Horsemanship.

1st, 6-in. by 4-in., Three knights in combat, one defending the other who is on his knees, from the attack of a third; two horses prancing at the back. 2nd, 6½-in. by 5-in., A man standing on two horses at full gallop, bearing two children on his shoulders; a child each side of him with a streamer in their hands, forming a graceful tableau. 3rd, 8-in. by 5½-in., Two acts of horsemanship; a man balancing himself on his head, on a bottle, on the back of a horse, who is leaping a five-barred gate; also another man on a horse, leaping over a gate, bearing a child on his head, who has a flag in each hand, the ring-master following; spectators at the back. 4th, 7-in. by 6-in., A female leaping over streamers and jumping through balloons, alighting on the back of a horse, which is at full gallop; ring-master, clown, and groom following. 5th, 7½-in. by 5½-in., A man standing on two horses at full gallop, bearing a youth on his shoulder, who is executing wonderful feats of posturing; a youth standing in front, with a foot on each horse; a little girl standing each side, clown and ring-master following; spectators at the back.

No. 519—Five Engravings of Horsemanship, 3-in. by 2½-in. each.

1st, A horse seated on his hind legs, ringing a bell, ring-master by his side. 2nd, Bacchus on horseback, with goblet and bunch of grapes. 3rd, A comic figure on horseback, standing straight up. 4th, A female dancing on horseback. 5th, A warrior on horseback, with bow and arrow.

No. 520—Three Engravings of Horsemanship.

1st, 3-in. by 4-in., A knight in full armour, on horseback, with lance. 2nd, 1½-in. by 1½-in., St. George and Dragon. 3rd, 2-in. by 2-in., A horse with wings.

No. 521—One Engraving of a balloon, 4-in. by 4-in.

Representing a balloon ascent at night, with four men in the car, from which is proceeding a brilliant illumination; crowds of people witnessing it.

No. 522—Two Engravings, La Trapeze and Double Globe, 2-in. by 3-in. each.

1st, A man supporting himself by a rope with his feet, bearing two men on his head, another man holding on by his legs turning a somersault. 2nd, A man lying on the ground, dancing a pole, with a globe at each end, with his feet.

No. 523—Five Engravings suitable for Acrobats.

1st, 4-in. by 3-in., Two youths throwing somersaults from a man's feet, who is lying on the ground; also another man bearing a youth on each hand. 2nd, 4-in. by 2½-in., A man lying on the ground, bearing a youth (who is standing on one leg) on each foot; another man throwing two youths in the air, who are turning somersaults. 3rd, 4½-in. by 5½-in., Two youths throwing somersaults from a man's feet, who is lying on the ground; a youth alighting to the ground. 4th, 4-in. by 5-in., A man throwing two youths in the air, who are turning somersaults. 5th, 5½-in. by 5-in., A man turning a somersault whilst playing a violin, alighting on a tight-rope.

No. 524—One Engraving, 6-in. by 4-½in.

A large fist (☞) with frame (blank space for word or figure), to catch the eye for anything of importance.

No. 525—One Engraving 3½-in. by 2-½-in.

A scaffold; a man in armour lying dead on a block, his head covered on the right is a boy lying dead; in the centre, a woman stabbing a boy; a man rushing up on the left; mob holding up their hands in astonishment.

No. 526—One Engraving, 3-in. by 2½-in.

An apartment in a palace; the king lying in state on a couch; a female dressed in black, with crown on her head, seated by his side, weeping.

No. 527—One Engraving of Dogs and Monkeys, 7½-in. by 5½-in.

In the centre is a monkey on a slack rope; another monkey balancing himself on his head on a dog's back; a double ladder; a monkey mounted on a dog, going up one side; a monkey balancing himself on his head on the top; on the other side is a dog coming down with a monkey on his back, with his head towards his tail, which he is catching hold of; a monkey balancing himself on his head on the top of a pole; on one side, in an oval frame, are three monkeys seated on a table, also a monkey dressed in livery, bringing a lighted candle and bottle to them; on the other side in an oval frame, is a man holding hoops, through which a dog is jumping; at the bottom, in an oval frame, is a dog walking on the top of a tub; on the top, in an oval frame, is a dog stretched out full length, on the back of two chairs; monkeys mounted on dogs, dressed as jockeys, representing a grand steeple chase, each side of the oval frames.

No. 528—Two Engravings of the drama of Wat Tyler.

1st, 3½-in. by 2½-in., Interior of Wat Tyler's smithy; the tax-gatherer rudely embracing Wat Tyler's daughter; Wat Tyler standing in a menacing attitude with a hammer in his hand; a tax-gatherer looking in at the door. 2nd, 6-in. by 3½-in., Interior of Wat Tyler's smithy; Wat Tyler embracing his daughter after having killed the tax-gatherer, who is lying dead on the floor; two others escaping by the door; a female kneeling by Wat Tyler's side, weeping.

No. 529—One Engraving, 4-in. by 3-in.

Public apartment in a tavern; in the centre is a Scotchman stabbing another man; several persons looking on amazed.

No. 530—One Engraving, 3-in. by 2½-in.

Gallery of a cathedral; in the centre is a man kneeling in an attitude of astonishment; another man looking in at the window; at the back is seen a procession of priests.

No. 531—One Engraving, 6-in. by 4-in.

An apartment; a woman bending over a man, trying to raise him, who is on the ground; three men at the back looking on in astonishment.

No. 532—One Engraving of Fair Rosamond, 3-in. by 2½-in.

Interior of Woodstock Bower; Fair Rosamond kneeling before the Queen in an imploring attitude.

No. 533—One Engraving 2-in. by 3-in.

Full length figure of a man dressed in cocked hat and wig, with tail, heavy coat, frills on wrists, long waistcoat, knee-breeches, shoes with buckles, sword by his side, and walking stick in hand. The costume of the last century.

No. 534—One Engraving, 5½-in. by 3½-in.

A forest; a man supporting a female who has sunk on her knees exhausted.

No. 535—One Engraving of Le Perche Globe, 4-in. by 10-in.

A man supporting a pole, at the top of which is another man dancing a globe with his feet.

No. 536—One Engraving of Lady Godiva, 3-in. by 2½-in.

A street in Coventry; Lady Godiva mounted on a horse, naked.

No. 537—Two Engravings of Alonzo the Brave.

1st, 3½-in. by 2½-in., Alonzo kneeling on the ground, presenting to Imogene a wreath of flowers. 2nd, 2½-in. by 2-in., Imogene seated in a chair of state; a man seated each side of her; a spectral figure in armour holding his hand towards her.

No. 538—One Engraving, 3-in. by 1-in.

Upon which are the following characters: Sir John Falstaff, Shylock, Lady Macbeth, Paul Pry, Romeo, and female with fan; a man viewing them through an eye-glass at table.

No. 539—One Engraving, 2-in. by 2½-in.

A forest; robbers attacking a coach; in the centre is a man presenting a pistol to the coachman's breast.

No. 540—One Engraving, 3-in. 2½-in.

A hall; a male and female hand-in-hand, in conversation; a man in a long robe at the back, looking at them; various groups in conversation.

No. 541—One Engraving of the Musical Glasses, 4-in. by 2½-in.

A man playing the musical glasses.

No. 542—One Engraving, House on Fire, 6-in. by 4-in.

A house on fire; female at a window in an imploring attitude; persons holding a sheet in order to assist her in making her escape; a man holding his hands up towards her.

No. 543—One Engraving of the Learned Pig, 2½-in. by 2-in.

Pig in centre, with a lettered card in his mouth, others placed around him; on the left are three children; on the right, a man with a stick in hand, talking to them.

No. 544—One Engraving, 4-in. by 3-in.

A blind old man seated at the foot of a tree; children playing around him, one crowning him with flowers. A very affecting scene.

No. 545—Two Engravings of Paul Pry.

1st, 3½-in. by 3-in., an apartment; a party of ladies and gentlemen, Paul Pry entering, with the following words: "Just popp'd in, hope as an old friend I don't intrude!" 2nd, 4-in. by 6½-in., Full length figure of Paul Pry, with umbrella under his arm, with the following words: "I hope I don't intrude!"

No. 546—Two Engravings, 3-in. by 4-in. each.

1st, Exterior of a tavern; a man seated on a horse, drinking out of a pot; a youth seated on a form, handcuffed; publican at the door. 2nd, A public room in a tavern; a recruiting sergeant seated at the table, with two men smiling at a youth intoxicated, with a pot in his hand.

No. 547—One Engraving of the drama of **Obi, or Three-fingered Jack**, 6-in. by 3½-in.

A mountain scene; in the centre is Obi with uplifted dagger, about to strike a female (in youth's attire) who is kneeling before him in an imploring attitude; on the left, is a slave, with sword in hand, coming to her rescue.

No. 548—Three Engravings, Marriage a la Mode, 4-in. by 3-in. each.

An apartment; a group of men seated at a table with papers and money before them; on the left is a man viewing himself in the glass; at the back is a male and female in conversation. 2nd, An apartment; a female seated at a table, in a passion, having overturned a chair in dismissing a lawyer, who is going out at the door; a man seated on a chair, on the left. 3rd, an apartment; an aged female holding a child to a female who is dying, the doctor holding her hand; at the back, is a man holding another by the collar of his coat.

No. 549—One Engraving, 4-in. by 3-in.

An old man with a long stick, holding a female by the wrist, who is pointing over a stile.

No. 550—One Engraving of May and December, 3½-in. by 4-in.

An old man leaning on a stick, arm-in-arm with a young female, who is smartly dressed.

No. 551—One Engraving, 5-in. by 5-in.

Ramparts of a castle; a monk pushing a man headlong down, from whom a dagger is falling.

No. 552—One Engraving, 3½-in. by 3-in.

Interior of a castle; a man in a Scotch dress, in an attitude of amazement, looking at a witch-like figure of a female with crooked stick, who is pointing at him.

No. 553—One Engraving, 4-in. by 3-in.

A female falling into a chasm from the top of a rock; a man on the top looking down.

No. 554—One Engraving, 4-in. by 3-in.

A forest, with distant view of a castle; a man in armour in the act of stabbing a youth, whom he is holding by the waist; another youth escaping.

No. 555—One Engraving, 4-in. by 3-in.

Room in a tavern; one ruffian with pistol in hand, attacking another, whom he is holding by the throat; a third holding him back.

No. 556—One Engraving, 5-in. by 3-in.

An elegantly-furnished apartment; a man in military uniform rushing towards a female who is lying dead; an old man kneeling by the side of her; a bouquet lying on the floor.

No. 557—Two Engravings of Jem Crow.

1st, 2-in. by 2-in., Full length figure of Jem Crow, in the act of singing the celebrated song of "Wheel about and turn about." 2nd, 1-in. by 1½-in., Ditto.

No. 558—One Engraving of the drama of **The Vagrant and his Family**, 8-in. by 6-in.

Represents in the back-ground a road-side cottage, winding-road, and waggon; in the fore-ground, a man dressed as a vagrant; child crying by his side; woman carrying a dead youth; a child clinging to her back.

No. 559—One Engraving, 5½-in. 4-in.

A stone apartment; on the left, a bed; on the right, a table, with candle and book upon it; a girl kneeling down; in the centre, is a male and female stabbing a soldier.

No. 560—One Engraving, 6-in. by 4-in.

A grave at the foot of a tree in the forest, upon which are the following words: "The Cossack's grave;" a man in a long dress, with lantern in hand, approaching with his head turned; another man behind a tree watching.

No. 561—One Engraving, 5½-in. by 4-in.

A forest; a man in the act of stabbing another, who is on the ground.

No. 562—One Engraving for a Pantomime, 4-in. by 2½-in.

A mountain lake ; a fairy with wand, rising out of the water; speaking to a knight standing with his arms outstretched towards her.

No. 563—One Engraving, 6½-in. by 4-in.

A ravine ; two men falling headlong down ; one grasping the other by the throat.

No. 564—One Engraving of No Followers, 3-in. by 3½-in.

An apartment ; two males and two females seated at a table eating ; a black servant peeping from under the table ; at the back, a screen ; also a female.

No. 565—One Engraving, 4-in. by 3-in.

A corridor ; a female kneeling before an old man, who is reading a paper ; two officers by her side ; at the back, is a male and female hand-in-hand, in conversation ; also a body of soldiers with their captain.

No. 566—One Engraving, Comic, 3-in. by 3½-in.

A library ; in the centre is a female fainting at the appearance of a man who is standing on the right, holding up his arm ; an old woman holding a long bottle to her nose ; on the left, is a lawyer with large wig, and stick in hand ; also a priest holding up a cross ; at the back, is a female embracing her child.

No. 567—One Engraving, 3-in. by 4-in.

A garden, in the centre of which is a bower ; a female in a long dress, and male in cloak, approaching it.

No. 568—One Engraving, 4-in. by 2½-in.

An apartment ; a man holding another by the throat, who is kneeling on the ground with sword in hand ; at the back an old man about to strike the uppermost one with a sledge hammer ; four females in imploring attitudes.

No. 569—One Engraving, 4-in. by 2½-in.

Exterior of a castle ; in the centre is a male and female kneeling before the king, attended by his nobles ; a page by his side, holding a crown on a cushion ; on the right, a group of persons doffing their hats, bowing.

No. 570—One Engraving of Robin Hood.

In the centre, is Robin Hood standing by the side of Maid Marian, who has shot a stag in the distance ; foresters seated on the ground, carousing ; Friar Tuck seated by the trunk of a large tree.

No. 571—One Engraving of the drama of **The King's Wager,** 2½-in. by 3½-in.

A street ; two ruffians capturing Sampson Tybbe, the night watchman, in mistake for Herbert Vane, under the guidance of Mirondelle.

No. 572—One Engraving of the play of **The Merry Wives of Windsor,** 4-in. by 2½-in.

Mrs. Page and Mrs. Ford putting Sir John Falstaff in the buck-basket, which they are covering with a cloth.

No. 573—One Engraving, Aladdin, 5½-in. by 4-in.

Interior of a cave ; a door open, through which is seen a flight of steps ; the magician belching forth fire and smoke from his mouth, in the act of raising a geni, who is on a pedestal ; aladdin about to run out amazed.

No. 574—One Engraving, 5½-in. by 3½-in.

A storm in the vicinity of some rocks, upon which are several spectators looking at a wreck in the distance.

No. 575—One Engraving, 5½-in. by 4-in.

A street ; on the right is a man standing at the foot of a ladder placed against the window ; in the centre is a gaily dressed cavalier, masked, with drawn sword, carrying off a lady, who is struggling in his arms;

No. 576—One Engraving, 4-in. by 3½-in.

An apartment ; two men seated at a table smoking and drinking, one of whom is holding a cup to a dwarf with large head, who is warming his hand by the fire.

No. 577—One Engraving of Hope, 3-in. by 4½-in.

An emblematical figure of Hope, leaning on an anchor ; a ship in the distance.

No. 578—One Engraving, 3½-in. by 4-in.

An apartment ; a male embracing a female, who is about to stab herself.

No. 579—One Engraving of the Seaman and the Secretary, 3½-in. by 2-in.

A hall in a castle ; Edwin, a page, asleep in a chair ; Will Steady, with purse in each hand, standing by his side ; a bottle and letter upon the ground.

No. 580—One Engraving, Comic, 3½-in. by 2½-in.

A soldier with walking-stick, in conversation with an old man, with large wig, long coat and waistcoat, knee breeches, and buckle shoes ; a cottage at the back.

No. 581—One Engraving, 2-in. by 3-in.

A plantation ; a slave owner holding a female by the waist, who is holding up her hands in an imploring attitude, at the back of whom is a man with whip in his hand.

No. 582—One Engraving of William Tell, 2-in. by 3-in.

In the centre is William Tell, with stretched bow, shooting the apple off his son's head, who is standing at the back ; soldiers looking on.

No. 583—One Engraving of the Waterman, 4-in. by 2½-in.

Blackfriar's Bridge ; a boat by the stairs, upon which is a waterman pointing ; distant view of St. Paul's.

No. 584—Five Engravings, suitable for Highwaymen's Pieces.

1st, 4-in. by 3-in., on the right is a highwayman, mounted on a horse, whipping another horse, upon which is an old man bound with his back towards the horse's head, having robbed him of his money.

2nd, 4-in. by 3-in., On the left is a highwayman mounted on a horse, presenting a pistol to a man also mounted on a horse, on the right, who has a belt around his waist, in which is a brace of pistols. 3rd, 4-in. by 3-in., A highwayman mounted on a horse, stopping a man who is riding in a chaise. 4th, 3½-in. by 2½-in., A highwayman dancing with a female enveloped in a cloak. 5th, 3½-in. by 3-in., A forest ; a priest warning a highwayman, who is mounted on a horse.

No. 585—One Engraving, Enlisting, 4-in. by 2½-in.

Exterior of a country ale-house ; soldiers seated before a table, drinking ; a soldier in conversation with a countryman, who is standing by the table ; on the left, a drummer and countryman in conversation.

No. 586—One Engraving, 3½-in. by 3-in.

A garden, with view of a castle at the back ; a male and female, hand-in-hand, in conversation.

No. 587—One Engraving of the Brigand, 4-in. by 3-in.

The brigand chief firing a pistol at an officer who is falling to the ground ; general conflict between brigands and soldiers.

No. 588—One Engraving, 5½-in. by 4-in.

A wretched apartment ; door partly open, through which is seen a flash of lightning ; a man stabbing another in the shoulder who is entering ; a female by a table at the back, upon which is a lighted candle, bottle, and glass, looking at him in amazement.

No. 589—One Engraving of Joan of Arc, 10-in. by 3-in.

In the centre is Joan of Arc seated on a horse, with shield and flag, at the side of which are two monks kneeling ; on the left a body of soldiers with banners, branches of palm, &c., doffing their hats and shouting ; on the right a body of females waving branches of palm ; city at the back.

No. 590—One Engraving, 4-in. by 5-in.

A garden ; a brigand disguised as a minstrel, with bagpipes, presenting a letter to a female who is looking over a balcony.

No. 591—One Engraving of the drama of **Love and Crime, or the Mystery of the Convent.** Embracing three of the principal tableaus, 4½-in. by 6½-in.

1st, Interior of a convent; a female kneeling before a cross, a monk with an uplifted dagger about to stab her in the back. 2nd, A knight with battle-axe, fighting with four men, one of whom he has beaten to the ground. 3rd, The ruins of an old abbey; a man on his knees horrified at the apparition of a female dressed in white, with a wound in her breast.

No. 592 - One Engraving, 6-in. by 4-in.

A stone apartment; a group of bravos seated at a table, one with a lighted torch; two bravos entering, bearing the senseless form of a female.

No. 593—One Engraving of the drama of **Mary, the Maid of the Inn,** 4-in. by 3-in.

In the centre is Mary concealing herself behind the ruins of an old abbey, with branch in hand, beholding her lover, whose hat has fallen off, assisting Harrop in carrying the dead body of a custom-house officer.

No. 594—One Engraving, 4½-in. by 2½-in.
Interior of a theatre, as seen from the stage.

No. 595—One Engraving, Charms and Counter-charms, 3½-in. by 4-in.
A male and female arm-in-arm; a female at the back watching them.

No. 596—One Engraving, 5½-in. by 4-in.

An apartment; a cavalier ordering the arrest of an old man by two soldiers; a hunchbacked dwarf, dressed as a court fool, with a wand, pointing at him.

No. 597—One Engraving, Military Punishment, 5½-in. by 5-in.

A square of soldiers; in the centre, a man being lashed; officers standing by his side; various soldiers being borne away, horrified at the sight.

No. 598—One Engraving, 4-in. by 5-in.

An apartment; in the centre, a female lying on a bed, a man kneeling by its side; an aged female seated by the side of the bed, weeping; on the left, a sailor with hat in hand, looking on.

No. 599—One Engraving, The Deserter, 7-in. by 4-in.
A file of soldiers about to shoot a deserter, who is kneeling at the back; various officers looking on.

No. 600—One Engraving, 6-in. by 7-in.
A female with a sheet thrown over her head, arms spread out, clouds behind her.

No. 601—One Engraving, The Waits, 4-in. by 2½-in.
A country road, with public-house; musicians playing outside; heavy fall of snow.

No. 602—One Engraving, 3½-in. by 3-in.
An apartment, looking into the grounds of a castle; a Scotchman with dagger in hand, seizing another closely enveloped in a plaid, making his escape by the door; a female seated on a chair, frightened.

No. 603—One Engraving, 3½-in. by 4-in.
A churchyard; a female looking amazed at a spectral figure of a knight in armour, who has his back turned towards her.

No. 604—One Engraving, 5½-in. by 4-in.
A cavern; an ogre half naked, with feathers on his head, large club in hand, and a lion's skin wrapped around him, standing opposite three figures, seated at a large stone.

No. 605—One Engraving, 7-in. by 4-in.
On the left, French soldiers; officer on horseback in centre, firing at a body of Arabs mounted on horses; the dead and dying scattered around in various directions.

No. 606—One Engraving, 4-in. by 3-in.
A library; a man seated at table reading a book; another man entering at the door.

No. 607—One Engraving, 3½-in. by 3-in.
A wild-looking man making his escape by wrenching a bar from the window, having fired the apartment, leaving a woman exhausted on the ground.

No. 608—One Engraving, 4-in. by 3-in.
A stable-yard; at the back, a coach, with door open; on the left, is a youth with bundle under his arm, looking back.

No. 609—One Engraving, 4-in. by 3½-in.
A corridor; a female with long dress, in conversation with a man smartly dressed, with frill round his neck, and sword by his side; a female at back.

No. 610—One Engraving, Punch, 2½-in. by 3-in.
Half-figure of Punch with stick in hand.

No. 611—One Engraving, 3½-in. by 3-in.
A ravine; two men falling headlong down; one grasping the other by the throat; at the top is a female looking down at them horrified; also a lighted torch and dagger.

No. 612—One Engraving, 7-in. by 4-in.
A garden; two men concealing bags of money under a stone; garden implements strewed about.

No. 613—One Engraving, 7-in. by 4-in.
A chamber; in the centre, a female in disguise, holding a goblet, in conversation with a cavalier seated in an easy chair by a table, behind which are two guards with long swords; on the right, seated at the other end of the table, is a man with goblet in hand, with his back turned.

No. 614—One Engraving, 7-in. by 4-in.
An elegantly furnished apartment; in the centre is a female seated on a sofa, holding a trinket in her hand, in conversation with another female; on her left, is a cavalier with hat in hand and a sword by his side.

No. 615—One Engraving, 7-in. by 4-in.
A gallery at the head of a flight of stairs; a man and woman seizing another man with dagger in his hand, having stabbed a female, who is falling.

No. 616—One Engraving, 6-in. by 4-in.
A lighted chamber; two men quarrelling, with daggers in hand; a woman between trying to separate them.

No. 617—One Engraving, 7-in. by 4-in.
The balustrades of a bridge; a man hanging by the ledge; another reaching through the rails, striking his fingers with the but-end of a pistol.

No. 618—One Engraving, 7-in. by 4-in.
An apartment with stone flooring; two men looking into an opening in the floor, one holding a light; placards on on the wall, upon which are the following words:—"Reward, £100!" "Lost!" "Stolen!"

No. 619—One Engraving, a Musical Emblem, 8½-in. by 3-in.
On the right are emblematical figures of musicians playing violins, double-bass, kettle-drums, &c.; on the left, a group of persons witnessing them, some with fans, opera glasses, &c.; in the centre, is the leader with hat and feather, sword by his side, and music in hand; an organ at the back.

No. 620—One Engraving, 7-in. by 4-in.
An elegantly furnished apartment; a female with fan in hand, seated at table with a young man in a fashionable dress of the last century; guitar and music books at the back.

No. 621—One Engraving of the drama of **Faust & Marguerite,** 7-in. by 4-in.
A garden; on the right is Marguerite reclining on a garden seat, covering her face with her hands; on the left, the demon standing by her side.

No. 622—One Engraving, 7-in. by 4-in.
A street (night); in the centre, a cavalier about to draw his sword, standing over the senseless form of a female, whom he is protecting; on the left, a cavalier holding another, who is masked, with drawn sword; two men in the distance.

No. 623—One Engraving, 7-in. by 4-in.
A hall of justice; on the left are two soldiers supporting a female, who has fainted; a man kneeling by her side, weeping; at the back, a judge, attended by his clerks, before a table.

No. 624—One Engraving, 7-in. by 4-in.

A garden; in the centre, a pair of large gates, partly open, from which a man, enveloped in a clonk, is seen; another man, with drawn sword, advancing towards him.

No. 625—Two Engravings, Ivanhoe, 7-in. by 4-in. each.

1st, The grand hall of the temple arranged in order of judgment, as for a trial; in the centre is Rebecca accused of sorcery; guards right and left; on the left, at the back, the grand master, preceptors, knights, &c. 2nd, Battlements of a castle; Ivanhoe holding Frondebœuf by the throat, about to stab him with a dagger.

No. 626—One Engraving, 7-in. by 4-in.

A chamber; in the centre, a man with cup in one hand, which he is offering to a female, who has fallen on her knees, covering her face from his gaze; a dagger in his other hand.

No. 627—One Engraving, 7-in. by 4-in.

A chamber; in the centre, a man in armour reproving a female, who is kneeling, with her face turned towards him, at the same time pointing to a female on his right, lying dead, with a dagger in her breast.

No. 628—One Engraving, 7-in. by 4-in.

A chamber; in the centre, a female standing by a table, upon which is a crucifix, book, and papers, holding documents in her hand, to which is attached a seal; a man kneeling by her side.

No. 629—One Engraving, 7-in. by 4-in.

An apartment; in the centre, a female with bonnet and shawl, standing before a table, holding some papers in her hand; on her left, an elderly man with his hands in his coat pockets, in conversation with her.

No. 630—One Engraving, 7-in. by 4-in.

Road in front of a mansion; man and boy stopping in amazement on beholding a dead body lying across the doorway.

No. 631—One Engraving, 7-in. by 4-in.

A churchyard; a man kneeling over a grave with his hands clasped together, a hat by his side.

No. 632—One Engraving, a Winter Scene, 3¼-in. by 2¼-in.

Cottage covered with snow; a pond frozen over.

No. 633—One Engraving, Deaf and Dumb Alphabet, 3-in. by 4-in.

No. 634—One Engraving, 7-in. by 4-in.

An apartment; in the centre, a cavalier introducing a young female to a lady, whom he is holding by the hand; on the left, a monk frowning and clenching his fist; at the back, are various figures seated at a table.

No. 635—One Engraving, 7-in. by 4-in.

A battle-field; on the left, a camp; in the centre is a female kneeling in an imploring attitude before an old Turk, who, with uplifted sword, is about to strike a young officer falling to the ground; soldiers charging in the distance.

No. 636—One Engraving, 7-in. by 4-in.

A chamber; in the centre, a man lying on the ground; on the right, a man thrusting him with a lance; a female looking on, with dagger in hand.

No. 637—One Engraving, 5¼-in. by 4-in.

An apartment; a man seated by a table in an attitude of grief; female entering from a door offering him a brace of pistols.

No. 638—Two Engravings, 6-in. by 4-in. each.

Each one portrays a picturesque representation of the various costumes of the Kaffir chiefs in their native country.

No. 639—One Engraving, 6-in. by 4-in.

A dense forest; a man supporting a fainting female, while defending himself against a brigand, who is armed with a staff in his right hand and holding a dagger in his left; brigands in the back ground rushing to aid their companion.

No. 640—One Engraving, 6-in. by 4-in.

Exterior of a prison, with town in the distance (by night); a man descending from the walls by the aid of a rope ladder.

No. 641—One Engraving, 8-in. by 5-in.

Representing the main deck of a man-o'-war, on which are preparations for the execution of three marines, who are kneeling with the ropes adjusted round their necks and their hands bound, surrounded by the officers and crew of the vessel; the captain in the act of giving the signal for the men to haul up the condemned.

No. 642—One Engraving, 6-in. by 4-in.

A garden scene; a young man standing, with hands clasped in an imploring attitude before a stern-looking man; on the right of whom is a female in handsome attire, smiling.

643—One Engraving, 6-in. by 4-in.

An open plain (with rising moon); a female, in Oriental costume, accompanied by a male, attired as a military officer, who is pointing to some object in the distance.

No. 644—One Engraving, 6-in. by 4-in.

Representing a dark and lonely street; a young female in white clinging in an imploring attitude to the arm of an aged man, who is attired as an officer of police; attendants behind, armed with guns, and holding lanterns, are looking on in amazement.

No. 645—One Engraving, 8-in. by 6-in.

A handsomely-furnished apartment leading on to a balcony (night); a female with writing desk before her and a letter in her hand, appearing as if anxiously awaiting some person; the moon brightly shining, its rays thrown through the open window.

No. 646—One Engraving, 8-in. by 6-in.

Representing Grace Darling and her father in the light-house boat, surrounded by the raging sea, gallantly rowing to the rescue of the crew of the "Forfarshire" steamer, which is seen in the distance, partially a wreck, being tossed about at the mercy of the mountainous waves.

No. 647—One Engraving, 6-in. by 4-in.

An open plain; engagement between French and English troops; a French officer in advance of his men deliberately shooting the English leader with a pistol; female on horseback, on the right hand cheering on the English troops.

No. 648—One Engraving, 5-in. by 4-in.

A street in Paris; on the right in the back ground, is a large concourse of men with their heads and faces covered with hoods, securely fastened round their necks, their arms bound behind; in the foreground, females of rank kneeling in imploring attitudes to a man with upraised sword, who has severed the head from the body of a female, richly dressed; a youth with drawn sword in the act of hastening to rescue the lady; a noble standing by his side stopping him.

No. 649—One Engraving, 7-in. by 4-in.

An apartment; a male and female in attitudes of grief.

No. 650—One Engraving, 6-in. by 4-in.

A street; knight on horseback taking leave of a female standing at an open door-way, in great grief; attendants looking on.

No. 651—One Engraving, 5-in. by 4-in.

Courtyard of a French prison; prisoners receiving religious consolation previous to being executed; the emblem of the crucifixion (the cross) being raised by a priest; one man lying down.

No. 652—One Engraving, 5-in. by 4-in.

An apartment, showing the death-bed of a young female; physician and two females looking on in grievous attitudes.

No. 653—One Engraving, 5-in. by 4-in.

A small field, surrounded with trees; a gentleman discharging pistol at a target; an old man in military uniform, and a youth looking on.

No. 654—One Engraving, 6-in. by 5-in.

A wood; an old woman making her way to a cottage; a man about to secrete himself behind a tree, watching her.

No. 655—One Engraving, 8-in. by 5-in.

A French court of justice; an advocate, in an excited manner, addressing the court.

No. 656.--One Engraving, 6-in. by 4-in.

A man being executed by torch-light ; great tumult among the crowd, who are attempting a rescue.

No. 657—One Engraving, 6-in. by 4-in.

A drawing-room ; military officer taking leave of his wife and child ; the wife kneeling in attitude of grief ; child by her side.

No. 658—One Engraving, 6½-in. by 4-in.

A country lane ; cottages on one side, hedge and trees on the other ; an old man with dagger about to stab a female enveloped in a dark veil, who is kneeling before him in an imploring attitude.

No. 659—One Engraving, 6-in. by 4-in.

A bed chamber ; a female in bed with clasped hands, dying ; a catholic priest giving her absolution, in the act of elevating the crucifix.

660—One Engraving, 6½-in. by 4-in.

A richly-furnished bed-chamber ; an elderly gentleman, with night-cap on, asleep ; two burglars in the room, one in the act of breaking open a large chest, the other, with thumb at the end of his nose, laughing at the sleeping man in derision.

No. 661—One Engraving, 7-in. by 4-in.

A poorly-furnished room ; an old four-post bedstead, with squalid mattress and pillow, on which is a dying youth ; a female poorly clad standing by the bed-side, with hand on his chest, gazing upon him in sympathy ; on the floor a man intoxicated lying asleep.

Nos. 662 & 663—Two Engravings for the drama of **The Black Doctor,** 6½-in. by 4-in. each.

1st, Fabian, the Black Doctor, kneeling to the Countess de la Reynerie, who is giving him money ; the Chevalier de St. Luce looking over her shoulder ; a lackey with large wax candle in his hand standing behind. 2nd, A drawing-room ; the Black Doctor standing with arms folded in a defiant attitude, looking towards the Chevalier de St. Luce and the notary, who have risen from their seats in attitudes of surprise.

No. 664—One Engraving, 7-in. by 4-in.

A fair in France ; booths, &c., in the back-ground ; in the foreground, a crowd of people listening to the harangue of an old woman who is standing on a stool.

No. 665—One Engraving, 7-in. by 4-in.

A street in Paris (night) ; officers of the watch challenging a man who is armed with pistols in his belt.

No. 666—One Engraving, 6½-in. by 4-in.

A woody glade, with rocky water-fall ; a young female with floral wreath encircling her head, reclining on a mossy bank ; a young military officer approaching her from the wood.

No. 667—One Engraving, 7-in. by 4-in.

A country lane ; two young females with gipsey bonnets on in conversation close to a rustic gate leading to a field.

No. 668—One Engraving, 7-in. by 4-in.

A dungeon, in which is a female in Turkish costume pleading to a Turk of ferocious aspect.

No. 669—One Engraving, 6-in. by 4-in.

A large tent ; Richard Cœur de Leon, in complete suit of armour, surrounded by knights and soldiers ; his queen, kneeling, supplicating for the lives of a large number of citizens, who are congregated before the opening of the tent, their countenances expressing great fear.

No. 670—One Engraving, 7-in. by 4-in.

The cloisters of Westminster Abbey ; a gentleman under an archway, listening to the conversation of two foreign gentlemen and a gipsy woman.

No. 671—One Engraving, 7-in. by 4-in.

A lady's boudoir ; a female lying dead on a couch, having discharged a pistol at her head, from which blood is flowing, her arm hanging by her side ; the pistol firmly clasped in her hand ; two males looking on in affright. Costume, Tudor period.

No. 672—One Engraving, 7-in. by 4-in.

Floral terrace on the turret of a castle ; figures of Romeo and Juliet in conversation.

No. 673—One Engraving for the drama of **The Wife of Seven Husbands,** 6½-in. by 4-in.

Interior of a court of justice intensely crowded ; usher of the court conducting the wife to a seat previous to her trial.

No. 674—One Engraving for the drama of **The Wife of Seven Husbands,** 6½-in. by 4-in. Illustrating the introduction.

No. 675—One Engraving, 6-in. by 4-in.

Represents the storming of Algiers by sea and land.

No. 676—One Engraving, 6-in. by 4-in.

A rocky eminence ; three persons in pursuit of a robber, who is seized at the throat by a dog.

No. 677—One Engraving, 6½-in. by 4-in.

France ; stone bridge over the Seine ; a storm by night ; the lightning having struck one of the arches it has fallen in, at the same moment a coach and pair with persons inside, and pedestrians from the opposite direction, are being precipitated into the waters beneath.

No. 678—One Engraving, 4-in. by 6-in.

Representing the burning of Joan of Arc.

No. 679—One Engraving, 6-in. by 7-in.

Represents the house in which Shakespeare was born.

No. 680—One Engraving, 6½-in. by 4-in.

A swampy moor ; a man on horseback, which has taken fright, is in the act of leaping over a wide ditch, the man holding by the horse's neck ; his hat blown away in the air.

No. 681—One Engraving, 7-in. by 4-in.

Figure of an Arab on the back of a full-blooded charger ; attendants in the back-ground.

No. 682—One Engraving, 7-in. by 4-in.

A street in France ; a man with whip, belabouring his horse, which is attached to a heavily-laden cart.

No. 683—One Engraving, 7-in. by 3-in.

Street in Bruges ; a man taking an affectionate leave of another, previous to being led to execution ; two horses in the foreground, from which the prisoner and an officer have alighted ; gallows and large concourse of persons in the distance.

No. 684—One Engraving, 7-in. by 5-in.

A view of Rome, with bridge spanning the river Tiber.

No. 685—One Engraving, 5-in. by 4½-in.

Room with large window, from which six persons are intently looking into the street below, their countenances expressive of pleasure at what they see.

No. 686—One Engraving, 5½-in. by 3½-in.

A rural landscape ; canal with lock-gates.

No. 687—One Engraving, 3½-in. by 3½-in.

An Elizabethian turreted mansion.

No. 688—One Engraving, 3½-in. by 2½-in.

Two ancient and dilapidated dwelling houses.

No. 689—One Engraving, 3-in. by 4½-in.

Sea shore and rocky cliffs ; a man on the sands in the distance, about to embark on board a small sailing-boat ; on the cliffs above is a comic figure of a man wrapped in an old cloak, watching the other.

No. 690—One Engraving, 4-in. by 3-in.

A French police court ; magistrate examining two sailors ; female recognising her son in one of them ; surprise depicted on the countenances of all.

No. 691—One Engraving, 4-in. by 3½-in.

Escape of Napoleon in his carriage after the battle of Waterloo ; represents him in the act of leaving the carriage by one door while at the other soldiers are endeavouring to capture him.

No. 692—One Engraving, 3¼-in. by 3¼-in:

A bed-room with bed ; a man leaning his head on his hands, seeming in great grief.

No. 693—One Engraving, 4¼-in. by 4-in.

A country road leading to a village church seen in the distance; in the foreground, a man with thimble-rig, surrounded by countrymen and sharpers.

No. 694—One Engraving, 4¼-in. by 3-in.

Interior of a tap-room of a sea-port town; sailors, soldiers, girls, &c., dancing, fighting, and singing; two fiddlers on a table.

No. 695—One Engraving, 4-in. by 3-in.

A wood ; brigands on the watch ; one discharging his carbine at a distant traveller who is falling from a rock.

No. 696 & 497—Two small Engravings, Naval and Military.

No. 698—One Engraving, 3¼-in. by 3-in.

Deck of a pirate ; the pirates betrayed.

No. 699—One Engraving, 2¼-in. by 4-in.

A heath ; the camp of Sir Robert Bruce ; Bruce and chieftains in conversation with two monks.

No. 700—One Engraving, 4-in. by 3-in.

Lord and lady of the 15th century.

No. 701—One Engraving, 4-in. by 3-in.

Engagement at sea between Admiral Blake and Van Tromp.

No. 702—One Engraving, 4¼-in. by 3¼-in.

A group of Peruvian Indians in their native wilds, males and females, surrounded by Spanish sailors and soldiers, one in the act of stealing a ear-ring by pulling it from the lobe of the ear of an Indian woman.

No. 703—One Engraving, 3¼-in. by 3-in.

A wood ; a male and female walking arm-in-arm, pointing to a mill in the distance.

No. 704—One Engraving, 6¼-in. by 5-in.

Fac-simile to No. 687, but on a larger scale.

No. 705—One Engraving, 4-in. by 3-in.

An allegorical engraving suitable for an almanack.

No. 706—One Engraving, 6-in. by 4-in.

Interior of the sultan of Turkey's seraglio ; the sultana surrounded by female slaves who are offering fruits, &c., to her.

No. 707—One Engraving, 5-in. by 3¼-in.

Representing the comic figure of a man dressed outre, with preposterously large cravat, his right arm extended, with a white hat in his hand ; this engraving is suitable for a farce.

No. 708—One Engraving, 5-in. by 9-in.

Representing a large Newfoundland dog lying down, small spaniel by his side.

No. 709—One Engraving, 5¼-in. by 3¼-in.

A market-place in Poland ; a man on the scaffold, receiving absolution from a catholic priest previous to being executed.

No. 710—One Engraving, 4-in. by 8-in.

A man sitting by the fire, holding umbrella over his head ; rain coming through the rafters.

No. 711—One Engraving, 2-in. by 2¼-in.

Bear attacking a man ; another man climbing a tree.

No. 712—One Engraving, 4-in. by 3-in.

Anchorite's cell ; anchorite gazing on the emblem of mortality, a skull.

No. 713—One Engraving, 6-in.

A fine engraving of tiger and

No. 714— Represents the two words "
of letters 2-in. ; length of the word are
circus 9-in. ; in each letter of the above
ceivable posture in which it is possibl

No. 715—A circular engr
Representing a lady in riding h
acts of equi

No. 716—An Engraving, 7
on the back of the great salam
by a grand pyrotechnic displa
kind ever witnessed in the ar

No. 717—A c
Representing a female eques
wreaths, the steed traversing t
represents the most daring act

No. 718—One Engraving, 8-
trian feat of a man in jockey co
horse while leaping over hurdle

The above four Engravings are
of daring e

No. 719—An Engraving, 8
tion of the field of battle, as
allied troops charging the e
men and horses in all dire
for a large company.

No. 720—An Engravi
French cuirassiers and
loo. This engraving i

ENDS
17

Database printout, as abstract of the Catalogue and alphabetical index to it

Title of play		Theme or genre	Description of engraving
449	A.E.I.O.U.	pantomime	figures with the letters
198	Abelard and Heloise	historical	characters in temple
445	Admiral Sam	maritime	fort exterior with escape
254	Adventures of a Gentleman	domestic	scenes including clergymen in cut-away house
10	Afloat and Ashore	maritime	naval action, survivors floating
442	Afloat and Ashore	maritime	6 action scenes, including much water
573	Aladdin	pantomime	magician and genie in cave
537	Alonzo the Brave [?]	supernatural	2 engravings of Alonzo the Brave, including spectre
443	Anchor's Weighed	emblematic	title with anchor
257	Angels and Lucifers	supernatural	man with lucifer matches
240	Antigone	burlesque (Greek)	characters before temple
125	Armstrong the Shipwright	maritime	Spithead scene, flogging
248	Artful Dodger	rustic	man on stile in front of village
220	Asmodeus	pantomime ?	Satan dressed in contemporary fashion
385	Assyrian Spy	foreign / Turkish	4 scenes
384	Azael	foreign / African	Spirit of the Desert appearing to Azael
250	Babes in the Wood	burlesque (folk tale)	robber threatens girl and comic boy
208	Barnaby Rudge	portrait (fictional)	Barnaby Rudge, full-length
306	Barnaby Rudge	adaptation	fancifully-attired youth with raven
355 b	Battle of Waterloo	military	field of victory, Wellington on horseback, Napoleon retreating
330	Battles of the East	emblematic	Spirit of Peace, English and French soldiers either side
277	Bedouin Arabs	crime	figure leaping from battlements, etc
278	Bedouin Arabs	acrobatics	men standing on each other's shoulders
287	Bedouin Arabs	acrobatics	three Arabs in acrobatic dances and action
332	Bedouin Arabs	acrobatics	gymnastic scene
127	Ben the Boatswain	maritime	combat action, and fire in hold
256	Black Cupid	burlesque (mythological)	burlesque dancer as Cupid
182	Black Doctor	historical	rock scenes above, Bastille dungeons below
662	Black Doctor	historical	doctor kneels to Countess and receives money
663	Black Doctor	historical	doctor defiant before chevalier
205	Black Swan	foreign / African	black lady
203	Blanche Herriot	historical	female clinging to bell
383	Blanche Herriot	historical	3 scenes
382	Blind Child of Africa	American / slavery	4 scenes
386	Bloomers	domestic	females in bloomers
195	Blue Beard	foreign / Turkish	head of Turkish chief
196	Blue Beard	foreign / Turkish	woman on tower, another about to be beheaded
187	Bohemians of Paris	historical	Parisian scenes of combat and crowds
38	Bottle	temperance	drunkard drinking, family pleading
183	Bottle	temperance	drunkards, pleading girls, gin demons
241	Boyhood of Bacchus	mythological	classical figures and grapes in landscape
214	Bridge of Life	riverine	girl crosses stream on human bridge
587	Brigand [?]	crime	brigand chief firing at officer, plus conflict
232	Bronze Horse	equestrian	man on horse riding in the air
483	Burlesque of Richard III	burlesque (Shakespeare)	Lady Anne pointing sword at Richard
392	Captain Hawk	crime	highwayman
189	Capture of Silesia	military	man falls from collapsing bridge into torrent, etc
456	Cato: or, the Dogs of the Plantation	dog-drama	two dogs rescue youth from stabbing
335	Charles O'Malley, the Irish Dragoon	military	Irishman with military accessories
595	Charms and Countercharms [?]	domestic ?	male and female arm-in-arm, another watching
441	Chesapeake and Shannon	maritime	cottage scene and scene of battle at sea
184	Christmas Carol	adaptation	figure of Christmas welcomes Scrooge
381	Christmas Carol	adaptation	3 scenes
149	Cinderella	pantomime	magic car, fairies
150	Cinderella	emblematic / pantomime	emblems of characters in scenes
50	Corsican Brothers	crime	the duel and the apparition

55	Courier of Lyons	crime	2 scenes
177	Crichton of Clunie	Scottish	hall, combat scene
46	Cricket on the Hearth	adaptation	[no description]
186	Cricket on the Hearth	adaptation	cottage scene with blind girl etc
225	Cricket on the Hearth	adaptation	cottage interior, vision in background
380	Crossroads	crime	3 tableaux
154	Dame Trot and her Comical Cat	pantomime	dame dancing with cat
236	Davis and Sally dear	foreign / African ?	African chief, youth kneeling to female
162	Demon Dwarf	pantomime	dwarf, victim, imps and creatures, etc
255	Deserted Mill	military	soldiers, fainting female, man hanging from rafter
291	Deserted Mill	crime	woman in cave, men shooting
388	Deserter	military	2 firing squad scenes
234	Deserter and his Dog	dog-drama	man before firing-squad, dog struggling
599	Deserter [?]	military	deserter about to be executed
178	Destruction of the Bastile	historical	destruction of the Bastille
191	Devil's Opera	pantomime ?	hall, devil rising from cauldron, onlookers, occult objects
463	Dick Turpin	crime	8 scenes of sequence of drama
76	Dog of Montargis	dog-drama	Dame Gertrude, dog with lantern
455	Dogs of St Bernard	dog-drama	dog rescuing exhausted youth
192	Don Cæsar de Bazan	historical	hall, ceremonial, etc
299	Don Juan	emblematic	statue of Guzman on horseback
446	Don Juan	pantomime	figure of Scaramouche
176	Dream of Life	crime	4 scenes in one, Gothic mansion, etc
223	Dream Spectre	supernatural	kneeling female protects man from hovering spectre
326	Dred	American / slavery	3 scenes
391	Dred	American / slavery	slavery scenes between letters of title
190	Drunkard's Children	temperance	6 scenes of children's progress and fall
393	Drunkard's Children	temperance	8 scenes of principal incidents
395	Dumb Man of Manchester	crime	Mrs Wilton stabbed, dumb man to rescue
202	Earl of Poverty	historical	old London houses and street
397	Earl of Poverty	historical	antique houses in old London street, with man
167	Earth, Air, Fire, & Water [?]	pantomime	cave, figures, demons and serpents, 'Earth'
168	Earth, Air, Fire, & Water [?]	pantomime	fairies, lovely female ascending, 'Air'
169	Earth, Air, Fire, & Water [?]	pantomime	car rising from fiery regions, with serpents, 'Fire'
170	Earth, Air, Fire, & Water [?]	pantomime	storm king and bride ascend from the deep, 'Water'
353	Eliza Fenning	emblematic	female
394	Eliza Holmes	rustic / romantic	4 scenes of country dance, gypsies, and spectre
398	Emigration	migration	travellers on mountain
350	Evil Eye	emblematic	large eye
351	Evil Eye	emblematic	no description [? eye]
352	Evil Eye	emblematic	no description [? eye]
82	Faust	historical	demon with scroll
85	Faust and Marguerite	historical	Marguerite, Faust, demon
621	Faust and Marguerite	supernatural	Marguerite and demon in garden
158	Fee-fo-fum: or, Harlequin te-to-tum	pantomime	magician
269	Fire Mill	rustic ?	man on windmill, fireworks
90	Fire of London	historical	man carrying fainting female down ladder
336	Fire of London	historical	6 scenes
379	Fire of London	historical	6 scenes
68	Fish and the Ring	pantomime ?	hall, lovers, grotesques
130	Flying Dutchman	maritime	phantom ship off the Cape
131	Flying Dutchman	maritime	crew boarding trader
434	Flying Dutchman	maritime	4 engravings of figures in action
121	Frank Hartwell	historical	tender off the Tower; combat scenes
439	Gallant Tom	maritime	5 action scenes
87	Gallant Tom [?]	maritime	stern of ship with caption, figures
201	Gathering of the Clans	Scottish	Highlanders assembling
281	Giles Scroggins	emblematic	portraits of the judge and jury club
216	Gin & Water	temperance	brutal husband, misery; happy group
26	Gin and Water	temperance	various tableaux
27	Gin and Water	temperance	gin and water (two scenes)
28	Gin and Water	temperance	various tableaux
29	Gin and Water	temperance	gin tableau
30	Gin and Water	temperance	water tableau

31	Gin and Water	temperance	tableaux: fire and quarrel
32	Gin and Water	temperance	tableaux of gin palace and Institution
57	Gin and Water	temperance	gin and water
215	Gin and Water	temperance	tableau of goblets and the Spirits of Gin and Water
375	Gin and Water	temperance	drunkard with children imploring, also a happy family
155	Goody Two Shoes	pantomime	cock crowing, with caption
172	Goody Two Shoes	pantomime	dame with shoes, harlequinade characters
173	Goody Two Shoes	pantomime	dame with broom by shoe
376	Guerillas	military	conflict between soldiers and guerrillas
377	Guerillas	military	5 scenes of combat
42	Guerillas: or, St Sebastian	military	combats, women praying
181	Guy Faux	historical	Guy Fawkes in dungeon
374	Guy Faux	historical	4 scenes
331	Hand of Cards	emblematic	hand holding cards
141	Hardiknute: or, the Wood Demon	pantomime	Hardiknute surrounded by figures of months and seasons, grotesques
145	Harlequin and Old Cocker	pantomime	10 boys with arithmetic emblems
156	Harlequin Georgy Barnwell	pantomime	Barnwell with blunderbuss, figure hanging in chains, imps
138	Harlequin Ice Queen	emblematic / pantomime	Queen Victoria and the late Prince Albert in a pavilion with portraits of public figures
161	Harlequin King Arthur	pantomime	figure with club, and attendants
165	Harlequin King Lud	pantomime	palace, king, attendants, star and firelight
325	Holly Tree Inn	crime	Isaac and Rachel with dagger
414	Holly Tree Inn	crime	attempted murder scene
417	Ice Fiend	pantomime	7 scenes of fiend and fairies
454	Idiot of the Cliff [sic]	crime	cottage in flames with action
218	Inundation	riverine	raft on floods, destruction
367	It's never too late to mend	adaptation	The Departure
368	It's never too late to mend	adaptation	prison scene
369	It's never too late to mend	adaptation	bridge and bushrangers, struggle, etc
370	It's never too late to mend	adaptation	The Return
625	Ivanhoe	adaptation	Rebecca being accused, another scene of Ivanhoe with Frondeboeuf on battlements
447	Jack and Jill	pantomime	fair scene and the hill
237	Jack in the Water	riverine	River Thames scene with characters
219	Jack Sheppard	crime	Sheppard cut down from Tyburn Tree
318	Jack Sheppard	crime	scenes on river in storm
319	Jack Sheppard	crime	Sheppard armed, in attitude
320	Jack Sheppard	crime	Sheppard interviewing mother in Bedlam
321	Jack Sheppard	crime	scene in well-shaft
322	Jack Sheppard	crime	5 scenes
420	Jack Sheppard	crime	5 action scenes
421	Jack Sheppard	crime	workshop interior
422	Jack Sheppard	crime	workshop interior, close-up of beam
423	Jack Sheppard	crime	Wilde interviewing Sheppard in prison
424	Jack Sheppard	crime	2 engravings of lettering
304	Jacob Faithful	adaptation	disconsolate man
333	Jane of the Hatchet	emblematic	female in armour with hatchet
419	Jane Paul	crime	5 action scenes
235	Joan of Arc	burlesque (historical)	Joan, full-length
589	Joan of Arc [?]	historical	Joan on horseback, surrounded by supporters
14	Johnny Horner	pantomime	tournament
418	Jolly Dick the Lamplighter	crime	5 action scenes
221	Jonathan Bradford	crime	various scenes in the George Inn
222	Jonathan Bradford	crime	vault with tomb and characters
148	King of the Castle	pantomime	hall, grotesques, nymphs, harlequinade figures
571	King's Wager	historical	ruffians capturing the night-watchman
146 a	Knight and the Sprite	pantomime	knights and lady with letter emblems
428	Knights of St John	historical	knight and Saracen, with banners
147	L.S.D.	pantomime	harlequinade figures, and goose, entwined around L.S.D.
507	L.S.D.	pantomime	3 scenes entwining the letters
448	Ladye Birde	pantomime	4 sensation scenes, including a dragon
425	Lamplighter	maritime	ship on fire, etc
122	Last Shilling	gambling	emblem; gambling scenes

120	Life of a Ship from Cradle to Grave	maritime	launching, storm, break-up; onlookers
129	Life Raft	maritime	escape on raft from foundering ship
245	Life's a Lottery	domestic	street marketing scene, with costermonger and donkey
298	Little Devil	emblematic	female figure
166	Little Yellow Man	pantomime	yellow man and tower, others
206	Lone Hut	crime	kneeling female about to be stabbed
123	Lost Ship	maritime	ship founders in storm, beacon rock, onlookers
591	Love and Crime	crime	engraving of three principal tableaux
290	Lucky Horseshoe	emblematic	large horseshoe
338	Lucky Horseshoe	domestic	5 scenes in border
426	Lucky Horseshoe	crime	woman targeting ruffian, with horseshoe border
427	Lucky Horseshoe	crime	6 action scenes
416	Lucy Woodbine	crime	court scene and capture scene
357	Macbeth	burlesque (Shakespeare)	dagger scene as comedy
340	Marco Sciarra	historical	6 scenes in border
396	Marco Sciarra	historical	6 scenes
193	Margaret Catchpole	crime	prison scenes, including messenger on horseback
204	Marriage a la mode	portrait	Hogarth and dog
400	Mary Clifford	crime	prison scene
401	Mary Clifford	crime	3 scenes featuring Mary and Mother Brownrigg
402	Mary Clifford	crime	5 scenes of Mary's sufferings
593	Mary, the Maid of the Inn	crime	Mary, concealed, watches lover deal with dead body
550	May and December [?]	emblematic	engraving of May (young female) and December (old man)
4	May Marsden	maritime	ship scene plus woman praying
6	May Marsden	maritime	rocks, mill in flames, fighting characters
285	May Marsden	crime / maritime	5 tableaux, of cottage, smuggling, mill in flames, ruined abbey, sailor escaping from prison
286	May Marsden	crime / maritime	sailors, mill, smugglers, disconsolate female
406	May Marsden	crime / maritime	5 engravings of sensational action
209	Mazeppa	equestrian	Mazeppa bound to horse
231	Mazeppa	equestrian	Mazeppa bound to horse under restraint
462	Mazeppa	animal act	3 scenes of horse etc, including wolves and eagle
253	Merchant of Venice	burlesque (Shakespeare)	trial scene
572	Merry Wives of Windsor	Shakespeare	wives putting Falstaff in buck-basket
399	Minnigrey [sic]	military	general on horse, with others
199	Mountain Cataract	historical	temple, tournament, etc
457 a	Mountain Guide	dog-drama	dog pursues robbers of female
39	Murder at the Old Crossroads	crime	inn exterior, shooting scene
407	My Poll and my Partner Joe	maritime	11 engravings of the action, including the slaver
408	Nicholas Nickleby	adaptation	6 engravings of the actions
564	No Followers [?]	domestic	engraving of 'No Followers', showing figures dining
242	Norma	burlesque (opera)	4 comic heads
265	Norma	burlesque (opera)	Paul Bedford as Adelgisa
258	Norval	Scottish	young Norval
547	Obi: or, Three-fingered Jack	crime	Obi striking kneeling figure
431	Ocean Monarch	maritime	between-decks and fire scenes
144	Old Bogie	emblematic / pantomime	Queen Victoria and Prince Albert centre, various scenes surrounding
174	Old Dame Trot	pantomime	head of cat
412	Old Fleet	crime	scenes relating to debtors' prison
295	Oliver Twist	adaptation	boy with stick and bundle over shoulder
323	Oliver Twist	adaptation	Bill Sikes with bulldog
324	Oliver Twist	adaptation	Sikes in action scene
409	Oliver Twist	adaptation	10 engravings of the action
251	Olympic Tarantella	burlesque (mythological)	Cupid and another dance mock tarantella
151	One O'Clock: or, Harlequin Wood Demon	pantomime	clock, harlequinade figures
249	Our Village	maritime / rustic	sailors dancing; shipwreck; country girl
185	Paul Clifford	crime	abbey ruins, combat scenes, horses
197	Paul Clifford	crime	footpads attacking coach
411	Paul Clifford	crime	action in abbey ruins
247	Pet of the Ballet	dance	opera dancer
457 b	Phantom Barque	dog-drama	dog seizes pirate firing at mulatto
410	Phœbe Hessel	gypsy	3 figures of Phœbe

179		Poor Susan	military	dead soldiers in forest scene, female searching
259		Pork Chops	domestic	man sleeping beside table, another enters with bag
194		Profligate	crime	brigands and combat, etc
126		Raby Rattler	maritime	sailors in combat, women on rock despatching sailor
243		Railway King	domestic	kitchen interior with characters
212		Richard the Third	burlesque (Shakespeare)	Richard III in costume with caption
213		Richard the Third	burlesque (Shakespeare)	Richard III in costume
143		Riddle me Ree	pantomime	emblem of heads around border
238		Road of Life	London	street scene by Temple Bar
239		Road of Life	London	street characters
413		Road to Transportation	crime	6 engravings of wrong-doing
484		Robert le Diable	supernatural	two men grappling, plus demons, snakes, etc
429		Rolla	historical	Rolla with sword and child
672		Romeo and Juliet	Shakespeare ?	Romeo and Juliet on castle terrace
404		Rye House Plot	historical	5 sensational engravings including execution
430		Sailor's Wife	maritime	3 action scenes, including one multi-stage
159		Saint Monday	pantomime	fairies etc in air, magic car, harlequinade characters
49		Sea of Ice	maritime	sea and ice, men and a child struggling on it
15		Sea Serpent	pantomime	mystic cavern, serpent, fiends
134		Sea, the Sea [? a song]	maritime	sailor on rope rescues woman and child from waves
339		Sealed Sentence	historical	5 scenes in border
579		Seaman and the Secretary [?]	maritime	Edwin and Will Steady in a hall
210		Shadow: or, the Mother's Dream	supernatural ?	shadow approaches man
359		Shylock: or, the Merchant ... Preserved	burlesque (Shakespeare)	trial scene as comedy
188		Silver Crescent	military / Turkish	Turks and Christian warriors in combat
200		Simon's Yat	riverine	female falling from top of rock
246		Sixteen String Jack	crime	highwayman scenes, including on horseback
5		Skeleton of the Wave	maritime	skeleton at sea
58		Skeleton of the Wave	maritime	5 engravings in border
435		Skeleton of the Wave	maritime	5 action scenes
437		Smuggler King	crime	action scene in cave
389		Soldier's Dream	military / Scottish	rustic vision appearing to kilted soldier
390		Soldier's Progress	military	6 scenes
157		Spirit of the Snow Drift	pantomime	coral cave, nymphs, knight and lady
387		Surgeon of Paris	historical	Madelon saved by surgeon in the Louvre
337		Three Musketeers	adaptation	combat scene in Calais
415		Tic-doloreux	crime	5 figures of females etc
260		Tinker Joe	rustic	tinker with accoutrements
124		Tom Trim	maritime	emblem; water scenes
211		Tower of London	adaptation	Guy Fawkes
373		Triumph of the Jews	historical	conflict in temple
45		Turpin's Ride to York	historical	Turpin on horseback, others
60		Uncle Tom and Lucy Neal	pantomime	the Garden of Freedom, with figures
405		Uncle Tom's Cabin	American	2 engravings, interiors
224		Vagrant and his Family	gypsy ?	vagrant family on road
558		Vagrant and his Family	gypsy ?	vagrants with wagon, beside cottage
51		Villikins and his Dinah	domestic	poison scene
528		Wat Tyler	historical	2 interiors of smithy with action
207		Water Witches	riverine	four women in cutter
583		Waterman [?]	riverine	boat beside Blackfriars Bridge
345		White Cat	emblematic	cat
132		White Squall	maritime	mutiny on deck
180		Whitefriars	historical	various scenes of combat and action; emblems
146	b	Whittington and Cat	pantomime	Whittington by milestone, plus cat
244		Whittington and his Cat	pantomime	youth on milestone with large cat
673		Wife of Seven Husbands	crime	wife in court
674		Wife of Seven Husbands	crime	engraving illustrating the introduction
35		Will and the Way	foreign / oriental	shooting scene
36		Will and the Way	foreign / oriental	border with figures of characters
47		Will and the Way	foreign / oriental	soldiers in victory ceremonies
54		Will and the Way	foreign / oriental	4 scenes
371		Will and the Way	foreign / oriental	4 scenes
372		Will and the Way	foreign / oriental	6 scenes
582		William Tell [?]	historical	Tell shoots apple off son's head
142		William the Conqueror	pantomime	Normans fight Saxons in grotesque costumes

457	c	Wonga	dog-drama	Indian and dog look out of box
328		Wreck of the Golden Mary	maritime	vision tableau
329		Wreck of the Golden Mary	maritime	iceberg disaster
436		Wreck of the Royal George	maritime	Royal George all but sunk
284		Zulu Kaffirs	foreign / African	songs and combat
137		["for a Nautical Drama"]	maritime	5 scenes of nautical desperation
378		[for a play, name not known]	crime	4 action scenes
118			acrobatics	man somersaults from tightrope firing pistols
119			acrobatics	female on tightrope with fireworks
477			acrobatics	human pyramid of 'the Quatre Wonders'
503			acrobatics	6 multiple engravings of acrobatic acts
523			acrobatics	5 acrobatic engravings
297			acrobatics ?	man on tub
52			American	Boston street, Uncle True, Gerty and kitten
271			American / slavery	Jem Crow singing
581			American / slavery	slavers molest female in plantation
103			animal act	figure of a monkey
282			animal act	Van Amburgh and lions
289			animal act	female on lion's back
313			animal act	man and lion boxing
458			animal act	the Learned Dog, with letters
496			animal act	4 engravings of Van Amburgh plus lions, tigers, leopards, lambs
543			animal act	the Learned Pig, with letters etc
80			animal act ?	forest, man grappling lion
160			animal act ? / circus	lion and clown
514			Arctic	icebergs and figures
23			ballooning	balloon with three persons in car
114			ballooning	balloon
266			ballooning	Nassau balloon and car arising at night
292			ballooning	male and female in car of balloon
365			ballooning	view of pleasure gardens with balloon ascent, etc
486			ballooning	3 engravings of balloons
521			ballooning	balloon ascent at night
93			biblical	Sampson and the gates of Gaza
317			biblical	death of Abel
522			circus	trapeze and pole dances
535			circus	pole dance with globe
37			crime	3 scenes, possible multi-set
48			crime	The Carpenter, others, shooting
86			crime	ragged man with lamp and dagger
89			crime	men quarrelling, man and child kneeling
108			crime	female prevents man from seizing gun
109			crime	house on fire, man on rafters, others point; sailor defeats ruffians before praying woman
279			crime	black man dressed in Spanish costume firing pistol
363			crime	man with pistols, ruffians, ballads
539			crime	robbers attacking coach in forest
553			crime	female falling into chasm, man watches
555			crime	ruffians with pistol in tavern
559			crime	complex scene of soldier being stabbed
561			crime	man stabbing another in forest
563			crime	man strangling another, falling down ravine
568			crime	men in combat, females imploring
584			crime	5 scenes of mounted highwaymen's action
588			crime	man stabbing another, female shocked, lightning
590			crime	brigand as minstrel, in garden with female
592			crime	bravos at table, two enter with female
607			crime	man escaping forcibly from apartment on fire
611			crime	one man strangling another, falling down a ravine
612			crime	two men hiding money in a garden
615			crime	a stabbing fracas at head of stairs
616			crime	two men quarrelling, with daggers, woman between
617			crime	man hanging from bridge, being struck by another
618			crime	men inspecting floor-trap, reward placards on wall
623			crime	Hall of Justice, with judge and other characters including fainting female

624	crime	cloaked man and swordsman advancing through garden gates
626	crime	man with cup and dagger, offering them to kneeling female
630	crime	man and boy finding dead body across doorway of mansion
636	crime	man being lanced by another, female looking on
637	crime	female offers pistols to grieving man
639	crime	brigand attacking man supporting fainting female
640	crime	man on rope ladder escaping from prison
644	crime	young female clinging to aged police officer with armed attendants
658	crime	old man with dagger stabbing kneeling veiled female
660	crime	two men burgle sleeping old man's bedchamber
676	crime	three persons pursuing robber seized by dog
683	crime	scene prior to execution, in Bruges
695	crime	brigands shooting at traveller
551	crime / historical	monk pushing stabbed man from castle ramparts
671	crime / historical	dead female on couch with pistol in hand, two men in affright (Tudor)
529	crime / Scottish	Scotchman stabs another in tavern
602	crime / Scottish	escape scene from castle apartment
668	crime / Turkish	female pleading with ferocious Turk in dungeon
102	crime ?	man chained to rock, attacked by eagle
105	dance	three-legged dancer
270	dance	Taglioni in 'pas', full-length
366	dance etc	casino interior, groups dancing
73	dog-drama	shooting man seized by dog
75	dog-drama	dogs seizing ruffians
233	dog-drama	scenes include dog seizing man
527	dog-drama	multi-action engraving of dogs and monkeys
77	dog-drama ?	forest, dog seizing man, monkey throwing coconut
78	dog-drama ?	murderer seized by dog
79	dog-drama ?	plantation, "Indians", dogs, man shooting
491	domestic	Mr & Mrs Caudle in bed
544	domestic	affecting scene of blind man and children
548	domestic	3 engravings, Marriage à la mode
549	domestic	old man and female in country scene
556	domestic	dead female with supporters in elegant apartment
566	domestic	'comic engraving' of figures in library
578	domestic	male embraces female stabbing herself
586	domestic	male and female conversing in garden
601	domestic	musicians outside inn, with snow, 'The Waits'
606	domestic	man reading in library
629	domestic	female with papers and elderly man
642	domestic	young man beseeching an elder, girl smiling
645	domestic	female with letter awaits a visitor at night
649	domestic	grieving male and female
652	domestic	physician and females at female deathbed
654	domestic	man hiding from old woman in wood
685	domestic	six persons looking out of window with pleasure
692	domestic	grieving man in bedroom
710	domestic	man at fireside being rained on through rafters
531	domestic / crime ?	woman raising supine man
534	domestic ?	man supporting female in forest
600	domestic ?	female with sheet over her head
608	domestic ?	youth and coach in stable yard
542	domestic!	female being rescued from house on fire
272	emblematic	characters at a Judge and Jury Club
280	emblematic	holly tree
293	emblematic	head of a judge
294	emblematic	figure of a tall man
300	emblematic	a flag
305	emblematic (Shakespeare)	Shakespeare supported by Muses
315	emblematic	man with 'Times'
348	emblematic	descriptive scene for game of Puff and Dart
349	emblematic	hat
362	emblematic	head of a judge
438	emblematic	figure of a sailor
450	emblematic	come-on with clown's head
451	emblematic	6 engravings of clowns

453	emblematic	6 engravings of harlequin figures
459	emblematic	8 figures of dogs and monkeys
460	emblematic	2 figures of monkey-action
461	emblematic	7 figures of monkeys differently dressed
471	emblematic	interior of an amphitheatre
474	emblematic	panoramic procession
475	emblematic	loyal ornamental border
480	emblematic	grand opera interior
481	emblematic	Royal family in theatre box
488	emblematic	grand processional car, drawn by 12 horses
489	emblematic	2 engravings of French and English flags
490	emblematic	engraving for 'General Notes of the Season'
492	emblematic	man in rags
494	emblematic (Shakespeare)	bust of Shakespeare
495	emblematic	9 engravings for Grecian statues
498	emblematic	train with passengers
499	emblematic	Thalia with mask
500	emblematic	man in temple with fireworks
502	emblematic	mansion door with liveried servant
505	emblematic	Figures for 'Ball of All Nations' in a border of grapes
516	emblematic	exterior of Exeter Hall
524	emblematic	large ding-bat fist
533	emblematic	man in 18th-century costume
538	emblematic (Shakespeare &c)	Shakespearean figures and Paul Pry
541	emblematic	man playing musical glasses
545	emblematic	2 engravings of Paul Pry, with words
577	emblematic	Hope leaning on an anchor
594	emblematic	theatre interior, seen from the stage
619	emblematic	musicians with instruments
632	emblematic	snow-covered cottage with frozen pond
633	emblematic	deaf and dumb alphabet
678	emblematic	representation of Joan of Arc burning
679	emblematic (Shakespeare)	Shakespeare's birthplace
684	emblematic	bridge over Tiber in Rome
686	emblematic	canal with lock-gates
687	emblematic	Elizabethan turreted mansion (see also 704)
688	emblematic	two ancient houses, dilapidated
700	emblematic	lord and lady (15th-century costume)
704	emblematic	Elizabethan turreted mansion, as 687, larger
705	emblematic	engraving for an almanac
707	emblematic	comic figure of man dressed in outré fashion
712	emblematic	anchorite gazing at skull in cell
713	emblematic	tiger (fragment)
714	emblematic	unknown caption for circus (fragment)
263	emblematic (Shakespeare)	bust of Shakespeare with classical figures
311	emblematic / African	Kaffir chief
312	emblematic / African	Kaffir queen
638	emblematic / African	2 engravings of Kaffir chiefs in costume
360	emblematic / circus	tall man being admired (Mr T. Good)
361	emblematic / circus	tall man being admired (Smith's giant barman)
708	emblematic / dog-drama ?	large newfoundland and small spaniel
355 a	emblematic / maritime	sailor
356	emblematic / Scottish	Scotchmen dancing with bagpipes
99	equestrian	3 views of horsemanship
107	equestrian	man on leaping horse, another man running
110	equestrian	tournament, horse-agilities, clown conjuring
112	equestrian	horseriding
464	equestrian	horsemanship (precipice scene)
465	equestrian	2 scenes of horsemanship with clown and balloon
466	equestrian	four armoured men on one horse
467	equestrian	9 various actions of horsemanship
468	equestrian	man leaping over twelve horses
469	equestrian	11 scenes with horses including some named characters
470	equestrian	a border of horses
472	equestrian	border of men on horseback
473	equestrian	a Fury with snakes on horse with winged hooves

517	equestrian	8 engravings of armoured horsemanship
518	equestrian	5 horsemanship engravings, 1 historical, 4 circus
519	equestrian	5 display engravings of horsemanship
520	equestrian	3 chivalric engravings of horsemanship
680	equestrian	man on bolting horse leaping ditch
681	equestrian	Arab on charger
715	equestrian	horsewoman in equitation acts (fragment)
717	equestrian	female equestrian act (fragment)
718	equestrian	jockey and horse over hurdle (fragment)
716	equestrian ?	act involving the great salam[ander?], plus fireworks (fragment)
711	foreign	bear attacking a man, another climbing a tree
98	foreign / African	African holds scroll
20	foreign / Egyptian	mummy, Roman models
682	foreign / French	man belabouring horse and cart
664	foreign / French	affair in France, woman haranguing
677	foreign / French	lightning strikes bridge over the Seine, coach and pair precipitated
702	foreign / historical	Peruvian Indians and the Spanish
267	foreign / Madrid	the Piaxa de Toros at Madrid, crowded
690	foreign / maritime	sailors being examined in French court, one recognised by mother
24	foreign / oriental	temple interior, man on elephant, others prostrating
262	foreign / oriental	temple at Rangoon, idol, Burmese scene
274	foreign / oriental	The Golden Temple in Rangoon, Burmese court
288	foreign / oriental	Burmese state carriage, elephants, peacocks
478	foreign / oriental	pagoda of Dagon, Rangoon
501	foreign / oriental	8 engravings for a Chinese collection
709	foreign / religious	man on scaffold receiving absolution in Poland
41	foreign / Turkish	sultan and Turks in combat
308	foreign / Turkish	scenes of Turks and Tartars
706	foreign / Turkish	seraglio interior, slaves offering fruit to sultana
22	gold rush	diggings, panorama from England to Australia
43	gypsy	figures in gypsy camp
261	gypsy	Miss Fanny Williams fortune-telling as The Little Gypsy
667	gypsy	two gypsy girls by rustic gate
670	gypsy	gypsy and men in Westminster Abbey cloisters
18	historical	tournament, spectators, two knights in combat
44	historical	woman as vivandière
84	historical	Virginius embracing daughter
106	historical	Guy Fawkes
273	historical	coronation scene in Westminster Abbey, knights in armour
301	historical	scenes of Roman gladiators
302	historical	Roman gladiators
316	historical	Roman temple with emperor and combat
525	historical	scaffold scene
526	historical	king dead, queen weeping
532	historical	Fair Rosamund kneeling to Queen
536	historical	Lady Godiva naked on horseback
554	historical	armoured man stabbing youth
567	historical	figures in garden bower
569	historical	suppliants kneel to king, before castle
570	historical	Robin Hood, Maid Marian, and Tuck
575	historical	cavalier carries off lady from laddered window
580	historical	'comic engraving' of soldier and old-fashioned old man
609	historical	old-fashioned figures conversing in corridor
613	historical	disguised female with cavalier, holding goblets, others
614	historical	two females in apartment with cavalier
620	historical	young man and woman of 18th century
622	historical	action with cavaliers over senseless female form
627	historical	armoured man reproving kneeling female beside female corpse
634	historical	cavalier, ladies, frowning monk, etc, in apartment
648	historical	complex Parisian revolutionary scene
650	historical	knight on horseback leaving grieving female
655	historical	advocate addressing French Court of Justice
656	historical	crowd surrounding torch-lit execution of man
665	historical	officers challenge armed man in Paris
669	historical	Richard Coeur de Lion in state in tent
540	historical / domestic	figures conversing in a hall

701	historical / maritime	naval engagement (Blake and Van Tromp)
691	historical / military	escape of Napoleon after Waterloo
596	historical / pantomime ?	cavalier and soldiers arrest old man with dwarf pointing
651	historical / religious	French prisoners receiving consolation from priest before execution
275	magical	wizard scene
276	magical	wizard scene
334	magical	levitation
487	magical	set of sleight-of-hand tricks
1	maritime	naval fight
2	maritime	naval fight
3	maritime	shipwreck
7	maritime	naval victory
8	maritime	ship on fire, bodies escaping
9	maritime	ship in flames
88	maritime	sea-shore with sailors and a female
128	maritime	ship on fire, running aground, survivors fired on by soldiers from shore
133	maritime	boat escaping from ship on fire; sailors drowning
135	maritime	combat scene in cabin, female pleading
136	maritime	sailor points to victory flag
252	maritime	effigy of Robinson Crusoe with parrot
264	maritime	shipping before Cronstadt, British tar, French soldier
346	maritime	pirate and sailor in combat
433	maritime	3 engravings of nautical combat, etc
440	maritime	boat in storm
444	maritime	ship at sea between rocks
508	maritime	press gang
509	maritime	death of Nelson
510	maritime	3 naval engagements
511	maritime	naval engagement, broadside from deck
512	maritime	2 figures of a full-rigged ship
513	maritime	ship on fire
515	maritime	crossing the line festivities
574	maritime	storm, rocks, shipwreck in distance
641	maritime	three marines about to be hanged on ship's main deck
646	maritime	Grace Darling and father in lighthouse boat, wreck of the Forfarshire in distance
689	maritime	cliffs, sea-shore, sailing boat
694	maritime	revellers in sea-port taproom
696	maritime	small naval engraving
698	maritime	pirates betrayed on deck
675	maritime / military	storming of Algiers by sea and land
598	maritime ?	characters kneel to female on bed, sailor watching
97	masquerade	masquerade
56	military	battle of the Alma
104	military	regulars fight guerrillas on a bridge
226	military	forest scene, soldiers fight brigands, couple escape
230	military	happy group in front of soldiers fighting brigands
403	military	battlefield scene
479	military	combat between Chinese and English soldiers
560	military	The Cossack's grave in forest, with figures
565	military	complex domestic scene of people and soldiers
585	military	soldiers enlisting in country inn
597	military	formal flogging scene, 'Military Punishment'
605	military	combat between French soldiers and Arabs on horseback
647	military	battle between French and English troops, female on horseback cheering on the English
697	military	small military engraving
719	military	Allied troops charge enemy men and horses (fragment)
720	military	French and British at ? Waterloo (fragment)
657	military / domestic	military officer taking leave of grieving family
83	military / Turkish	Turks and French in combat
485	military / Turkish	battle between French and Turks
635	military / Turkish	battlefield, female kneeling before old Turk, about to smite officer
21	minstrels	minstrels, bones, instrumentalists
309	minstrels	Ethiopian minstrels
310	minstrels	Ethiopian serenaders

314	minstrels	Jim Crow singing
476	minstrels	4 engravings of black minstrels
557	minstrels	2 figures of Jem Crow singing
307	mythological	Neptune scene with fountains
504	mythological	12 engravings of mythological gods and goddesses with properties
643	oriental	oriental female with military officer, pointing across plain
12	pantomime	coral cave, Britannia, fairies
13	pantomime	harlequin and other figures
16	pantomime	clown
17	pantomime	clown and pantaloon on horseback
59	pantomime	garden, fairy queen, fountain, fairies
61	pantomime	clown, pantaloon, men, all on donkeys
62	pantomime	ornamental frame with pantomime figures
63	pantomime	fairy queen, a youth, a grotesque
64	pantomime	coral cave, sailors, Nicholas, grotesques, and fairies
65	pantomime	transformation scene with figures
66	pantomime	double street, numerous figures, characters on geese
71	pantomime	three boys with "knowing" scrolls
72	pantomime	fairy queen drawn by swans, fairies
94	pantomime	Tom Thumb in Highland dress
95	pantomime	Tom Thumb as Field Marshal
96	pantomime	Tom Thumb in jockey dance
139	pantomime	clown with come-on placard
152	pantomime	crowned comic on plum pudding
153	pantomime	skating comic
163	pantomime	tableau for final scene in Palm Grove
164	pantomime	large clown's head
344	pantomime	character on ground, Spirit of Freedom over
358	pantomime	fairy grotto, Neptune, car as hansom drawn by doves
452	pantomime	fairy and water transformation scene
562	pantomime	fairy rising from lake, addressing knight
604	pantomime	ogre with club, others
116	pantomime / circus	small figure of a clown
117	pantomime / circus	figure of a clown
171	pantomime / circus	clown
576	pantomime ?	two men drinking with dwarf
268	Punch	Punch and further characters, including Toby
283	Punch	Punch
296	Punch	Punch in contemporary costume
610	Punch	Punch with stick in hand
228	religious	death scene, angels, ascension, people kneeling
530	religious	cathedral gallery with figures
628	religious	female with crucifix and papers and kneeling man
631	religious	man kneeling over grave in churchyard
659	religious	dying female in bed receiving absolution from priest
666	riverine	female reclining by waterfall approached by officer
693	rustic	thimble-rig act on country road
703	rustic	male and female in a wood
552	Scottish	Scotchman in castle looking at witch
699	Scottish	Sir Robert Bruce in camp
229	snowbound	scenes in snow-drift, including death
25	sporting	wrestlers
111	sporting	walking match
115	sporting	sparring
347	sporting	sparring
354	sporting	man firing at target
493	sporting	groups watching skaters
497	sporting	2 engravings of sparring
506	sporting	2 scenes of wrestling
653	sporting	man firing pistol at target watched by others
482	sporting ?	scenes concerning 'The Rat-catcher's Daughter', with rats and donkey
603	supernatural	female looking at spectre-knight in churchyard
546	temperance	2 scenes of drinking etc
661	temperance	dying youth, sympathetic female, man drunk in poor room

The following 27 engravings, with no description, are listed as 'destroyed':

11, 19, 33, 34, 40, 53, 67, 69, 70, 74, 81, 91, 92, 100, 101, 113, 140, 175, 217, 227, 303, 327, 341, 342, 343, 364, 432

Animals mentioned in Bath's catalogue of engravings

Dogs are mentioned in the following engravings:

73, 75, 76, 77, 78, 79, 204, 233, 234, 268, 323, 455, 456, 457, 458, 459, 527, 676, 708

Horses are mentioned in the following engravings:

17, 45, 99, 107, 110, 112, 185, 193, 209, 231, 232, 246, 355b, 399, 462, 464, 465, 466, 467, 468, 469, 470, 472, 473, 488, 517, 518, 519, 520, 536, 584, 589, 605, 647, 650, 677, 680, 681, 682, 715, 716, 717, 718, 719

Other animals, including birds, serpents, etc., are mentioned in the following engravings:

bear, 711
cat, 52, 146b, 154, 174, 244, 345
cock, 155
donkey, 61, 245, 482
dove, 358
dragon, 448
eagle, 102, 462
elephant, 24, 288
goose, 66, 147
lamb, 496
leopard, 496
lion, 80, 160, 282, 289, 313, 496
monkey, 103, 459, 460, 461, 527
parrot, 252
peacock, 288
pig, 543
rat, 482
raven, 306
salamander ?, 716
serpent, 15, 167, 169
snake, 473, 484
swan, 72
tiger, 496, 713
wolf, 462

Notes